GARY CHAPMAN

Happily
EVER AFTER
Six Secrets to a Successful Marriage

Tyndale House Publishers, Inc.
Carol Stream, Illinois

Visit Tyndale online at www.tyndale.com.

Visit Gary Chapman online at www.garychapman.org.

TYNDALE and Tyndale's quill logo are registered trademarks of Tyndale House Publishers, Inc.

Happily Ever After: Six Secrets to a Successful Marriage

Designed by Jacqueline L. Nuñez

Everybody Wins and *Home Improvements* edited by Dave Lindstedt

In-Law Relationships, Making Love, Now What?, and *Profit Sharing* edited by Kathryn S. Olson.

Library of Congress Cataloging-in-Publication Data

Chapman, Gary D., date.
  Happily ever after : six secrets to a successful marriage / Gary D. Chapman.
    p. cm. — (Chapman guides)
  Includes bibliographical references.
  ISBN 978-1-4143-6444-5 (sc)
  1. Marriage—Religious aspects—Christianity. I. Title. II. Title: Six secrets to a successful marriage.
  BV835.C4576 2011
  248.8'44—dc23   2011032095

Printed in the United States of America

17 16 15 14 13
7   6   5   4

Contents

Introduction

FOR MORE THAN THIRTY YEARS couples have been coming into my office seeking help. Almost without exception they come because of one of six things: an inability to resolve their conflicts without arguing, an ongoing struggle to negotiate some kind of personal change, challenges with money, readjustment to married life after having children, problems in the bedroom, or relationships with in-laws.

Sadly, in many cases, the couples have argued for so long that each partner already knows what the other is going to say before he or she says it. Their arguments have become predictable, yet resolution eludes them. Exhausted, they come to me for professional help.

I listen carefully and take notes, but as a counselor, I'm not as concerned with logic as I am about relationships. I know that in these couples' hearts they want more than a resolution to a disagreement. What they long for is a better relationship.

And why wouldn't they? Deep down, don't we all long for the "happily ever after" that we read about in fairy tales?

There is good news—that dream *is* attainable! In the three decades I've been counseling married couples, I've seen my share of marital struggles. But what I've also seen, time and time again, is the power of God completely transform even the most troubled relationships.

When two people commit to each other and commit to working together—openly, honestly, and without personal agendas—to solve their problems, positive change occurs!

Your marriage may be weeks, months, years, or decades old. It may be strong or struggling, stable or challenging. My prayer is that this book will encourage you, help you and your spouse better understand and communicate with each other, and provide practical takeaways for dealing with whatever conflicts you might face. You just may find that you have a new joy in each other and that you can indeed live and love . . . *happily ever after.*

—Gary Chapman

Part One

EVERYBODY WINS

Solving Conflicts without Arguing

WHEN COUPLES WALK INTO MY OFFICE looking for help, they inevitably come because of unresolved conflicts. They are seeking professional help, but I often sense that they view me more as a judge than a counselor, secretly hoping I will pronounce their spouse guilty of illogical thinking and unreasonable demands.

Because I am a counselor and not a judge, I begin the arduous task of listening to their complaints. They review their well-worn speeches for me, certain that I will see the logic of their respective positions. But I know that behind the frustration of unresolved conflicts is the desire for harmony.

Loving relationships are fostered by understanding, not by winning arguments. So I begin to ask a question such as, "How do you feel when those words come out of his mouth?" or "What happens inside you when you hear her make that comment?" I listen, take notes, and ask more questions, seeking to discover the feelings that lie beneath the conflicts. No conflict will ever be resolved successfully unless we first understand the underlying feelings.

I also ask couples questions about values: "Why is this so important to you?" The answer to that question often reveals the values that created a conflict in the first place. If I don't understand their values, I will never comprehend why they feel so strongly about the issues. As a counselor, I am doing for these couples what they have never learned to do for themselves. I am seeking to understand them. Understanding fosters resolution and harmony.

When I did the research for my book *The Four Seasons of Marriage*, I encountered hundreds of couples who admitted to having a "winter" marriage; that is, their marriages were characterized by anger, disappointment, loneliness, negativity, discouragement, frustration, and hopelessness. Their relationships were detached, cold, harsh, and bitter. They felt alone and betrayed. They had hunkered down in the igloo and hoped for spring, but for many, spring never came.*

Almost all of these couples started their marriages in spring. They had great visions of a happy life together. They intended to make their spouses supremely happy. Life would be beautiful. But some of these couples went straight from spring to winter, skipping summer and fall altogether. Others could look back on a former season in their marriages when the flowers bloomed and the sun was shining. Now they have to admit that the flowers have been dead for a long time.

What brought these couples from the anticipation of spring to the harshness of winter in their marriage relationships? Almost without exception, the process involved unresolved conflicts. Differences emerged, and some of these differences became divisive. The couples had no training in how to resolve conflicts, so they ended up trying to convince their spouses of the validity of their own perspective by means of carefully worded arguments. When the arguments were unconvincing, they repeated them with more intensity and blamed their spouses for being illogical and unreasonable. Eventually, tired of arguing, they withdrew from each other, and the coldness of winter settled over the marriage.

Couples have conflicts in all four seasons of marriage. Those who learn to resolve their conflicts spend more time in spring and summer. Those who fail to resolve conflicts inevitably drift to a fall or winter marriage. These unresolved conflicts create a sense of hopelessness for many couples. They see only two options: remain in the marriage and be miserable, or dissolve the marriage and hope that somewhere in the future they will find someone with whom they are "more compatible."

---

* The four seasons of marriage refer to the "climate" within a marriage relationship, not the "season of life" a couple is in or the literal season in which they were married. As I explain in my book *The Four Seasons of Marriage*, the natural seasons of the year provide us with an apt analogy for the changes that occur in a marriage relationship.

Those who choose the latter option fail to realize that no marriage is without conflict.

I believe there is a third option: Couples who learn how to resolve their conflicts without arguing turn the coldness of winter to the hope and promise of spring. Whatever the season of your marriage—spring, summer, fall, or winter—I believe that your relationship will be strengthened if you can learn the art of resolving conflicts in a positive way.

In this part, "Everybody Wins," my objective is to help you learn how to understand your spouse so that you can resolve conflicts rather than simply win (or lose) arguments. When you win an argument, your spouse is the loser. And we all know it's no fun to live with a loser. When you resolve a conflict, you and your spouse both win and your friendship is strengthened. Good marriages are based on friendship, not on winning arguments.

I wrote this section of the book particularly for the thousands of couples who will never seek the services of a professional counselor but who would desperately like to learn how to resolve conflicts. I have chosen to write in the language of everyday life, not with highly technical terminology or lofty theological concepts. My desire is that I can enhance the quality of your marriage by teaching you how to resolve conflicts without arguing.

1
WHAT'S SO BAD
ABOUT ARGUING?

LET'S START AT THE BEGINNING. In the dating phase of your relationship, chances are that you and your spouse were enamored with each other. You liked what you saw. You enjoyed spending time together. You could talk for hours. He or she was the most wonderful person you could imagine. In short, you were smitten. The courtship may have been long or short, but your positive feelings led you to the marriage altar, where you made a commitment "for better, for worse; for richer, for poorer; in sickness and in health; to love and to cherish, so long as we both shall live." The promises you made to each other were colossal, but at the time you fully intended to keep them. You were caught up in the current of love and it all seemed so effortless. You knew that you and your mate had differences, but you never thought that someday those differences would become divisive.

Unfortunately, the euphoric feelings of being in love have an average life span of two years.[1] Then we come back to the world of reality, where theoretical differences become actual. Some of these differences we come to view as assets. Alan likes to cook; Nancy doesn't. She likes to clear the table and wash dishes; he doesn't. These differences make

7

for a harmonious mealtime experience. Alan and Nancy work together as a team, each using his or her expertise for the benefit of the other. They experience the pleasure of harmony and may even express it with statements such as, "We were meant for each other," "We are a perfect match," "Life could not be better," and "I'm so glad I married you." When differences are viewed as assets, and husbands and wives work together in harmony, life is beautiful.

Other differences may become divisive. Bob likes sports and spends every Monday night watching football. Jill says, "Football is fine for the players, who are making millions of dollars by bashing their bodies against one another, but why would people want to waste their lives watching other people play a stupid game?" Surely the man she married is smarter than that.

"It's just my way of relaxing," Bob says.

"It's just your way of wasting your life," Jill replies.

"You have got to be crazy. Every man in the world watches *Monday Night Football*."

"Only the losers."

"Look, I work five days a week. Give me a break and let me watch football on Monday nights."

"Sure you work. So do I. But how about *us*? Why can't we spend a night together? It's football, baseball, basketball, car races. And if nothing else is on, you watch that dumb wrestling. There's never any time for *us*." Jill starts to cry and walks out of the room. Bob turns off the TV and now the real fight begins. *Monday Night Football* gives way to a verbal boxing match. Before the evening is over, Bob and Jill will argue themselves into an intense state of unhappiness.

What did an evening of argument accomplish? Some might say, "Nothing," but that answer would be naive. The argument accomplished a great deal. For one thing, it created greater emotional distance between a husband and wife who now view each other as an enemy rather than a friend. Each feels the other is unreasonable and, perhaps, irrational. Not only that, but they have also stimulated feelings of hurt, anger, and resentment, and troubling questions are rushing to their minds:

"What has gotten into him?"

"What is her problem?"

"I can't believe the things she said."

"How could he be so cruel?"

"What happened to our love?"

"Have I married the wrong person?"

They may even end up sleeping in separate bedrooms that night, or lying stock still and rigid in the same bed as they silently replay the argument in their minds. Yes, the argument accomplished a great deal. Unfortunately, the accomplishments were all destructive.

Perhaps the only positive thing that came from the argument was that Bob and Jill identified a point of conflict in their marriage. He discovered that she intensely dislikes his watching *Monday Night Football*, and she discovered that he finds great pleasure in watching football on Monday nights. But because the argument did not resolve the conflict, it now stands as an emotional barrier between them that will affect the way they process their relationship. Now, every Monday night, Bob will watch television with a conscious awareness that he is displeasing his wife. And every Monday night, Jill will say to herself, "He loves football more than he loves me. What kind of husband is that?"

We'll come back to Bob and Jill later, but first let me clarify what I mean by the word *argue*. It is a word that is best known in the legal arena, where attorneys present arguments to show that a defendant is either guilty or not guilty. These arguments are statements made by the attorneys based on available evidence. They are designed to appeal to a jury's sense of logic and reason. The implication is clear: Any reasonable person would agree with my argument. On occasion, an attorney may also appeal to the emotions of a jury by presenting aspects of the case designed to stimulate empathy for the attorney's argument.

In a courtroom, arguments are perfectly permissible. In fact, cases could not be tried without arguments from both sides. Both attorneys present evidence and their interpretation of the evidence, seeking to convince the jury that their position is the correct one. Witnesses can be cross-examined, and implications can be challenged. The judicial system is based on the assumption that by means of argument and counter-argument, we are likely to discover the truth about guilt or innocence.

We all know that the cause of justice is not always served in the courtroom, but at least the case is resolved. Defendants who are found not guilty go free. Defendants who are found guilty may pay a fine, be placed on probation, or go to prison, depending on the severity of the case. Or the case might be appealed to a higher court, whereupon more arguments would be presented at each level of appeal until a final judgment is handed down. In every case, somebody wins and somebody loses. Occasionally, one might hear an attorney make a statement such as, "I thought our arguments were good, but apparently the jury was not convinced." Or the winning attorney might say, "We made our case. The arguments were solid, and I think the jury recognized the truth."

When you choose to argue with your spouse, you are electing to use a judicial system to convince your spouse of the truth or validity of your position. Unfortunately, what works fairly well in a court of law works very poorly in a marriage relationship, because there is no judge available to determine whether you or your spouse is "out of order." Arguments quickly become charged with emotion and you may end up yelling, screaming, or crying; pouring out words that assassinate your mate's character; questioning his or her motives; and condemning his or her behavior as unloving, unkind, and undisciplined.

When you argue, your objective is the same as it would be in a courtroom: You want to win the case. You want your side to be vindicated and your spouse to be found guilty of your accusations. This is what is so gravely harmful about arguments. They ultimately lead to one of three results: (1) You win and your spouse loses; (2) you lose and your spouse wins; or (3) you argue to a draw. When an argument ends in a draw, both spouses are losers. Neither one is convinced by the other's arguments, and both parties walk away disappointed, frustrated, hurt, angry, bitter, and often despairing of hope for their marriage.

None of these outcomes is good. The winner may feel good for a few moments or a few days, but eventually, living with the loser becomes unbearable. The loser walks away from an argument like a whipped dog that goes away to lick its wounds. It's not a pretty picture, but it's a common experience. In fact, it's so common that we have a saying for it: "He's in the doghouse." Being in the doghouse means that one spouse has incurred the displeasure of the other and must live at a distance until he or she can once again find the spouse's favor. When conflicts are not resolved and both spouses walk away with stinging words of rebuke and condemnation ringing in their ears, they will typically withdraw from each other emotionally and hope for a better day. If a better day does not come in time, they may eventually seek a "better partner" or resign themselves to the coldness of a winter marriage.

Any victory won by means of an argument will be short lived. The loser will eventually come back with a new argument (or an old argument restated) in an effort to persuade his or her spouse. But the renewed argument will also end with a win, lose, or draw verdict. So you see, arguments never resolve anything; they only reveal conflicts. Once a conflict is revealed, a couple must find a way to resolve it with dignity and with respect for the other person. I believe there are thousands of couples who would like to learn how to resolve conflicts without arguing. That is the purpose of part one, "Everybody Wins."

●　●　●

Putting the Principles into Practice
1. List three issues you and your spouse have argued about within the past year.
2. What do you find most painful about arguments?
3. What have arguments accomplished in your marriage?
4. On a scale of 1–10, how strongly are you motivated to find a better way to resolve conflicts?

2

WHY IS IT SO IMPORTANT TO
RESOLVE CONFLICTS?

CONFLICTS GROW OUT OF OUR UNIQUENESS. Not only are males and females different, but each individual male and female is unique. Part of our uniqueness is genetically based. These genetic differences are most observable in our physical characteristics. No two fingerprints are exactly alike. Each person has unique facial characteristics. This is typically what allows us to recognize one another. Other differences are nonphysical. They sometimes fall into the category of what is commonly called personality differences. Though you can't observe these differences by simply looking at a person, they are just as real. When we use the words *introvert* and *extrovert*, we are describing a personality difference. Our differences also show in the way we perform the necessary tasks of daily life, such as loading a dishwasher, squeezing a tube of toothpaste, or hanging a roll of toilet paper. We have different ideas on how to raise children, how to drive a car, how to spend our leisure time, and a thousand other aspects of life. It is because of our differences that we experience conflicts, but I don't know anyone who would like to eradicate our differences and make us all clones.

The answer to conflict resolution is not in seeking to rid ourselves of our differences but in learning how to make our differences into assets rather than liabilities. The goal of a good marriage is for a couple to learn how to work together as a team, utilizing differences to make life better for both spouses. Resolving conflicts is one method by which we develop this teamwork. Sometimes, we don't even know what our differences are until a conflict arises.

When I use the word *conflict*, I'm not talking about simple disagreements such as her favorite color is blue, his favorite color is yellow. That is not a conflict; it is simply a difference of opinion or preference. Conflicts are disagreements in which both spouses feel strongly and their differing opinions affect their behavior, causing disharmony in the relationship. Now, if the wife's preference for blue and the husband's preference for yellow is applied to painting the bathroom, their strongly held differences might erupt into a conflict in which they try to convince each other to paint the room a particular color. Conflicts can erupt in any area of life: driving, eating, money, sex, in-laws, spirituality, leisure time, and child rearing, to mention a few. Conflicts are not necessarily bad—and they're inevitable in every marriage. For one simple reason, it is impossible to be married and not have conflicts: You are married to a person, and every person is unique. In marriage, our objective is not to get rid of conflicts, but rather to resolve conflicts and thereby learn how to work in harmony, as teammates, toward mutual objectives.

When I mentioned the conflict over what color to paint the bathroom, my mind flashed back to a young couple I counseled several years ago. Jerry and Iris had been married for two years and considered themselves to be in the spring season of their relationship; that is, until they decided to repaint their small apartment. They readily agreed upon the color for each room, until they came to the bathroom. He wanted blue and she wanted green. They were surprised to find themselves arguing passionately over something that they both realized was ultimately quite trivial. Yet they both felt so strongly about their opinions that, after a few rounds of argument, they agreed to go for counseling.

"We're actually ashamed to be here," Iris said. "This seems like such a trivial matter, but it has become very divisive in our marriage. And we don't want to end up fighting over what color to paint the bathroom."

With an apologetic shrug, Jerry said, "I bet you've never had a couple come to see you about what color to paint the bathroom."

I smiled and said, "Well, let's lay it on the table and look at it." Turning to Iris, I said, "I'm sure you've told Jerry all the reasons why you would like the bathroom painted green. So, why don't you share those reasons with me?" She ran through her list and I took notes. When she was finished, I said, "That makes a lot of sense. I can understand why you would feel that way." She seemed relieved.

Next, I turned to Jerry and said, "I'm sure you have equally valid reasons why you would like the bathroom painted blue. So, why don't you share those with me?" When Jerry had shared his reasons, I repeated my response: "What you're saying makes a lot of sense. I can understand why you would like to have the bathroom painted blue." Jerry seemed relieved that I would agree with him, but Iris looked perplexed. She said, "But you agreed with both of us, and that doesn't solve our conflict."

"You are right," I responded. "But I don't think either of you is actually looking for a solution. You are still in the arguing mode and have not yet moved to the resolution mode."

"What do you mean?" Iris said.

"How did you feel when I affirmed your list of reasons for painting the bathroom green?" I asked.

"It felt good," she said. "It felt like you were respecting my ideas."

I looked at Jerry and asked, "How did you feel when I affirmed your ideas as making sense and told you I could understand why you would like to have the bathroom blue?"

"I felt like you were hearing me," he said, "like what I said made sense to you."

"What I did for each of you is what you have not yet done for each other," I said. "You have each argued your own position, but you have not affirmed the other person's ideas." I turned again to Jerry and asked, "Can you honestly say to Iris what I said to her? 'What you're saying makes a lot of sense. I can understand why you would want the bathroom painted green.' I think her ideas made a lot of sense. Do you agree?"

"Yes," he said, "but I like my ideas better."

"That's understandable, but would you be willing to affirm her ideas by saying something similar to what I just said to her?"

"You mean now?"

"Yes, now would be a good time."

Jerry looked at Iris and said, "What you're saying makes sense to me. I can see why you would want the bathroom painted green. And besides that, I love you," he added with a smile. Both Iris and I smiled as well.

"Okay, that's a good start," I said. "And now, Iris, could you honestly make that statement to Jerry?"

She nodded at me and turned to face Jerry. "What you're saying also makes sense. And I can understand why you would want to have the bathroom painted blue. And I love you, too," she said.

"Now I think you are ready to look for a resolution," I said. "You are no longer enemies; you are two friends trying to solve a problem. So, what are the options?"

"We could paint it green," Jerry offered.

"Or, we could paint it blue," Iris said. "Or we could mix blue and green together and paint it aqua."

"I can think of another possibility," I added. "You could paint some walls blue and some walls green."

"I hadn't thought of that," Iris said.

"Neither had I," said Jerry.

"I've never seen a bathroom with two colors," said Iris.

"Neither have I," I interjected, "but it would be unique, wouldn't it? You would probably get lots of comments about it."

"I like that idea," Iris said. "What do you think, Jerry?"

"I think it's a great idea. We will have the most unique bathroom in the development. And when the neighbors ask us why the two colors, we can tell them about our conflict and how we resolved it."

"You might even save them a visit to a counselor," I said.

When a couple learn to resolve conflicts in this manner, when they work together to understand, encourage, and support each other, marriage becomes beautiful. The ancient Hebrew proverb "Two are better than one" becomes a reality.[1] Their deep, emotional need for companionship is met. They are connected with each other emotionally. They approach life with a sense of harmony and together will accomplish far more than either of them could accomplish alone.

On the flip side, unresolved conflicts become barriers to harmony. Life becomes a battlefield and husbands and wives become enemies. By means of verbal bombshells, they fight the same battles over and over again, inflicting injuries that push them even further apart emotionally. After an unrelenting series of unresolved conflicts, a husband might say, "We are just not compatible; we shouldn't have gotten married in the first place. We are like night and day. I don't see how we can ever get it together." His wife might respond, with tears flowing down her face, "How could it come to this when we enjoyed being with each other so much when we were dating? I don't understand where we went wrong." The academic answer to her question is simple: They never learned to resolve conflicts. Perhaps they never anticipated conflict. In the euphoria of the "in love" experience, couples seldom recognize differences and can hardly imagine serious disagreements.

The good news is that any couple can learn to resolve conflicts. I emphasize the word *learn*. The skill of conflict resolution does not come simply with the passing of time. As surely as you can learn to ride a bicycle, drive a car, or use a computer, you can learn how to resolve conflicts. It will require you to change some of your attitudes, learn to listen, treat your spouse with respect, and negotiate solutions, but it can be done. I'm not saying it will be easy, but the rewards for success are phenomenal.

Why is it so important to resolve conflicts? As one husband put it, "It's the difference between heaven and hell. For years, we were both miserable. But when we finally began learning how to resolve conflicts, I could see the light at the end of the tunnel. Now I know what it's like to be married and happy. I can't believe we waited so long to get help."

• • •

Putting the Principles into Practice
1. What are some of the *differences* between you and your spouse that have caused conflicts?

2. In what way might these differences become assets if you learn to resolve conflicts and work as a team?

3. Conflicts that are resolved in a positive way create intimacy. Can you think of a recent conflict that you resolved in a positive way? What made the resolution positive? If a recent conflict wasn't resolved in a positive way, what kept you from reaching a resolution?

3

IT'S ALL ABOUT ATTITUDE

Often the difference between resolving conflicts and arguing is *attitude*. Why do people argue? In one word, *rigidity*. We adopt a rigid attitude and dig in our heels. In essence we're saying, "My way is the right way, and if you don't do it my way, then I will make your life miserable." This is the attitude of an *arguer*, a person who insists on getting his or her own way.

Conflict resolvers have a different attitude. They say, in effect, "I'm sure we can work this out in a way that will be positive for both of us. Let's think about it together." Spouses who adopt this attitude are looking for a win-win resolution.

Let's revisit Bob and Jill from chapter 1, who were arguing about *Monday Night Football*. Obviously, each of them saw the other's position as unreasonable. They created a miserable evening by arguing and were left with a huge barrier between them. But with a different attitude, the outcome could have been totally different.

What if Jill had chosen an attitude of accommodation? She might have said, "Bob, I know you really enjoy *Monday Night Football*. It's a way for you to unwind from the stresses of the day. On the other hand,

I'm beginning to feel lonely and shut out of your life. That's not a feeling I want to have. So, at your convenience, I'd like for us to talk about it and look for a solution. I'm sure we can work it out. I love you very much, and I don't want this to come between us."

If Bob had chosen a conflict resolver's attitude, he might have responded, "Honey, you're right. I really do enjoy *Monday Night Football*, but I also value our relationship more than anything in the world. I want to meet your needs, and I'm sure we can find a solution that will be good for both of us. Why don't we talk about it at halftime?" The evening could have been pleasant for both Bob and Jill, and they likely would have found a solution that met their needs.

An Attitude of Respect

Finding a winning solution begins by choosing to believe that such a solution is possible and that you and your spouse are smart enough to discover it. It begins when you recognize that you are married to another human being who is created in the image of God and is thus extremely valuable. It begins when you choose to treat your spouse as a person of worth. Starting with an attitude of respect predisposes that a couple will find a resolution to their conflict rather than put each other down with condemning arguments.

We recognize that all human beings are unique and that our differences do not diminish our worth. Thus, we choose to treat our spouses with dignity and respect. This means we will not seek to convince our spouses to be like us, to agree with all our opinions. We will give them the freedom to think and feel differently, and we will always respect their thoughts and feelings. When we choose an attitude of respect toward our spouses, we are less likely to allow ourselves to get caught up uttering condemning, harsh, cruel words.

Remember Jerry and Iris, who were having difficulty resolving their conflict about what color to paint the bathroom? What they discovered in the course of our counseling together was the calming effect of respecting each other's opinions. Both Jerry and Iris articulated their opinions very clearly, and they genuinely felt that their opinions were more valid than their spouse's. It was not until they expressed respect for each other's ideas that they moved from *attack mode* to *resolution mode*. As long as couples put down each other's ideas and judge them as less worthy, they are not likely to find a satisfactory resolution. But when they choose an attitude of respecting each other's ideas, even though they disagree with them, they create a climate in which they can look for a resolution *together*.

An Attitude of Love

Another characteristic of conflict resolvers is that they choose an attitude of love. As one wife expressed it, "I am committed to my husband's well-being. I want to do everything I can to enrich his life and help him accomplish his objectives in life." If her husband has the same attitude toward her, then together they will find resolutions to their conflicts that will be beneficial to both of them. Selfishness is the opposite of love. Selfish people seek to impose their will on others. What is important to them is "getting my way." Lovers, on the other hand, seek to do those things that are most helpful for their spouses.

I saw an attitude of love graphically demonstrated when I visited John and Betsy. They had recently moved to our city and had visited our church. During our conversation, I discovered that they had lost a three-year-old son in a tragic boating accident a year earlier. They had two other children, who were now five and seven, and they told me that Betsy was now pregnant.

"Being a marriage counselor, Gary, I think you will find this interesting," Betsy said. "Our decision to have another child did not come easily. John really did not want another child, but I was strongly in favor of having another one."

I looked at John and he said, "The pain was so deep when we lost Josh that I couldn't bear the thought of going through that again. I was happy with the two children we had left and wanted to invest my time with them."

"I can understand that," I said.

Betsy continued, "I felt that my loss was so deep that I could never find healing without another baby. It was a real conflict between the two of us."

"So how did you resolve the issue?" I asked.

"We both respected each other's position," said John. "I knew that she really wanted to have another baby, and she knew that I didn't. And we knew that each of us was sincere."

"We prayed for God's wisdom," Betsy said. "One day while I was praying, God brought to my mind the story of Abraham offering his son Isaac on the altar to God. I knew that Abraham did that because of his deep love for God. Then a question came to my mind: 'Do I love John enough to offer my as-yet-unconceived child on the altar?' I've never loved anyone like I love John. He is a wonderful husband and father. I knew that my answer was yes. So I told John about my prayer and what God had brought to my mind, and I wanted him to know that I was willing to not have another child because I loved him so much."

"I cried like a baby when she told me that," John said. "Maybe it was the pent-up grief within me, but I sobbed uncontrollably for thirty minutes. I felt so overwhelmed by Betsy's love. I didn't say anything that night. I just cried and hugged Betsy. The next day, I went to work and reflected on what had happened. I was overcome by a deep sense of my love for Betsy, and I knew in my heart that I could never deprive her of having another child. I went home that night and told her that I wanted us to have another child. She was confused at first, because she knew how adamant I had been, but before the evening was over, she realized that my heart had sincerely changed and I wanted us to have another baby. So, as you can imagine," he said, "we're excited about the baby that is now inside Betsy's womb."

I nodded affirmingly as my eyes filled with tears. Finally, when I was able to speak, I said, "I don't know when I have ever seen such a deep demonstration of love. I think God has great plans for this child."

Love does not demand its own way but seeks the well-being of the one loved. It is an attitude of love that moves us toward resolving conflicts. The attitude of demanding our own way leads only to arguments.

An Attitude of Togetherness

In the world of sports, success depends on teamwork. Whether in football, basketball, or auto racing, every team member has a job. When team members coordinate their efforts, they are more likely to meet their goals. Marriage is a team of two: a man and a woman. From a Christian perspective, the purpose of marriage is to process life together for the glory of God. Marriage is not about "me and my happiness." Marriage is about two people discovering and accomplishing God's plans for their lives.

A husband and wife bring an assortment of abilities to their marriage. When they see themselves as teammates, they realize that their game plan is not to compete against each other but to cooperate. It is this attitude of togetherness that creates a climate in which conflicts can be resolved. Conflicts are inevitable, but if a couple is committed to working together as a team, they can tackle the problem and not each other. An attitude of togetherness says, "We will not let this defeat us. We will find an answer."

Chuck and Rhonda had a major conflict over the behavior of their two-year-old son, Caleb. Chuck thought that the best way to discipline Caleb was to spank him. After all, that is what his own parents had done with him, and he had turned out all right. Rhonda thought that spanking was barbaric. She never remembered being spanked by her parents. My first question was "Do you want Caleb to have two parents or one?"

"Well, two," said Chuck as Rhonda nodded affirmingly.

"Of course," I continued. "Do you want each of those two parents to do what is right in his or her own eyes, or do you want them to have the same game plan?"

"We've got to get on the same page," Chuck said. "What we've been doing is not working. It is destroying our marriage."

"It tears me apart when he spanks Caleb," Rhonda said.

"I don't want him to grow up to be irresponsible," Chuck said.

"I don't either," Rhonda replied.

"The two of you seem to have the same goal in mind," I observed. "You both want Caleb to grow up to be a responsible young man." Chuck and Rhonda both nodded in agreement. "The conflict lies in the method of reaching that goal. Can we agree that you are teammates and not enemies?"

"Lately we've been acting like enemies," Rhonda said, "but I think both of us want to be teammates."

"It's fundamental that the two of you affirm that attitude," I said, "because if you continue to be enemies, Caleb will likely grow up to be irresponsible. Now, I'd like for you to hold hands and repeat after me . . ."

They both seemed a little shocked, but Chuck reached over and took Rhonda's hand.

"We are teammates," I said.

Chuck and Rhonda repeated, "We are teammates."

"Do you believe that?" I asked.

"Yes," they said in unison.

"Then let's get started."

I gave them a reading assignment for the following week. They were to explore how other couples feel about spanking and to discover what child-development experts have written on the subject. After Chuck and Rhonda did their research and we discussed their findings at some length, Chuck came to understand that there is more than one way to discipline a child, and Rhonda learned that spanking administered in the context of love is not as barbaric as she had assumed. Ultimately, they decided on three levels of response to Caleb's disobedient behavior: Level 1 was verbal reprimand; Level 2 was loss of privileges; Level 3 was spanking. They agreed to observe which type of discipline seemed to work best in changing Caleb's behavior. They also agreed that they would continue reading and would attend a parenting class for parents of preschoolers that was offered at their church. It was the attitude of togetherness that provided the foundation on which Chuck and Rhonda were able to build a positive plan of discipline for their son. Without this attitude, they might still have been arguing when Caleb was twelve.

In summary, it is an attitude of respect, love, and togetherness that leads to resolving conflicts. The good news is that we can—and do—choose our attitudes daily. Unfortunately, our default mode is selfishness, which leads us to proclaim, "My way is the right way." By nature, we are all self-centered, and that is why arguments are so common in marriage.

However, with the help of God, we can choose an attitude of respect, love, and togetherness. Many of the couples I have worked with have found it helpful to put the following statements on an index card and post it in a prominent place in order to help them choose a winning attitude each day:

- I choose to respect my spouse's ideas, even when I disagree with them.
- I choose to love my spouse and do everything I can to help him or her today.
- I choose to believe that my spouse and I are teammates and that with God's help we can find solutions to our conflicts.

Choosing an attitude of respect, love, and togetherness leads us to listen carefully to one another. In the next chapter, we'll discuss how to listen empathetically.

•   •   •

Putting the Principles into Practice
1. Memorize the following and use it with your spouse the next time you have a conflict: "I'm sure we can work this out in a way that will be positive for both of us. Let's talk about it. What are your ideas?"
2. Expressing respect for your spouse's ideas creates a positive atmosphere. Memorize the following statement and use it with your spouse the next time you have a conflict: "What you are saying makes sense to me. Now, let me share my thoughts and see if they make sense to you."
3. Selfish people seek to impose their ideas on others. Loving people seek to do what is best for others. Rate yourself by placing an *X* on the line where it best indicates your attitude toward your spouse:

    Selfish _____ _____ Loving

4. Having an attitude of respect, love, and togetherness makes it possible to find win-win solutions to conflicts. How open are you to changing your attitudes?

4

CONFLICT RESOLUTION REQUIRES LISTENING

By its very nature, conflict reveals that two people have differing opinions and that they feel strongly about their own perspective. Along with every conflict comes a flag waving in the wind that reads, "Take time to listen." Conflicts cannot be resolved without empathetic listening. I use the word *empathetic* because most couples believe they are listening to each other, when in fact they are simply reloading their verbal guns. Empathetic listening means seeking to understand what the other person is thinking and feeling. It is putting ourselves in the other person's shoes and trying to look at the world through his or her eyes. It means that we have laid aside our verbal guns in favor of truly understanding the other person's point of view. Instead of focusing on how we are going to respond to what the other person is saying, we focus entirely on hearing what the other person is saying.

Affirm the Importance of Your Relationship

Empathetic listening begins when you affirm the importance of your marriage relationship. When conflicts arise, set the stage for resolution by carefully stating your objective: "I want to hear what you are saying because I know it is important to you and I value our relationship." I suggest that you write this sentence on an index card and read it out loud to yourself once a day until you memorize it, so that when a conflict arises, you will be ready to state your objective. Affirming the importance of your marriage relationship is a way of consciously choosing to put yourself in the role of *empathetic listener*—one who is seeking to discover your spouse's thoughts and feelings. If you don't consciously remind yourself that you are a listener, then you will likely revert to being an arguer.

I remember David, who said to me, "Your comment about choosing to be a listener was the most helpful thing for me. I went home and made myself a sign out of construction paper that read, 'I AM A LISTENER.' Whenever JoAnne and I have a conflict, I put the sign around my neck to remind myself of what I'm doing. My wife always smiles and says, 'I hope it's true.' The sign helps me remember to listen before I speak." By use of this simple device, David trained himself to be an empathetic listener.

Most people will need some training to become good listeners, because we are *responders* by nature. One research project found that the average person listens for only seventeen seconds before interrupting to give their own opinion. Such quick responses are what trigger arguments.

Natalie and Hunter had been married for fifteen years when they came to me for counseling. Natalie was on the verge of leaving the relationship. When I asked about the nature of the problem, she responded, "He never listens to me. All we ever do is argue. Nothing ever gets settled. I'm sick of arguing."

When I turned to Hunter, he said, "We don't argue all the time. We have some good times—in fact, more good times than bad times. It's just that when she gets upset about something, she wants me to agree with her. But I don't always agree with her, and so we argue. I don't think we argue any more than other couples."

"I don't care about other couples!" Natalie said. "I care about *us*. You don't even know who I am, because you don't listen long enough to find out. You are always right. You don't ever have time to hear my opinions. How could you possibly disagree with them?"

As I glanced back at Hunter, he said, "This must be more serious than I realized."

"What did you hear Natalie saying?" I asked.

"I heard her saying that I don't know who she is. And maybe she's right."

"Would you like to know who she is?" I inquired.

"I don't know," he said. "I might hear some things I don't want to hear."

"But if they are true," I probed, "would you rather hear them or would you rather have Natalie clam up in silence and never share with you what she's thinking and feeling?"

"I'd rather hear them," he said.

"Then why don't we use the next ten minutes as a listening session. You and I will listen to Natalie as she describes for us how she views your relationship. Neither of us will respond to anything she says. We will simply try to understand what is going on in her mind. You may not like what she says, and you may not agree with what she says, but for the moment, we're simply trying to find out what she's thinking and what she's feeling. I may ask her a question or two to stimulate her thinking, but I don't want you to say anything, Hunter. I want you just to listen."

For the next ten minutes, Hunter listened while Natalie spoke. It was the first of many "listening sessions" we were to have over the next three months. Through this process, Hunter took the first step in resolving their conflicts.

In the beginning stages of learning to listen, couples often find it helpful to establish a specific amount of time for each spouse to be the listener. Once they have developed the art of listening, they can remove the artificial time restraints, and the listening sessions will become more conversational. But they shouldn't jump the gun; first they must learn to listen.

Clarify What You Hear Your Spouse Saying

The second step in empathetic listening is to clarify what you hear your spouse saying. This is the classic technique of "active listening," in which you simply repeat to your spouse what you think he or she has said, without judging it to be good or bad. David, the husband who wore the "I am a listener" sign, said to his wife, JoAnne, "What I hear you saying is that you feel disappointed because I don't take the garbage out every day without your asking. I hear you saying that you wish I would take that responsibility seriously and that when you have to remind me, it makes you feel like you're my mother. And you don't want to be my mother; you want to be my lover. Actually, you didn't say that last part, but I get the feeling that's what you are saying. Is that right?"

JoAnne responded, "Yes, you're right. I do want to be your lover, and it's difficult when I have to remind you every day to do such a simple chore. I've got so much to do, especially since the baby came. That's just one thing I wish I didn't have to worry about."

David said, "I hear you saying that you feel overworked since the baby came. And if I would consistently take out the garbage without your asking, it would lighten your load."

"That's right," JoAnne said. "It's a little thing, but it means a lot to me."

"I can understand that," David said, "and I can do that. What time of the day would you like me to take it out?"

"Right after dinner each evening," JoAnne said, "before you get involved in other activities. If you wait till morning, it becomes smelly, and I don't like to start my day with a full trash can."

"Okay, I'll do it," David said. "I didn't realize it was that important to you."

"I've been telling you for months," JoAnne said.

"I know you have," David said, "but I guess I never listened. The next time you get upset with me, remind me to put on my listening sign so that I can really hear what you're saying."

David used clarifying questions to make sure he understood what JoAnne desired. Without asking these questions, he might never have known what his wife was truly thinking and feeling. He also learned why she had this desire and how it affected her emotions toward him. Once he clearly understood her thoughts and feelings, he was able to make an intelligent, considerate response. Taking the trash out on a daily basis without being asked was a small price to pay to enhance his marriage relationship. If David hadn't used these clarifying questions, he and JoAnne might have entered into an extended argument over the pros and cons of who should take out the garbage. The argument would have left them estranged, hurt, and resentful. Instead, empathetic listening brought their conflict to a healthy resolution.

Give Your Spouse Your Undivided Attention

The third aspect of empathetic listening is that you give your spouse your undivided attention. Don't try to watch television, read a magazine, or drink a Pepsi while listening to your spouse. One of the purposes of empathetic listening is to make sure that your spouse knows that he or she has been heard. When you lay everything else aside and give your spouse your undivided attention, you communicate that your relationship is more important to you than anything else. Without saying a word, you tell your spouse that you want to know what he or she is thinking and feeling. Focused attention is even more effective if you make eye contact with your spouse, nod your head affirmingly at appropriate moments, refuse to fiddle with a pencil or look out the window, and—whatever you do—don't walk out of the room while your spouse is talking.

If you're like some people, giving your spouse your undivided attention will be extremely difficult. I remember a woman who said to me, "I only have a couple of hours after dinner, after the children are in bed. I have a thousand things to do. If my husband has a problem, he wants me to sit down and listen to him. I tell him I can listen to him while folding the clothes. No, he wants me to look at him while I'm listening. Come to think of it, why doesn't *he* fold the clothes while I'm giving the baby a bath? Then maybe I could give him my full attention." For this wife, the sheer volume of household work made it difficult for her to give her husband her undivided attention.

On the other hand, many men pride themselves on being able to do three things at once. As one husband said, "I'm wired for multitasking. I can't imagine doing only one thing. When my wife insists that I sit down and listen to her, I feel like I'm in a straitjacket, like I'm wasting time. I could easily be listening to her while reading the report that I need to give the next day. It makes her furious when I try to do that. But I can honestly hear everything she's saying and read my report at the same time." This husband is being totally honest, but he exhibits little understanding of the dynamics of human relationships.

Here's what undivided attention communicates: "You are the most important person in my life. I want to hear what you are thinking and feeling because I value our relationship."

On the other hand, here's what listening while doing something else communicates: "You are one of my many interests. Please continue to talk; I'm listening." Distracted listeners are often surprised when their spouse stops talking, walks out of the room, goes to the bedroom, and starts crying. Empathetic listening requires that you give your spouse your undivided attention.

Share Your Own Ideas Only When Your Spouse Feels Understood

The fourth characteristic of empathetic listening is that you never share your own perspective until your spouse has assured you that he or she feels understood. The most common mistake couples make in communication is responding before they have the full picture. This inevitably leads to arguments. Listen for as long as your spouse has something to say. Use clarifying questions to make sure you understand what he or she is thinking and feeling. When your spouse assures you that he or she feels that you understand, it is time to give your own perspective. Often, determining this right time is best done with a series of questions:

"Do you feel that I understand what you are saying?" If your spouse says no, then let him or her continue explaining.

"Do you think I understand how you feel?" Again, if not, then let your spouse explain more fully.

When the answer to both questions is yes, then you can ask, "Can I tell you what I'm thinking and feeling?" If your spouse says yes, then you can proceed to share your perspective. Your spouse now becomes the listener.

The fact that your spouse now feels heard and understood makes it easier to shift from the arguing mode to the listening mode. Now your spouse can honestly say to you, "I'm ready to hear you because I feel as if you understand my concerns. I know that you have a perspective that is equally as valid as mine, and I want to hear it." Your spouse now gives you his or her undivided attention, repeating what you say and asking clarifying questions until you feel heard and understood.

Empathetic listening creates a positive emotional climate. Arguing creates a negative emotional climate. Conflicts are resolved more easily when the climate is friendly rather than adversarial.

Had David failed to practice empathetic listening when JoAnne first mentioned her concerns about the garbage, he might have said, "Okay, I'll take the garbage out. Don't bring it up again." The conversation would have been over, but the conflict would not have been resolved. It was because he fully heard her perspective before he responded that they were able to resolve their conflict easily. When people respond too quickly, they often respond to the wrong issue. They need to listen long enough—and ask enough clarifying questions—to discover what is really at the heart of their spouse's complaints.

Many times, the real conflict is not about football or which color to paint the bathroom walls but about personality differences or unmet emotional needs. For example, people with a controlling personality will feel emotionally unsettled if things are not done in a timely manner and with some degree of perfection. On the other hand, people with low self-esteem may feel condemned if their spouse expresses strong expectations. Feeling condemned may lead either to "fighting back," trying to prove their worth, or to withdrawing in silent suffering.

Empathetic listening allows us to hear what is going on beyond or underneath the words that are being said. Through empathetic listening, we seek to understand the feelings that lie behind the words and to discover why the other person feels so strongly about the issue. Understanding creates an emotional climate where conflicts can be resolved.

When Natalie told Hunter, "You don't know who I am," she finally got his attention. After Hunter learned the skills of empathetic listening, he said to me, "This has been the most insightful experience of my life. No one ever taught me how to listen. Why didn't I have a class on this in college? It could have saved me fifteen years of arguing. I can't believe how much pain I've put Natalie through over these years by not listening to her. I had come to believe that arguing was just part of life. I assumed that all couples argued as much as we did. It's amazing how close I feel to her now. I really feel like I know her. And what's more important, *she* feels like I know her." Hunter had learned the awesome power of empathetic listening.

Most of us have had little experience in empathetic listening. Thus, it will take effort and time to change argumentative patterns of communication. Empathetic listening requires a change of mind-set. It is a conscious choice to hear your spouse clearly. You create an atmosphere for empathetic listening when you say to your spouse, "I want to hear what you are saying because I know it is important to you and I value our relationship."

Having stated your objective, give your spouse your undivided attention. Put the book down, turn the TV off, and lay the pencil aside. When your spouse stops talking, repeat what you have heard him or her say, making clarifying statements such as, "What I hear you saying is . . ." or "I think what you said is . . ." "Is that right?" Continue to ask clarifying questions until your spouse assures you that he or she feels heard and understood. Although this approach to listening may be difficult to learn, it is extremely rewarding because it will lead you and your spouse to greater understanding.

• • •

Putting the Principles into Practice
1. Memorize this statement and use it with your spouse the next time you have a conversation or a conflict: "I want to hear what you are saying because I know it is important to you and I value our relationship."
2. Consider making a sign that reads: "I am a listener." Pick it up and hold it while your spouse is talking.
3. Try this response the next time your spouse shares an idea: "What I hear you saying is _____. Is that correct?"
4. When your spouse starts talking, put down the magazine or turn off the television, and give your spouse your undivided attention. Look into his or her eyes as you listen.

5. Do not share your own perspective until you get a positive response to these three questions:

   • "Do you feel as if I understand what you are saying?"

   • "Do you feel as if I respect your ideas?"

   • "Is this a good time for me to share my thoughts?"

6. After each conversation, using the scale of 1–10, rate yourself on how well you followed suggestions 1–5 above.

5

LISTENING LEADS TO UNDERSTANDING

JULIE AND BRIAN WERE ARGUING about going to see her parents.

"We were just down there two weeks ago," Brian said.

"I know," said Julie, "but Sunday is my mother's birthday."

"Then send her a card," said Brian.

"I don't believe you!" said Julie. "You are the most selfish person I have ever met."

"Well then, you haven't met very many people," Brian replied. "I don't know any man who wants to visit his in-laws every two weeks."

"I'm not asking you to go every two weeks," Julie said as she started sobbing and walked out of the room.

Brian and Julie have never learned how to listen empathetically. But now let's imagine that they had read the previous chapter and were now trying to be empathetic listeners. The conversation might have gone like this:

"Why do you want to go to your parents' again this weekend? We were just there two weeks ago."

"I know, but this Sunday is my mother's birthday."

"Are birthdays a big deal in your family?"

"Yes, they are. My sister and I have given Mom a birthday dinner every year since we were five years old. I still remember that first year, when Dad helped us make cupcakes and decorate them."

"So your sister is going to be there on Saturday?"

"Oh, yes, she wouldn't miss it."

"Is her husband also coming?"

"Unless he has to work. Some years, he has to work and can't get away."

"Do you want me to go with you? Or would you rather go by yourself?"

"I want you to go with me, Brian. It's a family thing and I want you to be a part of it."

"Okay, on a scale of one to ten, how strongly do you want me to go?"

"Ten."

"Okay, then I'll go."

"Oh, Brian, I love you so much."

Why did things turn out so differently in the second scenario? Because Brian listened empathetically before he responded. His listening led him to understand how important the birthday party was to Julie and how strongly she wanted him to participate.

On the other hand, Brian also has opinions. He wants his relationship with Julie to be authentic, so he says to her, "Would you like to know why I was hesitant at first about going to your parents' this Saturday?"

"I assume it was because we were just there two weeks ago."

"That's part of it, but there's more to it than that. Would you like to hear it?" (Brian is trying to help Julie get into the listening mode.)

"Yes," Julie says as she sits down on the couch and looks at him.

"I was invited to play on the all-star team of the church softball league. I was really excited about it—you know how much I love to play softball—but when I realized how important this was to you, I felt that being with you was more important than playing softball."

"Oh, Brian, now I love you even more. I can't believe you are willing to give up the all-star team in order to be with my family."

After a moment of reflection, Julie asks, "What time is the softball game?"

"Two o'clock. Why do you ask?"

"It just occurred to me that maybe you could play in the game and come to Mother's later. Dinner isn't until six. You might be a little late, but that would be all right. On a scale of one to ten," Julie says with a smile, "how strongly do you feel about playing in the game?"

"Do you really want to know?"

"Certainly," Julie says, still smiling.

"About a nine."

"Then, let's do it that way. I don't mind at all if you get there a little late."

"But that would mean driving two cars," Brian says. "And we wouldn't be together driving down and back."

"We'll make up for it when we get home."

"You're serious, aren't you?"

"Yes, I am."

"Julie, you are incredible. I love you so much."

In this scenario, it was Julie's efforts to listen empathetically that led her to understand how important the softball game was to Brian. Both Brian and Julie displayed an attitude of respect, love, and togetherness, which brought them to a win-win resolution of their conflict.

Many couples argue about conflicts rather than resolving them because they never come to understand each other's point of view. They spend their energy promoting their own perspectives rather than seeking to understand their spouse's perspective. Understanding involves the following four objectives, all of which can be obtained by empathetic listening:

1. *Know what your spouse is really saying.* This is not as easy as it sounds. In fact, one of the most common mistakes that couples make is responding to what they *think* their spouse is saying, without actually *listening* to what is being said. For example, Brian's initial interpretation was that Julie wanted to visit her parents a couple of times a month. This misunderstanding stimulated negative emotions

inside of him. However, he had not yet heard what Julie was actually saying. She was talking about a birthday dinner, a long tradition, and family values. Had Brian listened empathetically, he would have heard and understood what was really important to Julie.

2. *"Hear" your spouse's feelings.* In his initial encounter with Julie, had Brian been listening, he would have heard his wife expressing the emotions of hurt, disappointment, and anger. But because he was not listening empathetically, Brian did not hear these emotions. His failure to listen left Julie sobbing and the conflict unresolved.

3. *Discover what is truly important to your spouse—and why.* Had Brian listened empathetically, he would have discovered why it was so important to Julie to go to her mother's birthday dinner. It was a long-standing tradition, accompanied by warm feelings of family togetherness. Brian would have discovered that Julie's desire for him to be with her at this celebration hinged on the value she placed on family gatherings. Conversely, had Julie listened empathetically to Brian, she would have discovered why playing in the softball tournament was so important to him. It was an honor to be selected and had strong ties with his sense of self-esteem and his commitment to the team.

4. *Determine how strongly your spouse feels about his or her perspective.* Using a 1–10 scale is an easy way to determine how strongly your spouse feels about an issue. In fact, this is often the easiest place to begin when you are trying to understand your spouse. If you and your spouse are discussing Christmas shopping, for example, you might ask, "On a scale of 1–10, how strongly do you feel about my going shopping with you?" If your spouse responds with a number between 7 and 10 and your own desire is between 1 and 4, then you know that you must quickly shift into listening mode if you are going to resolve this conflict.

You might then ask, "When would you like to go shopping? How long would you like me to shop with you? What would you like my role to be in the process?"

These questions are designed to determine what your spouse truly desires. Then you might ask, "How would you feel if I decided not to go shopping with you?" or "How would you feel if I decided to go shopping with you?" The answers to these questions will reveal not only your spouse's feelings but also what impact your decision will have on your relationship.

Next, you can ask, "Why is my going shopping with you so important?" You may discover that the reason your spouse values your participation is that he or she sees it as a measure of the health of your marriage. Perhaps your spouse's parents always did their Christmas shopping together and it was an event that communicated, "We enjoy being together." On the other hand, you might discover that the reason it is so important to your spouse is that he or she feels very ill-prepared to select gifts for your parents and really needs your input. There may be any number of reasons why your spouse considers your participation so important. It is by means of empathetic listening that you will discover not only what your spouse is saying but also how he or she is feeling and why this issue is so important.

The sense of being understood and affirmed by one's spouse is a major step in creating an atmosphere where conflicts can be resolved. "I hear what you are saying, and it makes a lot of sense to me" is a million-dollar statement in resolving conflicts. It is what everyone longs to hear in conflict situations. We all want to be understood and affirmed.

Empathetic listening is the exact opposite of the argument approach, in which both parties are more interested in asserting their own opinions than in taking time to understand what the other is saying, thinking, and feeling. Asserting one's own opinion without first listening comes across as rejection and condemnation, which foster defensive feelings and resentment. That is why arguments lead to emotional distance. Empathetic listening, on the other hand, leads to understanding and affirmation.

Couples are not likely to resolve conflicts in a positive way if they do not understand each other. Understanding comes from listening and asking clarifying questions. When husbands and wives understand what their spouses are saying, why an issue is so important to them, how strongly they feel about it, and the emotions that accompany their desires, only then can they have intelligent and loving responses. Spouses who love each other by taking time to understand each other will be able to resolve conflicts in a healthy way.

• • •

Putting the Principles into Practice
1. Many couples argue about conflicts rather than resolve them because they never come to understand each other's point of view. Here are four questions to help you understand your spouse:

   • What is my spouse saying?

   • What is my spouse feeling?

   • Why is this important to my spouse?

   • On a scale of 1–10, how strongly does my spouse desire this?

2. Once you understand your spouse, you have an opportunity to give an intelligent and loving response. How intelligent and how loving was your response in your most recent conflict with your spouse?

6

UNDERSTANDING
LEADS TO RESOLUTION

Throughout this part of the book, we have indicated that conflicts are inevitable. There are no marriages without conflicts. However, conflicts need not be divisive. If you choose a "win-win attitude" and you sincerely listen to your spouse, you will come to understand what he or she is thinking, feeling, and desiring. You will also discover why your spouse has these opinions and how strong these opinions are. With this information, you are now in a position to resolve conflicts in a positive manner. You are ready to ask the question, "How can we resolve this conflict so that both of us will feel loved and appreciated?" The answer to this question will lead to positive resolutions. By asking this question, you are not demanding your own way and you are not seeking to manipulate your spouse into agreeing with you—you are seeking to find a resolution that will make both you and your spouse feel good.

A husband and wife who understand and love each other can focus on finding a mutually agreeable solution rather than condemning each other. They are friends, not enemies. Together they will find a positive solution.

Typically, resolutions fall into one of three categories: meeting in the middle, meeting on one side, or meeting later.

Meeting in the Middle

In this approach, the couple finds a solution approximately halfway between each of their original desires. Both spouses give up some of what they want, but both also gain some of what they want. Some people have called this approach "reaching a compromise." However, a compromise focuses on what both parties have given up. I prefer to focus on what they have gained. "Meeting in the middle" communicates to me that both parties have agreed on a solution that they feel is mutually loving and beneficial.

I met John and Brenda in Mobile, Alabama. They approached me after a seminar, and John said very excitedly, "This is our second time to attend your seminar. We attended last year when you were in Montgomery, and today we brought six couples from our church. We found it so helpful that we wanted to expose them to your teaching."

"Give me a specific example of how you found the seminar helpful," I said. Here is the story they shared with me:

John and Brenda knew that their old car, which had 215,000 miles on it, would soon need to be replaced. John wanted to buy a new car, and Brenda wanted to buy a used one. They realized they had a conflict over the issue one night when John came home and said, "I stopped by the Buick place today and priced some new cars."

"Why did you do that?" Brenda said. "We can't afford a new car."

"New cars are not much more expensive than used cars," John said. "Besides, they are much more reliable."

"Not if we get a late-model used car that has a warranty," said Brenda.

"I don't want to buy somebody else's junk," said John.

"I'm not talking about junk. I'm talking about finding a good, low-mileage used car," said Brenda.

With each exchange of words, the volume of their responses increased. When John realized that they were screaming at each other, he said, "I do believe that we have a conflict. I seem to remember hearing something about conflict resolution in that seminar we attended last month. Maybe we need to pull out our notes and see what was said."

"Better yet," Brenda said, "I've just finished reading the book *The Four Seasons of Marriage*. There's a chapter in there on empathetic listening. I remember thinking as I read it, *That's a chapter we need to discuss with each other*."

"I don't want us to get into a conflict over whether we should read the chapter or look at the notes," John said, smiling. "So why don't you review the chapter and I'll review the notes, and tomorrow night we'll share what we have learned about conflict resolution. I'm sure we're not the only ones who have wrestled with this topic, and I certainly don't think either one of us wants to get into a fight over this."

"Good idea," Brenda said. "But I don't want us to get ourselves in debt and do something we can't afford to do."

"I think we both agree on that," said John. "Obviously we don't agree on the question of new car vs. used car. But as smart as we are, I'm sure we can figure it out." He reached out and gave Brenda a hug.

"Okay," I said. "I can't wait to hear how you resolved the conflict."

Brenda spoke first. "Well, first we shared with each other some of the key ideas we had learned about how to listen. Then we tried to apply them to our situation. After we listened to each other, I realized that John had always wanted to have a new car. He had driven used cars all his life and had a number of experiences where he missed appointments and was inconvenienced by car troubles."

"And I learned," John said, "that Brenda was genuinely concerned about our finances. I didn't realize that she was living under so much pressure. That was one of the good things that came out of our listening to each other. Her dad had always bought reliable used cars, and she never remembered a car breaking down. I guess my experience was with older used cars that weren't very reliable."

"So how did you finally resolve the conflict?" I asked.

"After a lot of listening," John said, "and checking several options, we decided not to buy a car at all."

I'm sure John saw the puzzled look on my face, because he smiled as he continued, "We decided to lease a new car for three years."

"The monthly payments were just about the same," said Brenda, "and it was a payment that we both felt we could live with."

John continued, "At the end of three years, we hope to be in a better financial position, and then we can revisit the issue of buying a new car or a used car."

John and Brenda illustrate a positive approach to resolving conflicts by "meeting in the middle." John got to drive a new car and Brenda got a monthly payment that she felt they could afford. Both ended up feeling good about the resolution, and both felt loved and affirmed by the other. Many conflicts can be resolved by this "meeting in the middle" approach to conflict resolution.

Meeting on One Side

This approach involves the same process of empathetic listening and affirming each other's ideas and feelings as meeting in the middle. But the final resolution is made by one spouse choosing to meet the other on the other spouse's side.

Betty and Mark illustrate this approach to conflict resolution. They came to my office because they had been arguing for three months over Betty's desire to go back and finish her undergraduate college degree. She had dropped out of college after her junior year when she and Mark got married. They had moved cross-country at the request of his employer. Now, nine years later, they were back in their hometown. Mark had a good job, and they had two children, the youngest of whom had just started first grade. Betty now felt that this was an ideal time for her to go back and finish her degree. Mark felt strongly that for Betty to go back to school would be a waste of time, energy, and money. "I'm making all the money we need," he said. "She doesn't need to go back and get her degree. She doesn't really want to work, anyway, so what's the purpose in getting a degree? The kids need help with their homework, and I don't really have time to do that. It's going to put a lot of pressure on our family."

"He doesn't understand how important it is for me to finish my degree," Betty said. "All my brothers and sisters finished college, and I'm the only one who doesn't have a degree. It will take only a year, and

I can still help the children with their homework. Besides, Mark could help if he were willing to give up a little TV."

It was obvious to me that Betty and Mark not only had a conflict but also had spent considerable time arguing and were now at the point of throwing barbs at each other. It took a number of counseling sessions to help them come to respect each other's desires and to treat each other with dignity and love. Eventually, they learned to listen to each other empathetically. Mark was finally able to say, "I understand why it is so important for Betty to get her degree. I guess I was looking only at the financial side and the impact it would have on our family. I was not looking at her emotional need to finish her degree. I realize that I was self-centered and not willing to sacrifice in order to help her reach that goal. I have decided to support her enthusiastically in getting her degree. We've turned it into a family project. The kids are excited about it, and I realize now that this is going to have a positive effect on them. I hope that seeing Betty go back to finish her degree will motivate them to want to graduate from college themselves someday."

"How does this make you feel, Betty?" I asked.

"I feel very loved and affirmed by Mark," she said. "I'm sorry it took us so long to get here, but I think that he genuinely understands my desire. I really appreciate his love and support. I think it's going to make our marriage much stronger."

Mark and Betty's conflict was resolved by his choice to "meet on one side"—in this case, hers. The process of empathetic listening led them to understanding, and understanding led to a resolution they both agreed on. The conflict was no longer a barrier; it was genuinely resolved by Mark's choice to meet Betty on her side. Many conflicts can be resolved by this positive approach.

Meeting Later

A third approach to resolving conflict is "meeting later." In this approach, a couple cannot honestly find a place to meet in the middle, nor can one spouse conscientiously move to the other side. Therefore, they "agree to disagree" with respect and love. This approach may resolve a conflict temporarily or permanently, depending on the nature of the disagreement. First, I'll illustrate how this approach works as a temporary resolution.

It is almost midnight on a Tuesday. Brad and Renee have been arguing for the past two and a half hours about whether he should go fishing at the end of the month with a group of guys from work. Brad really wants to go. He feels it is important for building rapport with his coworkers and that it would be good for him in terms of job security and possible promotion. Renee is resisting the idea because her perception is that most of Brad's coworkers are not the kind of guys he should be hanging out with. "Half of them are unfaithful to their wives," she says, "and almost all of them drink in excess. I just don't think it's a healthy climate."

It's well past their usual bedtime and both of them are fatigued. Their arguments have gotten them nowhere, and they now have a decision to make. Either they can continue to argue through the night and both face the new day emotionally and physically drained, or they can call a truce, acknowledging that the conflict is not resolved but that both of them need a break. In short, they can agree to disagree—temporarily. In essence, they are saying to each other, "We know this conflict is not resolved, but because it's late and we're both tired, we're going to put it on the shelf and agree that we will pick it up again tomorrow or at some other agreed-upon time. In the meantime, we will both give thought to how we might approach the issue in a more constructive manner, and we agree not to throw any more bombs at each other." They have agreed to a truce, and they both know that the truce is temporary.

If Brad and Renee do not learn to listen empathetically and seek to understand each other before they sit down to talk again, their next session may be as frustrating and unproductive as the last, and resolution may still elude them. However, if they do learn how to listen empathetically and understand each other's desires, they might create a much warmer atmosphere in their relationship. Through empathetic listening, they will learn to appreciate each other's point of view, even if they still honestly disagree. Instead of arguing, they'll now be able to express respect and love for each other. Renee may not be able to bring herself to meet Brad on his side, and Brad may be equally unable to meet Renee on her side, but they can still communicate amicably with each other. This means they will not treat each other harshly or allow distance to come between them. They will go on with life in a positive way, realizing that they simply have a conflict that is not yet resolved.

Sooner or later, of course (before the end of the month), they must move to a solution. If they fail to "meet in the middle" or "meet on one side," the day for the fishing trip will arrive and Brad will either go or stay at home. If he stays at home with resentment toward Renee, it will show up in his behavior and the unresolved conflict will have a detrimental effect on their relationship. If he goes on the fishing trip without regard to Renee's thoughts and feelings, her hurt and anger will be revealed by her behavior and the relationship will be damaged. Therefore, in this illustration, the decision to "meet later" is only a temporary solution that requires additional empathetic listening and understanding.

In other cases, the decision to "meet later," or to "agree to disagree," can be a permanent resolution of the conflict. For example, Nina and Tyler have a conflict over toothpaste. She is a middle squeezer and he squeezes from the bottom. For the first year of their marriage, they exchanged friendly but frank objections to the way the other squeezed the tube. Eventually, they got around to talking about it with some level of openness. They both agreed that, from an engineer's perspective, squeezing from the bottom made more sense. But from the perspective of Nina's sanguine personality, always squeezing from the bottom was a discipline that seemed impossible for her to learn. Neither Nina nor Tyler seemed able to consistently squeeze the way the other desired. Instead, they agreed to buy two tubes of toothpaste and let both of them squeeze the way they pleased. This solution will work for a lifetime—or until they discover the pump! They agreed to disagree, and neither held any animosity toward the other. They were simply no longer irritated by the other's behavior. They found a mutually satisfactory solution in choosing to agree to disagree.

Many of the common conflicts experienced in the early years of marriage can be resolved by "agreeing to disagree." I remember that when Karolyn and I were first married, we argued numerous times over how to properly load the dishwasher. I contended (and still do) that if you place like things together—plates with plates, cups with cups, and so on—they will come out cleaner and be less likely to get broken in the dishwasher. Karolyn argued that such organization was a waste of time. Dishwashers are designed to wash whatever is in them, no matter how or where the dishes are placed. After many months of arguing, we were left with anger and resentment.

When we finally learned to listen empathetically and sought to understand each other rather than seeking to win the argument, we ultimately agreed to disagree. The practical solution was that when Karolyn loaded the dishwasher, she could load it her way, and when I loaded the dishwasher, I would load it my way. Because I was the one who unloaded the dishwasher each morning, I agreed to clean the spoons that had been cradled together with peanut butter between them and to occasionally toss a broken glass into the trash. It was a small price to pay for marital harmony, and this solution has served us well for more than forty years.

Most conflicts can be resolved by "meeting in the middle," "meeting on one side," or "meeting later." Conflict resolution is much easier when we feel understood and loved and when we have reached the decision without coercion. We realize that we are on the same team and are working together to use our ideas, desires, and emotions to reach win-win solutions to our conflicts.

Each of these three patterns of conflict resolution requires empathetic listening, understanding, loving attitudes, and openness to change. The reason that many couples do not resolve conflicts is that they never learn to follow the process of listening, understanding, and loving. They are stuck in a pattern of selfishly demanding their own way. But listening, understanding, and loving is what creates a climate for mutually satisfying conflict resolution.

● ● ●

Putting the Principles into Practice

1. Memorize this question and use it with your spouse next time you have a conflict: "How can we resolve this conflict so that both of us will feel loved and appreciated?"

2. In this chapter, we discussed three positive ways of resolving conflicts:

   • "Meeting in the middle"

   • "Meeting on one side"

   • "Meeting later"

   Did you use any of these strategies in resolving a recent conflict? Did you and your spouse both feel loved and appreciated?

3. Can you think of an illustration where "meeting later" or "agreeing to disagree" became a permanent solution to one of your conflicts?

4. In your opinion, how well are you and your spouse doing in reaching win-win solutions? What do you need to change, or continue, in order to improve?

7

RESOLUTION
LEADS TO HARMONY

At the beginning of a seminar in Chattanooga, Tennessee, my associate Rick Pierce asked couples who had been married for forty years or longer to raise their hands. Several hands were raised. He then narrowed the field to those who had been married for at least forty-five years, and then fifty. When Rick said, "Okay, fifty years or longer," only one couple's hands were still raised.

"So, how long have you folks been married?" Rick asked.

"Fifty-two years." I made a mental note to talk to this couple during the lunch break.

When I met up with James and Mildred, I asked, "To what do you attribute your long marriage?"

James replied, "We made a commitment early in our marriage that whenever we had a disagreement, we would listen to each other and try to find a solution that we both thought was right. As you can imagine, we had a lot of differences, especially in the early years. We spent a lot of time listening and looking for solutions. But it all paid off, because we've lived in harmony for fifty-two years. We have four children, all of whom are happily married. Mildred and I could not have asked for a better life."

I turned to Mildred and asked, "Would you like to add anything to that?"

"Well, I think he's right," she said. "The only thing I would add is that we made a commitment also to love each other, no matter what happened, and to be there for each other. I came down with multiple sclerosis a few years ago. Physically, things have gotten worse for me, but James has been there for me through the whole time. I could not have asked for more support."

"And what brought you to my seminar?" I asked.

"For years, we've made it a practice to attend a marriage enrichment weekend every year," Mildred replied.

"We read your book on the five love languages a few years ago," James added, "and we decided that if you ever came to Chattanooga, we would come to hear you."

"I'm glad you came," I said. "I hope you will find it helpful." As I turned to walk away, I added, "I wish every couple in the country could hear what you have just told me. If every couple made the commitment to listen to each other and resolve their differences, to be supportive of each other no matter what happens, and to continue growing by attending marriage enrichment events and reading books on marriage, we would see a radical change in the marriages of this generation."

James responded with a laugh and said, "Feel free to put our comments in your next book, and maybe the whole world will hear it."

"Maybe I'll do that," I said. And so I have.

I am always thrilled to meet couples like James and Mildred, who have learned how to resolve conflicts and walk together in harmony over a lifetime. On the other hand, I have been deeply pained by the many couples whom I have observed arguing with each other, verbally berating each other, and destroying their dream of what marriage should be.

James and Mildred epitomize the mind-set that leads to conflict resolution rather than arguing. First, they were committed to resolve conflicts, and to do so in a way that respected both spouses' ideas. Every unresolved conflict stands as a barrier to marital harmony. Every resolved conflict brings a deeper sense of intimacy. The decision to seek resolution is a decision to build marital harmony.

Second, they built harmony in their marriage by committing to love each other no matter what happened and to be there for each other. Many couples do not understand that love is a choice and not a feeling. It is a decision to look out for the best interests of their spouse. It begins with an *attitude* and expresses itself in *behavior* that seeks to make life easier for the other person. It is a willingness to *give* so that they can *build up* the life of their spouse. Couples who fail to understand that love is an attitude rather than a feeling may never find marital unity. If we simply follow our feelings, we will treat each other kindly when we have positive feelings, and we will treat each other harshly when we have negative feelings. Husbands and wives who allow their emotions to control their behavior will forever be arguing. On the other hand, those who choose an attitude of love and seek to implement it on a daily basis will create a climate where conflicts can be resolved in a way that respects the opinions and feelings of both spouses.

The third bit of wisdom that James and Mildred shared was the understanding that marriage is perpetually in process. We must continue to grow and learn throughout the years. The fact that James and Mildred attended my seminar after fifty-two years of marriage indicates that their mind-set was one of continual learning. Mildred said, "For years, we've made it a practice to attend a marriage enrichment weekend every year." And James told me that they regularly read books on marriage as a couple.

There are many ways of stimulating marital growth. Marriage enrichment weekends and books about marriage were the two that James and Mildred shared. A couple might go for marital counseling, watch a recorded marriage enrichment seminar on VHS or DVD, or listen to such a program on CD. Many churches also offer marriage enrichment classes that meet weekly or monthly. Many couples have found these to be extremely informative and supportive.

Couples who build their marriage on this three-part foundation— the decision to seek reconciliation, the commitment to love and support each other no matter what, and the dedication to continually involve themselves in activities that stimulate marital growth—will succeed in resolving conflicts without arguing.

I've never met a couple who enjoyed arguing, but I have met thousands of couples who argue regularly. Arguing is based on the unspoken assumption that "my way is the best way." Arguing seeks to prove that the spouse's ideas are inferior. Arguing stimulates negative emotions. Arguing communicates condemnation and strikes at the other person's self-esteem. To sum it up, arguing creates disunity between husbands and wives.

Arguments, by their very nature, create an atmosphere of antagonism. Couples quickly become adversaries rather than friends. I have never known a couple who argued themselves into harmony, but I have worked with many couples who have argued themselves into hopelessness.

Marital conflicts are inevitable, but arguing is an option—an unhealthy option. Arguments never resolve conflicts; they simply intensify them. Unresolved conflicts over a period of months or years have led many couples to the conclusion that they are not compatible. In their minds, if they were, they wouldn't have so many conflicts and would be able to resolve them easily. But the truth is that every couple has conflicts, and conflict resolution is not easy. Because we are all egocentric, we believe that any sane and mature person would agree with our opinions. Conversely, anyone who disagrees with us needs to be educated—so we set about educating our spouses. But they too have an egocentric worldview, and they are trying to educate us. The result is argument and disunity.

In part one of this book, "Everybody Wins," I have sought to point to a higher road. Marital conflicts can be resolved, but it requires that we get off our stallions of superiority and view each other as human beings who are uniquely crafted in God's image. Because we are all individuals, our thoughts, feelings, and desires will be different from one another's. However, along with our individuality comes a deep need for intimacy. Marriage is designed to meet that need. A husband and wife come together with their differences to form a team where each will use his or her strengths to help the other, and together they will use their abilities to make the world a better place to live. Each of us is uniquely crafted by God with certain interests and abilities to accomplish positive purposes when we cooperate with God and with each other. In a healthy marriage, the partners work together as a team to help each other accomplish the objectives and goals that each believes he or she is destined to fulfill. When the team works together in harmony, marriage becomes all that it was designed to be.

Conflicts give us an opportunity to demonstrate our love, respect, and admiration for each other. When we accept conflicts as a normal part of marital team dynamics, we will create time to listen to each other. We will learn how to listen effectively so that we understand our spouse's thoughts, desires, and feelings. And together, we will find solutions that allow us to work together as a team, supporting each other rather than allowing our differences to divide us.

Conflict resolution is one of the most fundamental aspects of marital success. The bottom line is that unresolved conflicts accompanied by arguing destroy marriages. Conflicts that are resolved by listening to each other, respecting each other, and negotiating solutions will strengthen our marriages. It is my desire that you will learn how to resolve your marital conflicts without arguing.

●　●　●

Putting the Principles into Practice

1. James, who had been married fifty-two years, said, "We made a commitment early in our marriage that whenever we had a disagreement, we would listen to each other and try to find a solution that we both thought was right." Have you and your spouse made a similar commitment? If not, why not?

2. Mildred said, "We made a commitment also to love each other no matter what happened, and to be there for each other." Have you and your spouse made a similar commitment? If not, why not?

3. James and Mildred made it a practice to attend a marriage enrichment weekend every year and to read books on marriage. Have you and your spouse made a similar commitment? If not, why not?

4. If your spouse will not join you in making these commitments, don't despair. You can have a positive influence on your spouse by learning and practicing the techniques we have been discussing. In fact, your most powerful influence will be your example. As you

change your approach from "arguer" to "solution seeker," you will enhance the emotional climate in your marriage.

• • •

Closing Thoughts on Everybody Wins

The ideas I have shared in this part of the book were not devised in an ivory tower. They grew out of thirty years of listening to couples who had spent hours arguing and had come to the point of desperation. They also came from more than forty years of experience in my own marriage. What I have shared with couples in counseling, I now share with you. But I am fully aware that knowledge alone is not enough. In order to be helpful, knowledge must be applied to life. Now that you have read part one, "Everybody Wins," I want to challenge you to read it again, this time with your spouse. Share your answers to the questions at the end of each chapter. Your answers will reveal your thoughts, feelings, and desires related to the topic of the chapter. Then, as conflicts arise in your marriage, seek to apply the principles you have read and discussed with each other.

Argumentative patterns from the past will not die quickly, but you can learn a better way. It will take time and effort, but it is effort well invested. If the two of you can learn to resolve your conflicts without arguing, you will experience the joy of working in harmony as a team. This is what marriage is all about: a husband and wife using their unique ideas, emotions, and desires to strengthen each other's lives. Resolving conflicts in a healthy manner deepens a marriage relationship. You can learn to resolve conflicts without arguing.

If you find these techniques helpful, I hope you will share them with a friend. If you have stories to share with me, I invite you to select the Contact link at www.garychapman.org.

• • •

Some Ideas Worth Remembering

- When you win an argument, your spouse is the loser. And we all know it's no fun to live with a loser.

- Arguments accomplish a great deal. Unfortunately, the accomplishments are all destructive.
- As surely as you can learn to ride a bicycle, drive a car, or use a computer, you can learn how to resolve conflicts.
- The answer to conflict resolution is not in seeking to rid ourselves of our differences but in learning how to make our differences into assets rather than liabilities.
- Finding a winning solution begins by choosing to believe that such a solution is possible and that you and your spouse are smart enough to discover it.
- Arguments never resolve conflicts; they simply intensify them.
- Three winning attitudes:

  1. I choose to respect my spouse's ideas, even when I disagree with them.
  2. I choose to love my spouse and do everything I can to help him or her today.
  3. I choose to believe that my spouse and I are teammates and that with God's help we can find solutions to our conflicts.

    - Conflicts cannot be resolved without empathetic listening. I use the word *empathetic* because most couples believe they are listening to each other, when in fact they are simply reloading their verbal guns.
    - Empathetic listening requires that you give your spouse your undivided attention.
    - The most common mistake couples make in communication is responding before they have the full picture. This inevitably leads to arguments. . . . When people respond too quickly, they often respond to the wrong issue.

Part Two

HOME IMPROVEMENTS

Negotiating Change with Your Spouse

AFTER THIRTY YEARS AS A MARRIAGE COUNSELOR, I have drawn one firm conclusion: All married people wish their spouses would change. Sometimes, these desires go unexpressed but are refined and deepened in the process of daydreaming. The husband pictures his wife as having made the changes he desires, and he relishes this new creation. The wife dreams of a husband who will take out the garbage without being asked. These secretly nurtured visions of the perfect spouse become barriers to intimacy in the real world.

At the other extreme are husbands or wives who overtly declare their demands for change, usually in the heat of anger. Harsh language and brutal behavior reveal the intensity of their desire for change. One wife reported that her husband pushed her against the wall, and when she complained, he said, "When you start acting like a wife, I'll start treating you like one. Until then, you get what you deserve." Behind the words "start acting like a wife" were no doubt specific expectations he had that would require a change in her behavior. A wife who screams, "I am sick and tired of picking up after you; it's time you grew up," is revealing her expectations for change.

In between the two extremes of silent desire and brazen demands, thousands of couples live with unfulfilled expectations. If only their husband or wife would change, life would be so different. Sometimes they attempt to express their desires; other times, they simply give up in frustration.

What's the problem? Why is the desire for spousal change so universal, and yet the reality of change so rare? I believe the answer lies in three factors:

- We start at the wrong place.
- We fail to understand the power of love.
- We lack the skills to effectively communicate our desire for our spouse to change.

This part of the book, "Home Improvements," will answer the question, "How do I get my spouse to change—without manipulation?" In the next few pages, I will show you the right place to start, how to leverage the power of love, and how to develop the skills for requesting change.

I believe that what you are about to read has the potential of bringing about the changes you desire in your spouse. It will not be easy to apply the principles I will teach you, but if you do, they will bear much fruit. In all my years of counseling, I have never known anyone who sincerely applied these principles who did not see significant change in the spouse's behavior.

Part two, "Home Improvements," is divided into three chapters, each addressing one of the key issues mentioned above. I am going to talk to you as if you were sitting in my counseling office, and I am going to share with you what I have shared with hundreds of couples over the past three decades. If you're ready, so am I. Let's get started.

1

STARTING AT THE RIGHT PLACE

INVARIABLY, PEOPLE WHO WANT THEIR SPOUSE TO CHANGE start at the wrong place. A young man named Robert was one such person. He came alone to my office and told me that his wife, Sheila, would not come with him.

"What seems to be the nature of the problem?" I asked.

"For one thing, my wife is so disorganized. She spends half her life looking for her car keys. She never knows where to find anything because she can't remember where she put it. I'm not talking Alzheimer's—she's only thirty-five. I'm talking totally disorganized. I've tried to help her. I've made suggestions, but she's not open to anything I say. She says I'm controlling her. I'm not trying to control her. I just want to help make her life easier. If she would get more organized, it would certainly make my life easier, too. I waste a lot of time helping her find things she's lost."

I jotted some notes while Robert was talking, and when he was done, I asked, "Are there other problem areas?"

"Money. I have a good job. I make enough that we should be able to live comfortably, but not the way Sheila spends it. I mean, she makes no attempt to shop; she pays full price for everything. Like her clothes—if she would just buy them at the right season, they would be half price. We've gone for financial counseling, but she won't follow the financial planner's advice. Right now, we owe $5,000 on our credit card, and yet Sheila won't stop spending."

I nodded my head as I listened. "Are there other problem areas, Robert?"

"Well, yes. Sheila is just not interested in sex. I think she could live without it. If I didn't initiate it, we would never have sex. Even when I do, I'm often rejected. I thought sex was an important part of marriage, but apparently she doesn't feel that way."

As the session continued, Robert shared a few more of his frustrations about his wife's behavior. He said he had made every effort to get her to change, but he had seen few, if any, positive results. He was frustrated and at the point of hopelessness. He had come to me because he had read my books and thought that perhaps if I were to call his wife, she might talk to me and maybe I could get her to change. I knew from experience, however, that if Sheila came to my office, she would tell a different story than the one I'd heard from Robert. She would tell me about her problems with him. She would probably say that instead of being understanding, Robert is demanding and harsh with her. She would say, "If Robert would treat me with a little kindness and be a little romantic, I could be interested in sex." She would say, "I wish I could hear one compliment from him about some purchase I have made, rather than always condemning me for spending too much money." In essence, her perspective is "If Robert would change, then I would change."

Is there hope for Robert and Sheila? Can they get the changes they desire in each other? I believe the answer is yes, but first they must radically change their approach. They are starting at the wrong place.

Ancient Wisdom

In my counseling practice, I have discovered that most of the relationship principles that really work are not new. Many are found in ancient literature, though they've often been overlooked for years. For example, the principle of starting at the right place can be found in a lesson that Jesus taught, commonly known as the Sermon on the Mount. I will paraphrase the quote to apply the principle directly to the marriage relationship: "Husband, why do you look at the speck of sawdust in your wife's eye and pay no attention to the plank in your own eye? Or, wife, how can you say to your husband, 'Let me take the speck out of your eye,' when all the time there is a plank in your own eye? You hypocrite, first take the plank out of your own eye, and then you will see clearly to remove the speck from your spouse's eye."[1]

The principle is clear: The place to start is getting the plank out of your own eye. Notice carefully that Jesus did not say, "There's nothing wrong with your mate. Leave him or her alone." In fact, he indicated that there is something wrong with your mate when he said, "Once you get the plank out of your own eye, then you can see more clearly to get the speck out of your spouse's eye."

Everyone needs to change. There are no perfect spouses—although I did hear once of a pastor who asked the question, "Does anyone know of a perfect husband?" One man in the back of the church raised his hand quickly and said, "My wife's first husband." My conclusion is that if there were any perfect husbands, they're all dead. I've never met a real live husband who didn't need to change. Nor have I met a perfect wife.

The most common reason people do not get the changes they desire in their spouse is that they start at the wrong place. They focus on their spouse's failures before they give attention to their own shortcomings. They see that little speck in their spouse's eye and begin to go after it by tossing out a suggestion. When that doesn't work, they overtly request a change. When that approach meets with resistance, they turn up the heat by demanding that their spouse change—or else. From there they move on to intimidation and manipulation. Even if they succeed in bringing about some change, it comes with deep resentment on the part of the spouse. This is not the kind of change that most people desire. Therefore, if you really want to see your spouse change, you must start by dealing with your own failures.

Getting the Plank out of Your Own Eye
Dealing with our own failures first is not the way most of us have been trained to think. We're more likely to say, "If my spouse weren't like

that, then I wouldn't be like this." "If my spouse didn't do that, then I wouldn't do this." "If my spouse would change, then I would change." Entire marriages have been built on this approach. One wife said, "If my husband would treat me with respect, then I would be able to be affectionate; but when he acts like I'm his slave, I want to run away and hope he'll never find me." To be honest, I empathize greatly with this wife; however, "waiting for my spouse to change" has led thousands of couples to an emotional state of hopelessness, which often ends in divorce when one or both spouses conclude, "He (or she) will never change; therefore, I'm getting out."

If we're honest with ourselves, we have to admit that waiting and hoping has not worked. We have seen little change unless it has been the result of manipulation—external pressure, either emotional or physical, that was designed to make a spouse uncomfortable enough to want to change. Unfortunately, manipulation creates resentment, and the marriage ends up worse after the change than it was before. If this has been your experience, as it was in the early years of my own marriage, then I hope you will be open to a different approach, one that works without creating resentment.

Learning to deal first with your own failures will not come easy. If I were to give you a sheet of paper, as I often do to those who come to me for counseling, and ask you to take fifteen minutes to make a list of the things you would like to see changed in your spouse, chances are you could make a rather formidable list. However, if I gave you another sheet of paper and asked you to take fifteen minutes to make a list of your own failures—things that you know need to be changed in the way you treat your spouse—my guess is that your list would be very short.

The typical husband's lists will have twenty-seven things wrong with his wife and only four things wrong with him. The wives' lists are not much different. One wife came back with a list of seventeen things that she wanted her husband to change, but the page of her own short-comings was blank. She said, "I know you are not going to believe this, but I honestly can't think of a single thing I'm doing wrong."

I have to confess I was speechless. I had never met a perfect woman before. I thought about calling my secretary to bring in the camera: "Let's get a picture of this lady."

After about thirty seconds of silence, she said, "Well, I know what *he* would say."

"What's that?" I asked.

"He'd say that I am failing in the sexual area, but that's all I can think of."

I didn't say it, but the thought did run through my mind: *That's pretty major, even if it's the only thing you can think of.*

It's not easy to get the plank out of your own eye, but let me give you three steps that will help you do it:

Step 1: Ask for Outside Help

Most people will not be able to identify their own flaws without some outside help. We are so accustomed to our own ways of thinking and acting that we fail to recognize when they are dysfunctional and negative. Let me suggest some sources of help in identifying the plank in your own eye:

TALK TO GOD

For some people, this might be uncomfortable, but I suggest you ask God's advice if you want some good insight. Your prayer might go something like this: "God, what *is* wrong with me? Where am I failing my spouse? What am I doing and saying that I shouldn't? What am I failing to do or say that I should? Please show me my failures." This simple prayer (or one like it) has been prayed and answered for thousands of years. Take a look at this prayer from the Hebrew Psalms, written in approximately 1000 BC by King David, Israel's second king: "Search me, O God, and know my heart; test me and know my anxious thoughts. Point out anything in me that offends you, and lead me along the path of everlasting life."[2] We can be certain that when we pray a prayer like this, God will answer.

If you're ready, take fifteen minutes to ask God to show you your failures in your marriage, then list whatever he brings to your mind. These may not be major moral failures, but could be words and actions that have not been loving and kind. Whatever things come to mind that have been detrimental to your marriage, write them down.

Here are the lists that one couple compiled after praying this prayer. (I suggest you complete your own list before looking at these.)

HUSBAND

I watch too much TV.
I need to be more helpful with things around the house.
I don't use my time wisely.
I don't listen to her like I should.
I don't act kindly to her at times.
I don't talk things out with her.
I don't listen to her ideas.
Our time of sharing is sparse.
I have made her afraid to voice her views.
We don't pray together like we should.

WIFE

I fail to encourage him.
I put myself and my needs above his needs.
I put him down at times.
I am not affectionate enough.
I expect him to do things the way I would.
I am sometimes rude and harsh in my speech.
I spend too much time on the computer.
I am not sensitive to my husband's love language.
I don't like to admit when I'm wrong.
I don't spend enough time with God.
I focus more time and energy on our son than on our marriage.
I hold on to wrongs from the past and use them in arguments.
I need to stop looking at his faults and look at mine.

TALK TO YOUR FRIENDS

In addition to talking with God, I suggest that you talk with a couple of friends who know you well and who have observed you and your marriage. Tell them that you are trying to improve your marriage and you want them to be completely honest with you. Tell them you are focusing on areas in which you need to improve in your own life. Ask them to give you honest feedback on whatever they have observed in your life, particularly the ways you respond to your spouse. Tell them that you will still be friends after they give you the truth—in fact, it's because of your friendship that you know you can trust them to be truthful with you. Don't argue with your friends. Simply write down whatever they tell you.

One friend said to a wife who had asked for input, "Do you really want me to be honest?" When the wife said yes, the friend said, "You are critical of your husband in front of other people. I have often felt sorry for your husband. I know it's embarrassing for him." The truth may be hard to hear (in some cases, it will be *very* hard), but if you don't hear it, you'll never take the necessary steps to change and you won't accomplish your goal of a better marriage.

A friend said to a husband who had asked for feedback, "My observation is that you often try to control your wife. I remember that just last week she was standing in the lobby of the church talking with another lady, and you walked up and said, 'We've got to go.' It was like you were her father telling her what she needed to do." Friends will often give you perceptions of yourself you have never imagined.

TALK TO YOUR PARENTS AND IN-LAWS

If you are really courageous, and if your parents and your in-laws have had a chance to observe you and your marriage, you might ask them the same questions you asked your friends. Begin the conversation by telling them that you are trying to improve your marriage and you are focusing on the things that *you* need to change. Again, please don't argue with their comments. Simply write them down and express your appreciation for their honesty.

TALK TO YOUR SPOUSE

Now, if you really want to get serious, ask your spouse for the same information. You might say, "Honey, I really want to make our marriage better. I know that I have not been a perfect spouse, but I want to get better in the areas that are most important to you. So I want you to make a list of the things I've done, or failed to do, that have hurt you the most. Or perhaps it's things I've said or failed to say. I want to deal with my failures and try to make things different in the future." Don't argue with your spouse's list or rebuff the comments you are given. Simply receive them as information and thank your spouse for helping you become a better person.

Step 2: Reflect on the Information You Have Gathered

When you have collected all the lists, what you will have in your hands is valuable information—about yourself and the way you relate to your spouse, from God's perspective and from the perspective of the people who are closest to you. Now it's time for you to come to grips with this information. This is not a time to develop rationalized defenses to the comments you've received. It is a time to accept the possibility that there is some truth in all these perspectives. From the lists you have received, make your own list of things that you agree are wrong in the way you treat your spouse.

I suggest that you personalize each sentence, starting with the word *I*, so that you are honestly reporting your own awareness of the flaws in your behavior. For example, "I recognize that I often lose my temper and say hurtful words to my spouse." Starting your sentences with *I* will help you keep it personal. Include statements about things that you should be doing but aren't, as well as things you are doing that you shouldn't. For example, in addition to the statement above about losing your temper and saying hurtful things to your spouse, you might also say, "I do not give my spouse enough positive, encouraging words."

In this time of reflection, be as honest as possible with yourself. You might even ask God to help you honestly evaluate your failures. Trying to justify yourself or excuse your behavior based on your spouse's behavior is a futile attempt at rationalization. Don't do it. You will never get the plank out of your own eye as long as you are excusing your failures.

Step 3: Confession

We have long known the emotional and spiritual power of confession. Confessing the things we've done wrong liberates us from the bondage of past failures and opens us up to the possibility for changed behavior in the future. I suggest that you begin by confessing your failures to God. Here is King David's confession, written after God showed David his failures. Your own confessions may not be expressed as poetically as David's, but you may find that his words of confession will help you express your own.

Have mercy on me, O God,
    because of your unfailing love.
Because of your great compassion,
    blot out the stain of my sins.
Wash me clean from my guilt.
    Purify me from my sin.
For I recognize my rebellion;
    it haunts me day and night.
Against you, and you alone, have I sinned;
    I have done what is evil in your sight.
You will be proved right in what you say,
    and your judgment against me is just.
For I was born a sinner—
    yes, from the moment my mother conceived me.
But you desire honesty from the womb,
    teaching me wisdom even there.
Purify me from my sins, and I will be clean;
    wash me, and I will be whiter than snow.
Oh, give me back my joy again;
    you have broken me—now let me rejoice.
Don't keep looking at my sins.
    Remove the stain of my guilt.
Create in me a clean heart, O God.
    Renew a loyal spirit within me.

Do not banish me from your presence,
    and don't take your Holy Spirit from me.
Restore to me the joy of your salvation,
    and make me willing to obey you.

PSALM 51:1-12, NLT

The word *confession* means, literally, "to agree with." When we confess to God, it means that we agree with him that what we have done or failed to do is wrong. Confession is the opposite of rationalization. Confession makes no attempt to minimize our wrongdoing but openly admits that our behavior is inexcusable.

The God who is revealed in the Bible is a God who stands ready to forgive those who admit their sins. Here is one brief quote: "If we confess our sins [to God], he is faithful and just and will forgive us our sins and purify us from all unrighteousness."[3]

The New Testament tells us that the reason God can forgive our wrongdoing and still be a God of justice is because Christ has paid the penalty for our failures. The ultimate penalty for wrongdoing is death. Because Christ took that penalty in our place, God is willing to forgive us. The penalty has already been paid by Christ. That is the central message of the Christian faith.

However, confession of wrongdoing needs to be broader than simply admitting your failures to God. You also must confess to the person you have wronged. In marriage, that is your spouse. Having confessed to God, you should now have the courage to confess to your spouse. Your confession might go something like this: "I've been thinking about us, and I realize that in a lot of ways I have failed you. I sat down the other day and made a list of the things I feel I have done that are wrong. I have asked God to forgive me for each of these things, and if you have a few minutes, I'd like to share my list with you and ask if you would forgive me, as well. I really want the future to be different, and I think this is where I need to start."

Most spouses will be willing to forgive when they hear an honest confession. If there has been a drastic violation of your marriage vows, it may take time for trust to be rebuilt. But the rebuilding process starts with an act of genuine confession.[4]

If you have gone to your parents or in-laws to ask for their input about your failures in your marriage, you might also want to confess your failures to them and ask for their forgiveness. Such confessions will go a long way toward rebuilding trust, respect, and a positive relationship with them. Even if you did not ask for their input but you know they are aware of your marital failures, I would encourage you to confess to your parents and in-laws.

Common Questions about Starting at the Right Place

Having read these ideas about starting at the right place, you may have questions floating in your mind. When I present this concept at my marriage seminars, I hear some common questions. For example, a wife in the Midwest said, "I understand what you are saying. I know that I need to get the plank out of my own eye, but I don't think you fully understand my situation. What if your spouse really *is* the problem?"

I thought for a moment and responded, "Let's assume that your husband is 95 percent of the problem. That would leave only 5 percent for you. But even if the problem is mostly with your spouse, you wouldn't say that you are perfect, would you?"

"Oh no," she said. "No one is perfect."

"Well, if we're not perfect, then we're imperfect, right?"

"Right . . ."

"So let's assume your husband is 95 percent imperfect and you are only 5 percent imperfect. What I'm suggesting is that if *you* want to improve your marriage, and if *you* want to see changes in your husband, the place for you to start is with *your* 5 percent. Your marriage will immediately be 5 percent better, and you will be freed from the guilt of past failures and emotionally liberated to be a positive influence on your husband."

I'm not sure she was totally satisfied with my answer, but she did nod her head and say, "Okay, that makes a lot of sense."

Rob, a middle-aged husband from Birmingham, asked me another question: "If I confess my failures to God and to my wife, do you think she will come back in a few days and confess her failures to me?"

I wish I could have answered affirmatively and with confidence, but in all honesty, I had to say, "I don't know. But that would be nice, wouldn't it?"

Rob nodded as tears coursed down his cheeks.

"I'm not even certain that your wife will forgive you," I continued. "I wish I could guarantee that, but the fact is we can't predict human behavior. She may be so deeply hurt and angered that she cannot honestly forgive you at the moment. You must be patient with her and give her time to process your confession."

What I did guarantee Rob, and can guarantee you, is that when you confess your failures in your marriage, you have removed the first barrier to marital growth. Confession creates a climate that fosters positive change. You cannot erase your past failures, but you can agree that what you did, or failed to do, was wrong, and you can sincerely ask for forgiveness. In so doing, you are starting at the right place.

"But if she doesn't forgive me," Rob said, "how can there be hope for change?"

I reminded him that confession of one's failures is only the first step in seeking change. Your spouse's immediate response may not be the ultimate response. A woman who initially said to her husband, "I don't know that I can ever forgive you; too much has happened, and the hurt is too deep," three months later said, "I didn't know that I would ever be able to forgive you, but today I want you to know that the past is the past. I no longer hold it against you." What happens after the confession will have an impact on whether or not your spouse chooses to forgive you, but we'll discuss what comes next in the following chapter.

The process we've described in the current chapter will obviously take some time. I doubt that the confession phase can be completed in less than a month. However, I want you to read the rest of "Home Improvements" (through page 109) now because I want you to see where we're going. I can assure you that, in the end, I am going to give you the key to getting your spouse to change without manipulation.

After your confessions have been made, you have taken the first step in creating an atmosphere for requesting change from your spouse. I was honest with you from the beginning when I said that the road to change is not easy. I am fully aware that confessing your failures to God and to your spouse is a major accomplishment. However, few things are more important than confession for maintaining both mental and marital health. When you confess your failures, it is like emptying your conscience and cleansing it of all the guilt that goes along with those failures. Living with a clean conscience will keep you mentally and relationally alert, and it will free you from the bondage of past failures. After you have confessed, you will feel better about yourself, and your spouse will begin to look at you with more respect and dignity because you have been strong enough to deal with your own failures.

After confession, you will likely feel emotionally elated because a burden has been lifted and because you are being authentic with your spouse. There is something exhilarating about being honest and dealing with our failures. However, please don't jump to the conclusion that you can now request change and expect your spouse to comply. There is another major ingredient that must be added before you are ready to take that step. It has to do with the power of emotional love. Read on.

●　●　●

Putting the Principles into Practice

1. In the past, what has been your approach to your own failures in your marriage?

    ___ blame them on my spouse

    ___ deny them

    ___ admit them, but refuse to change

    ___ say, "I'll change when you change."

    ___ fully confess my failures and ask for forgiveness

    ___ other

2. If you are willing, say to God, "I know I'm not perfect, so where have I failed in my marriage?" Make a list of what comes to your mind.

3. If you are willing to seek outside help, write the date you asked for input from the list that follows.

_____ God

_____ close friends

_____ parents

_____ in-laws

_____ spouse

4. Admitting your failures and asking forgiveness may be difficult, especially if you believe that your spouse is 95 percent of the problem. But would you be willing to *start at the right place* and see what happens? If so, write the dates when you made your list (_____) and verbally confessed your failures to your spouse (_____).

2

LEARNING THE POWER OF LOVE

YOUR DESIRE TO SEE CHANGE IN YOUR SPOUSE is most likely correlated with a desire to meet some need in your own life. Regardless of culture, human beings are by nature egocentric. We think the world revolves around us. Meeting our own needs is the motivation behind much of our behavior. Robert wanted Sheila to become more organized so that she would not spend so much of her time looking for things, but he also admitted that part of his motivation was that he did not want to waste his own time helping her. He wanted her to be more interested in sex because his needs were not being met. He wanted her to spend less money so that he would feel that he was a good provider and they could live within their means. On the other hand, Sheila desired to hear from Robert words of affirmation in order to enhance her own self-esteem. His condemning words cut deeply at her self-respect.

A concern for one's own well-being is natural and healthy. In fact, if we did not feed ourselves and get proper sleep and exercise, we would not be able to live. We are responsible for seeking to meet our own physical and emotional needs. At the same time, we are also designed for relationships. Those who live in isolation will never reach their full potential in society. Relationships call us to get outside of ourselves. If meeting our own needs becomes the central theme of our lives, we will never have good relationships.

Successful relationships require that we become interested in the well-being of another person. It is taking our natural desire to meet our own needs, turning it outward toward someone else, and using the same amount of energy to meet his or her needs. The word to describe this other-centered attitude is *love*. In this sense, the song is true: *Love makes the world go round.*[1] Without love, society would not continue. In a marriage relationship, I know of nothing more important than love. Where there is love, change is inevitable. Without love, positive change seldom occurs.

Reflect on the stage of life when you and your spouse were "in love." Is it not true that you were willing to do anything for your lover's benefit—climb the highest mountain, swim the deepest ocean, stop smoking, learn to dance? Whatever desire he or she expressed, you were willing to attempt. Why were you so open to change? I believe it was because your emotional need for love was being met so fully. It is true that *love stimulates love.*

In time, however, the emotional obsession you had for each other faded, and your egocentric natures took over. Both you and your spouse began focusing on getting your own needs met. Ironically, the result was that neither of you was satisfied. The nature of egocentric living is disappointment and hurt, which leads to anger, resentment, and bitterness. Such is the plight of thousands of married couples. In order for this to change, there must be a return to love—not the euphoric state of being "in love," but the conscious choice to look out for the best interests of the other person. Love requires a fundamental change of perspective. It goes against our natural bent toward selfishness, but it is the most powerful weapon in the world for good. It radically changes the climate of a marriage.

The attitude of love must find behavioral structures through which to be expressed. In my own marriage, these structures were formed by asking my wife the following questions:

"How may I help you?"

"What can I do that would make your life easier?"

"How can I be a better husband to you?"

When I was willing to ask those questions and let Karolyn's answers guide me in how I expressed my love to her, our marriage was reborn.

Through thirty years of marriage counseling, I have helped hundreds of couples discover how to connect with each other emotionally by choosing to walk the road of love. In 1992, I wrote a book called *The Five Love Languages*, which has helped literally hundreds of thousands of couples to reconnect and create a positive emotional climate in their marriages.[2] Of the five love languages, everyone has a primary love language. One of these styles of communication speaks more deeply to each of us emotionally than the other four. We like all of them to varying degrees, but there's usually one we prefer above the others, one that we wouldn't give up for anything. That is what makes us feel genuinely loved. When our spouses "speak" to us in our primary love language, our love tanks fill up and we feel secure. The key is to discover your spouse's primary love language and give him or her heavy doses of it while sprinkling in the other four love languages as cherries on top of the sundae. I have never seen a marriage that was not improved when one spouse or both chose to follow this path.

To help you get started, I will briefly summarize the five love languages and illustrate why it is so important to learn your spouse's primary love language:

Love Language #1: Words of Affirmation

For some people, words of affirmation are what make them *feel* loved. Choosing to focus on the positive and to verbalize affirmation for those things you appreciate about your spouse will tend to motivate him or her to noble behavior. If your spouse's primary love language is words of affirmation, look for even the slightest opportunity to offer some simple, affirming words such as those that follow.

"You look nice in that dress."

"Oh, do you ever look sharp tonight."

"I really appreciate the meal."

"Thanks for taking out the garbage."

"I want you to know I do not take you for granted."

"I really appreciate the fact that you cleaned the kitchen tonight."

"Thanks for mowing the grass; the yard really looks nice."

"I appreciate your putting gas in my car. And thanks for getting the bugs off the windshield."

Affirming words may also focus on your spouse's personality traits:

"I noticed how you spent time with Rebecca last night. She seemed to be upset. I really appreciate the fact that you take time for people."

"I don't think I've told you this lately, but I really appreciate the fact that when I come home, you are always so encouraging and excited about my being here. That means a lot to me."

"I appreciate the spontaneity of your personality. You make my life interesting."

"The methodical way in which you attack problems is such a gift. I appreciate the way you make my life easier by solving so many of my problems."

Words of affirmation may also focus on the person's physical characteristics:

"Your hair looks nice."

"I love the twinkle in your eye."

"Have I told you lately that your breasts are beautiful?"

"Look at those muscles. Wow!"

"The blue of your eyes reminds me of a calm lake in the mountains."

Affirming words give life; condemning words bring death. Many couples have destroyed their marriage by using condemning, judgmental, harsh, cutting words. That can be changed when one spouse chooses to stop the flow of negativity and begin the flow of loving words.

Love Language #2: Gifts

My academic background is in anthropology, the study of cultures. No one has yet found a culture in which gift giving is not an expression of love. A gift says, "He was thinking about me. Look what he got for me." Gifts are a physical, visible token of thoughtfulness and care.

A gift need not be expensive. After all, it's the thought that counts, right? Actually, it is more than the thought left in your mind that counts; it is the thoughtful gift that results from the thought in your mind that makes the difference. Most of us could learn a great deal from observing our children. Children are masters of gift giving, and most of the time it costs them nothing. They make imaginary strawberry pies and ask you to join them in eating. They make cars out of paper towel tubes and buttons and give them to you as a gift. They run to you with a flower, present it with a smile, and say, "I got this for you." Where along the way to adulthood did we lose this spirit of gift giving?

I believe that anyone can learn to give gifts. It requires an awareness that gift giving is one of the fundamental languages of love, and you must decide to speak that language to your spouse. It's not what the gift costs but your thoughtfulness that matters. Make your wife a love card out of the various colored papers that come across your desk. Write words of affirmation on the card and give it to her on Valentine's Day—or better yet, on an "unspecial" day. Of course, not all gifts should be free. Listen to your spouse's comments about things he or she might like. If your spouse expresses a desire for something, make a note of it. Three weeks later, surprise your mate by presenting it to him or her after dinner.

Love Language #3: Acts of Service
"Actions speak louder than words." For some people, that is certainly true. Doing something that you know your spouse will like is a deep expression of love. Cooking meals, washing dishes, vacuuming the floors, mowing the lawn, washing the cars, doing laundry, cleaning the bathroom, changing the baby's diaper—all these are acts of service. Yes, they require time, effort, energy, and sometimes skill, but if your spouse's primary love language is acts of service, you will strongly communicate your love whenever you do something that you know your spouse will like.

In household responsibilities, we tend to be creatures of habit. We fall into patterns of behavior—he cooks, she washes dishes; she does the laundry, he mows the grass; he keeps the cars filled with gas, she makes sure the clothes are clean. We find our niche and stick with it. Of course, there is a positive aspect to all this. Typically, we will do the things that we feel best equipped to do, and if we do them with a positive spirit for the benefit of each other, we are speaking the language of love.

If the chores and responsibilities are already well established at your house, you can enhance your expression of love to your spouse by doing something that is not normally on your list. Be advised that your spouse might not understand or fully appreciate your efforts, as depicted in the following dialogue:

"Honey, would you like me to clean the bathrooms tonight?"

"Are you saying that I'm not keeping the bathrooms clean?"

"No, I think you're doing a great job. I just thought it might be nice if I did something to help you."

Be prepared that your spouse might not be overly enthusiastic at first. Perhaps he or she is still wondering if you are telling the truth. But once you have completed the task, you are likely to hear some words of affirmation.

Love Language #4: Quality Time
Quality time is much more than being in the same room or the same house with your spouse. It involves giving your spouse your undivided attention. It is sitting on the couch with the TV off, looking at each

other and talking. It's taking a walk down the road, just the two of you. It is going out to eat and looking at each other and talking. Have you ever noticed how in a restaurant you can almost always tell the difference between dating couples and married couples? Dating couples will look at each other and talk; married couples sit quietly and eat. For the dating couple, it is quality time; for the married couple, it is meeting a basic physical need. Why not turn your mealtimes into expressions of love by giving each other your undivided attention, talking and listening?

Begin by sharing the events of the day, but don't stop there. Talk about things that might be troubling your spouse, or desires that he or she has for the future. Once our spouses sense that we are interested in what they are thinking and feeling, they will not only talk more freely but also feel loved.

If you would like to shock your spouse with an expression of quality time, the next time your spouse walks into the room while you are watching TV, hit the mute button and turn and look at your spouse, giving him or her your undivided attention. If your spouse starts talking, flip the TV off and engage in conversation. If he or she walks out of the room without talking, you may go back to your TV program, but the simple act of making yourself available for quality time communicates that your spouse is more important to you than anything on television. Quality time is a powerful language of love.

Love Language #5: Physical Touch
We have long known the emotional power of physical touch. All research indicates that babies who are affectionately touched fare better emotionally than babies who are not touched. The same is true of adults. If you have ever walked the halls of a home for the elderly, you have seen the outstretched hands of people who are longing to be touched. A handshake, a hug, a pat on the back would fill the love tank of many a lonely person.

In marriage, physical touch is one of the fundamental languages of love. Holding hands while you give thanks for a meal, putting your hand on your spouse's shoulder as you sit watching television, embracing each other when you meet after being apart, sexual intercourse, kissing—sometimes a peck, sometimes with passion—any touch, as long as it is affectionate, is a deep expression of love.

I remember a woman who said to me, "Of all the things my husband does, nothing is more important than the kiss on the cheek he gives me when he comes home from work. It doesn't matter how bad his day has been or how bad my day has been. When he comes to greet me with a kiss before going to the television or the refrigerator, everything seems better." A man at one of my seminars said, "I never leave the house without getting a hug from my wife, which she initiates. And when I return, the first thing she does is give me a hug. Some days, her hugs are the only positive thing that happens, but they are enough to keep me going."

Discovering Your Primary Love Language

In order to discover your primary love language, ask yourself what you complain about most often to your spouse. Your complaints reveal your love language. If every so often you say to your spouse, "We never spend any time together. We are like two ships passing in the night," you are communicating that your love language is quality time. If your spouse returns from a trip and you say, "You mean you didn't bring me anything?" you are revealing that your love language is gifts. If you hear yourself saying to your spouse, "You don't ever touch me. If I didn't touch you, I don't think we would ever touch," you are revealing that your love language is physical touch. If you often say to your spouse, "I don't ever do anything right," you are revealing that your love language is words of affirmation. If you hear yourself saying, "You don't ever help me around here. I mean, I have to do everything. If you loved me, you would do something around here," your primary love language is acts of service. If you have no complaints, it means that your spouse is speaking your primary love language, even though you may not know what it is.

How do you discover your spouse's primary love language? Listen to his or her complaints. Typically we get defensive when our spouse complains. If a husband says, "I don't understand why you can't keep this house halfway decent. It looks like a pigpen," his wife is likely to explode in angry words or burst into tears. However, her husband is giving her valuable information about his primary love language—acts of service.

Listen to your spouse's complaints and you will learn what makes him or her feel loved.

The key to creating a positive emotional climate in a marriage is learning to speak each other's primary love language and speaking it regularly. My wife's love language is acts of service. That's why I vacuum floors, wash dishes, clean blinds, and fold clothes. I am not by nature a doer; I would much rather talk or listen. But I know that, for my wife, actions speak louder than words.

The other day, my wife said in passing, "The blinds are looking pretty dusty." I got the message, and I made a mental note. Two mornings later at about six o'clock, before I left to lead a marriage seminar, I was in the dining room vacuuming the blinds when Karolyn walked in and asked, "What are you doing?"

I said, "Honey, I'm making love."

She responded, "You have got to be the greatest husband in the world."

My primary love language is words of affirmation. Karolyn filled my love tank while I filled hers. It took thirty minutes and a little effort to vacuum blinds at six o'clock on Friday morning, but it was a small price to pay to live with a happy woman. Her response to me took less than six seconds, but for me those words of affirmation meant more than a thousand gifts.

From time to time, someone complains to me: "But what if my spouse's love language is something that just doesn't come naturally for me?" I always respond, "So?" Learning to speak a second language may not be easy, but the effort is well worth it. To be honest, vacuuming floors, washing dishes, and dusting blinds do not come naturally for me, but I have learned to speak my wife's love language because meeting her emotional need for love is important to me.

So where do you begin? I suggest you start where you are. If you grew up in a family that was not touchy-feely and you are married to someone whose love language is physical touch, start by touching yourself. Put one hand on top of the other, or rest your hand on your elbow or shoulder. Touch your knee or pat yourself on the thigh. When you become comfortable touching yourself, imagine putting your arm on your spouse's back for three seconds, or giving your spouse a small pat on the back. Practice these motions alone. Picture yourself touching your spouse casually and naturally. Then, one day, with all the courage you can muster, walk up to your spouse, pat him or her on the back, and see what kind of response you get. Your spouse may be surprised, but you will be on your way to mastering your spouse's love language. The next time—and the time after that—will be even easier.

If your spouse's love language is words of affirmation and you are not a verbal person, get a notebook and begin to write phrases and sentences that express positive affirmation to your spouse. If you can't think of anything, listen to what other people say and emulate that. Read magazines and books and record the expressions of love that you find. Next, stand in front of the mirror and read these things aloud to yourself. Become comfortable hearing these words come out of your mouth. When you're ready, pick one of these statements, walk up behind your spouse, and speak your chosen words of affirmation. You will have "broken the sound barrier" and made it progressively easier to speak words of affirmation. By the fourth or fifth time, you will start to become comfortable looking your spouse in the eye when you speak these words of affirmation.

If you decide to make the effort, you can learn to speak your spouse's primary love language. When you do, it will meet his or her most basic emotional need in the most effective way possible. Once you start speaking your spouse's primary love language, you can sprinkle in the other four languages as well for extra emotional credit.

You may be thinking, *So, what does all this talk about love have to do with getting my spouse to change?* I'm glad you asked, because unless you understand the answer to that question, you are not likely to see significant changes in your spouse. All of us have basic emotional needs, including the need for security, significance, freedom, self-worth, and love. When these emotional needs are not met, we become emotionally frustrated. This frustration may express itself in depression, anxiety, resentment, or withdrawal. In a state of emotional frustration, we are almost never open to our spouse's suggestions or requests. Typically, we interpret such requests as criticism. We may explode, retaliate, or withdraw, but we are not likely to change.

The most fundamental of all emotional needs is the need to feel loved. When we feel unloved, the whole world looks dark. Conversely, when our love tanks are full and we genuinely feel loved by our husband or wife, the whole world looks bright. Life becomes an adventure, and we don't want to miss out on the excitement. In this positive state of mind, we are open to change, and the person to whom we are most responsive is the person who is filling our love tanks.

When your spouse's love tank is full, he or she will be much more open to the changes that you desire, especially if you are the one who is filling your spouse's love tank. You have created a climate where change is not only possible but also likely.

Will it be easy to learn to speak your spouse's primary love language? Probably not, but the results are worth the effort.

When I met Brian and Joanne, they had been married for thirty-three years—but not thirty-three happy years. In fact, in Brian's words, "The last twenty years have been utterly miserable. We have lived in the same house and tried to be humane, but we really haven't had a marriage for the last twenty years."

With that revelation, I was looking at Brian rather somberly, until he said, "That all changed six months ago. I was visiting with a friend and told him how miserable I was in my marriage. He listened to my story and then gave me a copy of *The Five Love Languages*. He said, 'Read this. I think it will help you.'

"I went home and read it, cover to cover. As I read, it was like light-bulbs kept coming on in my brain. When I finished the book, I said to myself, 'Why didn't someone tell me this twenty years ago?' I realized that neither of us had been speaking the other's primary love language for at least twenty years. I gave the book to my wife and asked her to read it and let me know what she thought. The next week, we sat down and I said to her, 'Did that book make any sense to you?' She responded, 'I wish I had read it thirty years ago. I think it explains what went wrong in our marriage.' So I said to her, 'Do you think it would make any difference if we tried now?' to which she responded, 'We don't have anything to lose.' 'Does that mean you are willing to try?' I asked. 'Sure, I'll try,' she said.

"We discussed what we believed to be our primary love languages and agreed that with the help of God, we would seek to speak each other's primary love language at least once a week, no matter how we felt about each other. If anyone had told me that in two months I would have strong love feelings for my wife, I would have said, 'No way.' But I do."

At that point, Joanne broke into the conversation and said, "If anyone had told me that I would *ever* have love feelings for Brian again, I would have said it was impossible. But I do. It's like we are on a second honeymoon. Last month, we took the first vacation we have taken together in twenty years. It was wonderful. We enjoy being with each other again. My only regret is that we wasted twenty years. I realize now that both of us had such deep needs for love, and yet neither one knew how to meet the other's needs. I wish every couple could discover what we have discovered. It makes all the difference in the world."

Brian and Joanne speak for thousands of couples who have discovered that speaking their spouse's primary love language created a radically different atmosphere between the two of them. When they genuinely felt loved by their spouse, they were much more open to suggestions and requests.

It will be obvious that filling your spouse's love tank will take time, but not as much time as you might imagine. For Brian and Joanne, after living with empty love tanks for twenty years, the emotional climate changed within two months. You will not be ready to start requesting change until your spouse has lived with a full love tank for a few weeks. I cannot tell you how long it will take, but I can tell you how to know when you've arrived and are ready for the next step.

Several years ago, I devised a little game that has helped thousands of couples. It is called Tank Check. Here's the way you play the game: After you have been speaking your spouse's primary love language consistently for one month, ask your spouse, "On a scale of 0 to 10, how's the level in your love tank?" Wait for your spouse to give you a reading. If he or she says anything less than 10, you say, "What can I do to help fill it?" When your spouse gives you a suggestion, do it to the best of your ability. Play this game once a week. When you start getting responses of 8, 9, or 10 consistently, you will know you are ready for the next step, which is explained in the next chapter. I want you to read chapter 3 now so you can see where you're headed, but please don't try to implement the next step until you have completed the challenges of the current chapter as well as rereading chapter 1 of this part.

• • •

Putting the Principles into Practice

1. In your marriage, what do you complain about most often?
2. What does your spouse complain about most often?
3. With these answers in mind, guess which of the following love languages are most desired by your spouse. (Rank the following in order of importance, with the most desirable being number 1 and the least desirable being number 5.)

   ___ Words of Affirmation
   ___ Gifts
   ___ Acts of Service
   ___ Quality Time
   ___ Physical Touch

4. Now, using the same scale, indicate which love languages you would most like to receive:

   ___ Words of Affirmation
   ___ Gifts
   ___ Acts of Service
   ___ Quality Time
   ___ Physical Touch

5. If your spouse is willing, ask him or her to complete steps 1–4 above. Discuss your answers in order to discover each other's primary and secondary love languages. Choose to speak each other's primary and secondary love languages for the next month and see what happens.
6. If your spouse is not interested in participating in the exercises in this chapter's "Putting the Principles into Practice," don't be

discouraged. Instead, simply start speaking his or her primary and secondary love languages, based on your "best guesses" in number 3, on the previous page, and see what happens over the next month. Remember, love stimulates love.

3

REQUESTING CHANGE

HOW CAN I GET MY SPOUSE TO CHANGE, without manipulation? When you started reading part two, "Home Improvements," I assume this is what you really wanted to know. Perhaps you thought, *I'd even be willing to manipulate if I thought I could really get my spouse to change.* I understand the thought, but I really don't think that's what you want to do. Change that comes from manipulation is always accompanied by resentment. Resentment pushes people apart, and that is not what most couples want in their marriage.

Manipulation reduces a marriage relationship to the level of a contract negotiation: "If you'll do this, then I'll do that." At its worst, manipulation is simply an attempt by one spouse to control the other: "You will do this, or else." Perhaps the "or else" will induce enough fear in the spouse that he or she will acquiesce, but the change will be external and temporary. Real change comes from within, not from manipulating circumstances.

So how can you get real change? If you have read and applied what we've discussed in the first two chapters of "Home Improvements," you are now ready to request change from your spouse. The method of requesting change that I am about to describe will be effective only when you have genuinely dealt with your own past failures and you are expressing love in your spouse's primary love language. However, once you have established the proper foundation in your marriage relationship, real change is possible.

First, make a list of a few things you would sincerely like to see your spouse change. (Please see pages 352–357, where I have included separate lists of how husbands and wives have responded when asked the question, "What would you like to see your spouse change?") It's important to be specific; generalities won't work. For example, "I want you to talk more" is too general and much too difficult to measure. If increasing your communication is the desired goal, say, "I want to request that we spend twenty minutes each evening—Monday through Friday—talking and listening to each other as we share our thoughts and feelings related to the events of the day." This request is specific, understandable, achievable, and measurable.

"I wish you would stop nagging me" is also far too nebulous. Pick one area in which you feel your spouse is nagging you and make a specific request related to that area. For example, you might say, "As you know, I have accepted the responsibility to take out the garbage. I would like to request that, in the future, you will not remind me of that task. I may not take it out on your timetable, but I will get rid of the garbage. When you keep reminding me, I feel like you are my mother and I am a child. I don't like that feeling, and I don't think it is good for our marriage. Therefore, I am requesting that you refrain from mentioning the garbage."

If you are the wife who hears this request, perhaps you would like to say to me, "Yes, but he won't take the garbage out. If I don't remind him, it will sit there for a week." My response to that is, "If you want to be married to a child, then continue to nag him about the garbage; but if you want to be married to an adult, then treat him like an adult. He will never act like an adult as long as you remind him of his responsibilities. And please, don't take the garbage out for him; that is an even greater insult. Spray the garbage with air freshener, but don't touch it. You will be amazed at what will happen."

All right, now that you have your specific requests in mind, are you ready to learn how to make requests of your spouse? Here are three suggestions for doing it right: Choose your setting, don't give an overdose of criticism, and precede your request with compliments.

Choose Your Setting

When you get ready to request a change from your spouse, it is extremely important that you choose your time and place and be sensitive to your spouse's emotional state. The time should be after a meal, never before a meal. When we are hungry, we are irritable—and when we are irritable, it is difficult to take suggestions. Have you noticed that when the family is on a trip together and everyone is hungry, everyone tends to be more argumentative? That the children are at each other's throats, and you find yourself yelling a lot more? That's because hunger and irritability are companions. When you are about to do something as important as requesting change from your spouse, be certain that it is not when he or she is hungry.

The place to make your request should always be in private, never in public. When you mention something you wish your spouse would change, and you do it in front of other people, it is a put-down, even if you couch it with humor. "My wife is not exactly a gourmet cook. Her specialty is hard-cooked, soft-boiled eggs." Everyone in the group may laugh, but your wife gets the barb. I hope you don't expect a soft-boiled egg anytime soon. It is more likely she'll want to throw a raw egg in your face when you walk into the kitchen the next morning. Put-downs only stimulate resentment and revenge.

If you want your spouse to accept your request, make it in private. Here's how one husband made a successful request after dinner one night: "Honey, I really appreciate the fact that you boil my eggs three mornings a week. I really like boiled eggs. My request is that on Wednesdays you try to make them soft boiled. I looked in a cookbook and it suggested that cooking the eggs for three minutes from the time the water starts boiling will produce a soft-boiled egg. If it would be helpful, I would be willing to buy a timer. It would mean a lot to me if one morning a week I could have my eggs soft boiled." This husband got his soft-boiled eggs.

A third part of the setting is your spouse's emotional state. Is he or she emotionally ready to receive a suggestion tonight? Some nights, we're emotionally drained. If everything we've done all day long has gone wrong, and if everyone we've met has been harping on us about something, the last thing we want when we get home is for our husband or wife to ask us to change something about ourselves. Even the simplest request can cause us to explode. Why? Because the request is the straw that breaks the camel's back.

How do you find out if your spouse is emotionally ready to receive a suggestion? The best way I know of is simply to ask. Say, "Honey, would this be a good night to make a request of you?" Even if your spouse says no, I can almost guarantee that he or she will be back in less than an hour, saying, "About that request. What did you have in mind?" He or she will be dying to know! But you say, "No, honey. It's not necessary tonight. We can do it on another night when you are feeling ready. You just let me know when you are feeling like it." Your spouse is likely to respond, "Well, I'm ready now." If that happens, then go ahead, because you have helped your spouse to get ready emotionally to receive your request. Don't ever hit your spouse broadside with a request for change. Always find out if he or she is emotionally ready to receive a suggestion.

Don't Give an Overdose of Criticism

Couples who don't have a system for requesting change will typically hold things inside that bug them, until the pressure gets so strong that they erupt in destructive criticism. A husband says, "I don't know why you can't record the checks that you write. Trying to balance the checkbook when half the records are missing is the most frustrating thing in the world." After launching this opening salvo, he continues, "And another thing: Why can't you leave my desk alone? I'm tired of trying to find things that you have moved. And while I'm at it, you left the garage door open again this morning. Can you imagine how much heat that wastes? And on the days when I'm out of town, does it ever cross your mind to bring in the mail? The box was stuffed last night when I opened it." Such overdoses of criticism almost never result in positive change.

Hostility gives birth to hostility. An overdose of inflammatory, condemning words will likely bring some return fire from the other spouse. "You're not exactly perfect yourself, you know. I can never depend on you for anything. You promised to bring me a sweatshirt the next time you went to Nashville, but you forgot it again. And I'm sick and tired of doing all the work around here. You don't ever lift a hand to help me. It's like you think I'm your slave. And I don't know how you have the gall to talk to me about leaving the garage door open when you never close a drawer in the bedroom."

Nothing constructive came of this conversation. The husband verbally shot his wife four times, she shot him back three times, and both spouses went away wounded and defensive. You can be certain that no positive changes will occur. Overdosing on criticism destroys the motivation for change.

I remember a husband who came to me a number of years ago and said, "I didn't come in here to get counseling. I came to tell you that I'm leaving my wife. I wanted you to hear it from me. I know that when I'm gone, she's going to call you, because she respects you. We've been married eight years, and I can't remember a single day in eight years that she hasn't criticized me. She criticizes the way I comb my hair, the way I walk, the way I talk, the way I dress, the way I drive. She doesn't like anything about me. I have finally concluded that if I'm all that bad, she deserves something better."

Later that day, when the wife called and came to my office, I shared with her what her husband had told me. She burst into tears and said, "I was just trying to help him."

Trying to help him? She decimated him. None of us can emotionally handle overdoses of criticism. All of us want change from our spouses, but overdosing on criticism is not the way to get it.

I suggest that you never make more than one request for change per week. That's fifty-two changes per year, and that ought to be enough. Some people are too emotionally fragile to handle even one request per week. For them, it may need to be one every two or three weeks. As you begin to develop the art of making requests, you may want to alternate weeks with your spouse. One week, you might make a request, and the next week it would be your spouse's turn. In fact, on the off weeks,

I suggest that you *invite* your spouse to share something that he or she would like to see you change. When you and your spouse are home in the evening, after you've had dinner, you can say, "This would be a good night for you to give me a request for change. Tell me one thing that would make me a better spouse." Because you're the one who is initiating the conversation, you've predetermined your emotional state, and all that remains is to choose the right time and place to ask your spouse for a suggestion on how you can improve.

Personally, I find I can respond to one request per week from my wife, if it is made after a meal, in private, and when I am feeling emotionally stable. I want to be a better spouse and I can work on one thing a week, but more than that becomes overwhelming. Give me an overdose and I'm not likely to work on changing anything.

Perhaps you grew up in a home where you received overdoses of criticism. Every day, your parents told you what was wrong with you and what you needed to change. They seldom gave you compliments, but they filled your ears with condemning statements. Now that you're an adult and married, you may be giving your spouse overdoses of criticism without even realizing what you're doing, because you're just so used to it from your upbringing. You may want to ask your spouse, "Do you feel that I give you overdoses of criticism?" If he or she says yes, then I suggest that you apologize. Say that you're sorry and that you didn't realize what you were doing. After you've cleared the air, agree with your spouse that you will limit yourself to asking only once a week (or once every two weeks) for something you would like to see changed. And, of course, your spouse will have opportunities to make requests, as well.

Some couples have found the following technique helpful: If one partner starts to make a second request in the same week, the other person simply holds up two fingers and says, "Two, babe, two." Both agree that, when reminded, they will hold their second request until the next week. If you have a lot of things that are bugging you, you may want to get a little "request for change" notebook where you can write them all down. Each week, you can pick out one request to share with your spouse. Learning to limit the number of your requests makes the possibility of change more likely. When we are overwhelmed with requests, we tend to become resentful or angry, and these emotions do not foster change. Breaking the cycle of overdosing on criticism could save your marriage.

Precede Your Request with Compliments

Mary Poppins had it right when she sang, "A spoonful of sugar helps the medicine go down."[1] Compliments make the requests for change more palatable. I suggest a three-to-one ratio. Tell me three things you like about me, and then tell me one thing that you would like me to change.

Let's say that this week my wife is going to request of me that, before I leave the bathroom, I get the hairs out of the sink. Hairs in the sink bug her, and this is her week to make a request. But before she makes her request, she says to me, "Wait a minute, honey. First of all, I want you to know how much I appreciate the fact that you hang up your clothes. I have talked to other wives who tell me that their husbands leave clothes all over the house. Their wives have to pick up after them like they were children. You have always hung up your clothes. I guess your mother trained you—I don't know. But I like it.

"Second, I want you to know how much I appreciate the fact that last night you got the bugs off my windshield. I love it when you get the bugs off my windshield.

"And third, I want you to know how much I appreciate the fact that on Thursday nights you vacuum the floors. When you vacuum the floors, it is next door to heaven for me. One . . . two . . . three . . . are you ready, babe? Those hairs in the sink just bug me to death."

Now, I can work on cleaning up the hairs in the sink, and I probably will. Why? Karolyn likes me! Look, I'm already better than some guys (who can't pick up their clothes), and I want to be a better husband. I've seldom met a man who didn't want to be a better husband. I did meet one a while back. He said, "My wife doesn't deserve anything better." Perhaps, but most men would like to be better.

I'm suggesting that if a husband will take one request from his wife each week and will work on it to the best of his ability, he'll be amazed by how much better of a husband he'll become in three months. The same is true with wives who are willing to take a request from their husbands each week and seek to improve. In fact, I'll make a little prediction. If you will try this plan for requesting change, you'll walk in the door one day, maybe four months from now, and when you say to your spouse, "I'm ready for my suggestion of the week," your spouse will reply, "I think I'll pass this week."

Wow! Won't that be progress! From that point on, your spouse may not have a request every week. In fact, several weeks may pass between requests. But you'll always give your spouse a chance to make a request of you, to tell you something that would make you a better spouse.

Here's an important point: When you make a request and your spouse goes to work on it, don't forget to *notice* and *praise* the effort. Without compliments, your requests may sound like nagging. As one husband said, "I worked so hard at improving, and what did she do? Gave me another criticism! Once in a while, I'd like to know that I'm doing something right." By recognizing your spouse's efforts to improve and praising his or her positive qualities, you will motivate your spouse to make additional changes.

Think about It

When we get married, we discover all those things about the other person that we didn't know before. Some of those things really irritate us. They are flies in the ointment of our marital unity.

Perhaps you found out that when your husband takes a shower he leaves the washcloth in the bottom of the shower stall, sopping wet. When you walk by, you ask yourself, *Who does he think is going to pick that thing up?* Or maybe you discovered that your wife's clothes don't know how to get on hangers and her shoes don't know how to get to the closet.

You discover that he cannot brush his teeth without getting white spots on the mirror. When she replaces the bathroom tissue, she always puts it on backward. He always leaves the seat up. She squeezes the toothpaste in the middle, instead of on the bottom like she ought to. One husband told me, "I put a sign on our toothpaste: 'Squeeze my tail.' Didn't work!" he said.

What are you going to do about these irritations and the hundreds more that crop up over the years? I'm suggesting that once a week you request a change. And if it's something you're doing or not doing, and you can make a change, why not? Guys, if she wants the towels folded under and over, how long does it take to fold a towel under and over? Two seconds. A small price to pay for a happy wife. So your mother didn't fold towels under and over. You're not married to your mother. I believe we should change everything we can change to please each other. As we change, we make life easier for each other and we walk together in marital harmony.

What about the Things Your Spouse Does Not Change?

It would be unfair of me to leave you with the impression that, if you follow the plan we have been discussing, nine months or a year from now your spouse will do everything you request. In reality, there are some things your spouse cannot or will not change.

I can best illustrate this from my own life: Karolyn and I had been married for some time when I realized that she knew how to open drawers but didn't know how to close them. She also knew how to open cabinet doors but didn't know how to close them. And all these open drawers and doors bugged me.

One day, before I learned the things I have shared with you, I said to her, "Karolyn, if you don't mind, when you finish in the kitchen could you please close the cabinet doors? I hit my head on these things if I'm not careful. And in the bathroom, when you finish, if you don't mind, would you please close the drawers? I catch my pants on these things when I walk through the room." To me, these were simple requests. The next day when I came home, I walked into our little apartment and glanced into the kitchen—and cabinet doors were open. I went into the bathroom, and drawers were open.

"Okay, it's a habit," I reasoned. "It will take her a while to change a habit so I will give her a few days."

I did. I gave her a week. But every day that week, I did my door check and my drawer check, and every day they were open.

At the end of the week, I thought to myself, *Maybe she didn't even hear what I said. Maybe she was having a bad day and really didn't get the message.* I was in graduate school in education, so I figured I'd just use a little education.

When I got home, I went into the bathroom, took everything out of the top drawer, and called Karolyn in for a demonstration. I opened the drawer and showed her how it worked. "This little wheel fits in this groove here. Marvelous things, these drawers. You could actually close this drawer with one finger." I demonstrated. Then I took Karolyn to the kitchen and said, "Now, if you get this door close enough, this little magnet here will grab it and close it for you."

I knew she got the message that day. When you use visual aids, you communicate, right? (I can hear all the wives booing me right now—and rightly so. But remember, I was young and foolish.)

The day after my little demonstration, when I came home from work, I walked into our apartment and glanced into the kitchen—and cabinet doors were open. I went into the bathroom, and drawers were open. Again I thought, *Okay, it's a habit. It will take her a while to change a habit. I'll give her a few days.* So I did; I gave her a month. But every day that month, I ran my door check and my drawer check, and every day they were open. At the end of a month, I gave Karolyn an angry lecture. I said, "I don't understand you. You're a college graduate. You are an intelligent woman. You are a deeply spiritual person, and yet you can't close drawers. I don't get it."

The problem persisted for nine months. I followed two approaches. For about a month or so, I would go on a "slow burn," which means I wouldn't say anything to Karolyn, but inside I was asking myself, *What is wrong with this woman?* Then I would switch and I would give her angry lectures for about a month. But it really didn't matter whether I gave her lectures or held it all inside; she did not close the drawers or the doors.

After nine months of this, I came home one night to find that our daughter, who was eighteen months old at the time, had stitches near the corner of one of her eyes.

"What happened?" I asked Karolyn. Amazingly, she told me the truth.

"She fell and cut herself on the corner of an open drawer."

I could not believe my ears. I thought to myself, *If I were you, I would not tell me that the baby fell onto an open drawer. Tell me anything else, but don't tell me she fell on an open drawer.* But Karolyn told me the truth.

I was so proud of myself for not overreacting. *I will not pour salt in the wound,* I said to myself. *I will not say, "I told you so."* But in my heart I was thinking, *I bet she'll close the drawers now!* And the other thought I had was, *She wouldn't listen to me. Now God is working on her.* But you know what? She still didn't close the drawers, even after that!

Two months later (this is now eleven months down the road), it finally dawned on me: *This woman will never close drawers.* I'm a slow learner, but I finally got the message. As my mind absorbed the full impact of this latest revelation, I went to the college library, sat down at my graduate study desk, and did what I had been trained to do. Have you heard this plan? When you don't know what to do about a problem, get a sheet of paper and write down all the thoughts that come to your mind—good thoughts, wild thoughts, crazy thoughts, helpful thoughts. Write them all down. Then go back and pick out your best alternative. That's what I did.

The first thing that came to my mind was this: *I could leave her.* I had thought about that before. On the heels of that idea came this thought: *If I ever get married again, the first thing I'm going to ask is, "Do you close drawers?"*

The second idea came in stages. I thought it through very carefully before I wrote it down: *I could be miserable—every time I see an open drawer—from now until the day I die, or she dies.* I thought it, so I wrote it.

The third possibility, and the last one I could think of, was this: *I could accept this as something she will never change, and from now on I could close the drawers myself.*

Since that time, some people who have heard the story have made other suggestions. One man told me that you can get springs that close the drawers automatically. (I didn't know that.) Another man told me that he had taken the cabinet doors off altogether. (That thought never crossed my mind.)

When I was done, I looked at my list and marked off number 1 immediately. I was in seminary, studying to be a pastor. I thought, *If I leave her, I'll never get a pastorate.* So I marked that one off quickly. I read number 2 and also marked it off. I thought, *Why would a grown man choose to be miserable about something for the rest of his life?* That didn't make sense.

Well, that left me with number 3. I could accept the fact that my wife would never change, and from this point on I could close the drawers myself. Then I asked myself, "How long would it take me to close the cabinet doors in the kitchen?"

One . . . two . . . three . . . four seconds.

"How long would it take me to close the drawers in the bathroom?"

One . . . two . . . three seconds.

"Four plus three equals seven. *Seven seconds.* I believe I can work that into my schedule."

When I got home, I said to Karolyn, "About those drawers . . ."

She quickly responded, "Gary, please don't bring that up again!"

"No," I said, "babe, no, no, I've got an answer. From now on, and for as long as I'm alive, you will never have to close the doors or the drawers again. From now on, I'll close the doors, I'll close the drawers, and you won't ever have to worry about it."

Do you know what she said?

"Fine."

And she walked out of the room. It was no big deal to her, but it was a major turning point in my life. Ever since that day, open drawers have not bothered me. I have no emotion when I see an open drawer. In fact, if you were to walk with me into our bathroom most nights, you'd see that the drawers are open. But when I walk in, I close them—because that's my job!

What am I saying? I'm saying there will be a few things that your spouse either cannot or will not change. I don't know which it is, and it really doesn't matter. I have an incredibly wonderful wife. She has made many changes for me. I have often thought that maybe it's something genetic that prevents her from closing drawers. It's possible! But whether it's *can't* or *won't*, the point is that your spouse will never fulfill all your requests.

So, what are you going to do about the things your spouse won't change? I believe that love accepts these imperfections.[2] Wouldn't I be foolish, after all these years, to still be mumbling and grumbling about open drawers? Instead, I choose to thank God for all the positive changes that Karolyn has made, and I choose to accept the things that she either cannot or will not change.

Some of you men have been running behind your wives for fifteen years mumbling about the lights. "I don't understand why you can't turn off the lights when you leave a room. The switch works both ways, you know. And it just takes one finger. If you would turn off the lights, I could buy you a new coat." I don't want to discourage you, guys, but if she hasn't turned off the lights for fifteen years, she may never. Maybe you need to understand that she is the "light turner-onner" and you are the "light turner-offer." Love accepts some imperfections. (And aren't you glad?)

By now you realize that I'm not promising you that your spouse will change everything to your satisfaction. What I am saying is that if you will implement the three-step plan I've outlined, your spouse will make significant changes. I have never seen the plan fail. Here is a recap:

Step One: *Confess your own failures and ask forgiveness.* This sends a clear signal that you realize you have not been a perfect spouse in the past. It indicates that you are thinking seriously about your marriage and that you want the relationship to improve. Whether or not your spouse is able to forgive you immediately, he or she is now aware that something significant is happening in your mind. This awareness plants a seed of hope.

Step Two: *Learn to speak your spouse's primary love language.* When confession is followed by new expressions of unconditional love in your spouse's primary love language, you are watering that seed of hope. You are meeting your spouse's emotional need for love in the most effective way. In due time, the sprout of new life will emerge. Those expressions of love will stimulate emotional warmth and change the climate in your marriage. You may begin to see a new sparkle in your spouse's eyes and a more positive attitude toward you and your marriage. Eventually your spouse will begin to reciprocate by expressing love to you in your primary love language. That's when you'll discover that nothing holds more potential in human relationships than the power of unconditional love.

Step Three: *Now you are ready to begin making specific requests.* Because your spouse has already forgiven you for your past failures, and because your spouse already feels your love, he or she will be far more open to your requests. Most people are willing to make changes when they feel loved.

What has been interesting to me through the years is that couples who implement this plan often find their spouse making positive changes even before they are requested. Because of past complaints, they already know many of the changes that their husband or wife desire. Now that they are living in an atmosphere of forgiveness and are experiencing their spouse's expressions of love, they are motivated to do things that they think their spouse will appreciate—without even being asked.

"I couldn't believe it," one husband said. "For years, I had asked my wife to walk the dog one night a week while I attended the Elk's club. She never did it. I always hated coming home on Tuesday nights at nine thirty and having to walk the dog. I was about six weeks into the 'love phase' of this new strategy when I came home one Tuesday night and discovered that she had already walked the dog. I hadn't even gotten around to requesting it. I was blown away. I told her how much I appreciated it. From that night on, she has always walked the dog on Tuesday nights. I know it's a little thing, but it means a lot to me."

Little changes or big changes, they are all easier when past failures have been confessed and love has become a way of life. Now that you have read part two, "Home Improvements," and have a clear picture of how to get your spouse to change without manipulation, I want to challenge you to implement the program. Read chapter 1 of this part again, and begin the process of identifying and confessing your past failures. Don't rush the process. Take time to get outside help, as described in the chapter. Make your confession thorough and genuine. Then reread chapter 2, discover your spouse's primary love language, and begin speaking it regularly. Two weeks into the process, start to sprinkle in the other four love languages as well. Then play the Tank Check game with your spouse. When you are receiving consistent scores of 8, 9, or 10, you will know that you are ready to begin making your requests for change.

When you start to see positive changes in your spouse, I would love to hear your story. Visit www.garychapman.org and select the Contact link. I hope to hear from you soon.

• • •

Putting the Principles into Practice

1. Think of times in the past when you or your spouse gave each other overdoses of criticism. How did you feel? How do you think your spouse felt?

2. Think of times in the past when your spouse verbalized something that he or she wanted changed, but did it in the presence of other people. How did it make you feel? Or, if you were the one who verbalized something about your spouse, how do you think it made him or her feel?

3. In the future, if your spouse agreed to make his or her request in private, after a meal, and after giving you three compliments, how often would you be willing to receive a request?

___ one request for change per week
___ one request for change every two weeks
___ other (please specify): _____

4. If your spouse is willing, ask him or her to complete steps 1–3 above. Discuss your answers and begin following the plan for requesting change suggested in this chapter.

5. If your spouse is not interested in participating in steps 1–3 above, don't be discouraged. Simply tell him or her that you would like to work on becoming a better mate and would like for him or her to give you one suggestion each week (or every other week) for something you could change that would make your spouse's life easier. (When your spouse sees that you are taking the requests for change seriously, he or she is likely to begin reciprocating.)

6. Make a list of a few things you would sincerely like to see your spouse change. (At the end of the book, I have included sample lists of how husbands and wives have responded when asked the question, "What would you like to see your spouse change?")

7. Now, go over your list and make sure your requests are specific, understandable, and achievable. The more specific, the better. (You may want to read pages 352–357 again.)

8. Remember:

- Never make more than one request per week (or according to your agreed-upon schedule).
- Never make a request when your spouse is hungry.
- Always make your request in private.
- Ask if your spouse is emotionally ready for you to make your request.
- Precede your request with at least three compliments.

• • •

Closing Thoughts on Home Improvements
In my own life and in the lives of hundreds of couples I have counseled, the principles in part two, "Home Improvements," have brought real change. It is my hope that you will now do the hard work of implementing this threefold approach. You have the plan. It has worked for other couples, and I'm encouraging you to try it in your own marriage. You have nothing to lose and everything to gain. And if it works for you, I hope you will share it with your friends. In today's cultural climate, successful marriages are more difficult than ever to effect. I believe the ideas shared in this part of the book have the potential for helping thousands of couples move down the road of marital intimacy with greater harmony. If that happens, I will be greatly pleased.

You will want to see the additional helps related to part two on pages 352–357 in the back of the book: "How to Get Your Spouse to Change without Manipulation—A Three-Step Plan"; "What I Wish My Wife Would Change"; and "What I Wish My Husband Would Change."

• • •

Some Ideas Worth Remembering
- The most common reason people do not get the changes they desire is that they start at the wrong place.
- Most of us have lived by the philosophy, "If my spouse would

change, then I would change." If most of us are honest, we will
have to admit this approach has not worked.

- Confessing wrong liberates us from the bondage of past failures
and opens up the possibility for changed behavior in the future.

- Confession of wrongdoing needs to be broader than simply
confessing to God. You also need to confess to the person you
have wronged. In marriage, that is your spouse.

- We cannot erase past failures, but we can agree that what we
did or failed to do was wrong, and we can sincerely ask for
forgiveness. In so doing, we are starting at the right place.

- One of the fundamental languages of love is to speak words
that affirm the other person. Affirming words give life, while
condemning words bring death.

- A gift is a physical, visible token of thoughtfulness. Any adult
can learn to give gifts.

- For some people, "Actions speak louder than words." Doing
something that you know your spouse would like for you to
do is an expression of love.

- Quality time is much more than being in the same room or the
same house with your spouse. It involves giving your spouse your
undivided attention.

- All requests for change should be specific, understandable,
doable, and measurable.

- Tell me three things you like about me, and then tell me one
thing you would like for me to change. Compliments make the
request more palatable.

- I believe we should change, everything we can change to please
each other. As we change, we make life easier for each other and
we walk together in marital harmony.

Part Three
PROFIT SHARING
Making Money an Asset in Your Marriage

COULD WE SURVIVE WITHOUT MONEY? Well, it depends on where you live. My academic background is anthropology, the study of cultures. There are a few primitive cultures in the world where people live without money. The men hunt for meat, while the wives and children work the gardens. Everyone in the village shares the food. When a couple get married, the men of the village build them a thatched-roof house. Clothing, such as it is, is made from the skins of animals. Thus, the basic needs for food, clothing, and shelter are met without any need for money.

However, you do not live in this kind of moneyless society. In the modern industrial world, most couples do not build their own houses, grow their own food, or make their own clothing. We are a society of specialists: Some of us build houses, others make clothing, and others produce and distribute food. We each receive money for the work we perform. With this money, we then buy from others the things we desire. This system of production and distribution is complex, but for the most part, it works fairly well. In the United States, most people manage to obtain food, clothing, and shelter.

Why then is money often the number-one source of conflict in American marriages? The poorest couples in America have abundance compared to the masses of the world's population. I am convinced that the problem does not lie in the amount of money that a couple possess but rather in their attitudes toward money and the manner in which they handle it. The problem is not really money; it is their relationship with

money. If they could find a more wholesome perspective on money—
that is, change the way they think about money—and find a positive
way to handle money, then money would cease to be an area of conflict
and would become an asset to their marriage.

This part of the book focuses on marriage and money. For over thirty
years as a marriage counselor, I have been listening to couples argue
about money. Here are some of the complaints I frequently hear:

- "He could get a better job if he would try."
- "She spends more money than we both make, and we both have
  good jobs."
- "I never know how much money we have because he won't let
  me see the checkbook."
- "He makes investments that are foolish. He has lost thousands
  of dollars."
- "Her parents keep giving her money; I don't like that."
- "Why can't we save something? We've been married for ten years
  and don't even have a savings account."
- "All I ask is that she record the checks that she writes. Balancing
  our checkbook is a nightmare."
- "He doesn't understand that when you put things on a credit
  card, eventually you have to pay for them. We're ten thousand
  dollars in debt, and all we're able to pay each month is the
  interest."
- "She bought a $300 dress. Do you know how much food $300
  would buy?"
- "He pledged $5,000 to the church building fund. I don't know
  where he thinks that money is going to come from."
- "She keeps telling me that she grew up with a different lifestyle.
  Well, I'm sorry. I'm not her father. I don't go to work in a shirt
  and tie every day."
- "He bought a new car and didn't even discuss it with me."
- "How can we afford to invest when we don't have enough money
  to buy the baby's milk?"
- "She keeps buying lottery tickets. Do you know the chances of

ever winning the lottery? It's like throwing our money out the window."

Perhaps you could add a few comments yourself—things you've said or heard your spouse say regarding money. The purpose of this book is to help the two of you learn to work as a team in obtaining and managing money so that you are working together rather than against each other. Teamwork produces profit sharing. Each of you is a benefactor. Money becomes not a battleground but a means of helping you obtain things that will enhance your marriage.

I hope that the time you invest in reading this part of the book will produce huge dividends in your marriage.

1

IT ALL BEGINS WITH ATTITUDE

BEFORE WE LOOK AT THE VARIOUS DYNAMICS related to handling money in marriage, we must first of all put money into its proper perspective. Some couples live as though the accumulation of money and the acquisition of material possessions are the focus of life. These couples live to get. A new purchase brings momentary pleasure. Between acquisitions, they experience emotional lows while anticipating the next moment of pleasure. I don't need to tell you that such an attitude does little to create marital satisfaction.

Jesus lived a rather simple lifestyle, but he impacted human history more than any person who has ever lived. I shall never forget the day I read this statement spoken by Jesus: "A man's life does not consist in the abundance of his possessions."[1] It changed my perspective on money forever. It also resonated with my experience. Hundreds of well-to-do couples have sat in my office over the past thirty years and made statements like this: "We sold our souls for the acquisition of *things*, and now we are bankrupted spiritually and emotionally. We have things . . . but life is empty."

Relationships, Not Things

Real satisfaction is found not in money (any amount of it) but in loving relationships with God, our spouse, our children, and our friends. Loving relationships are our greatest asset. This is most often realized in moments of crisis. Many times I have stood outside the room of a hospital intensive-care center when a child was in critical condition because of an automobile accident or a life-threatening illness. What matters to the parents at that point is not how much money they have or the size of their house, but the friends who come to stand with them in the midst of deep pain. In the experience of physical and emotional crisis, all humankind stands on level ground—some have friends and some do not. Money is no replacement for friendships.

If you believe that more money and more material possessions will bring you marital happiness, you have the wrong attitude. Money can be used to provide more creature comforts, but money will not create a successful marriage. It is righteous living, love, patience, gentleness, and compassion that build meaningful relationships. It is treating each other with dignity, respect, love, and care that creates a happy marriage. This can be attained in the poorest of circumstances as well as in the homes of the affluent. If you are telling yourselves, "We'll be happier when we get more money," you are deceiving yourselves. Some of the happiest couples I know live near the poverty level. I am not saying that they do not aspire for more; they do. But they are under no illusion that more will automatically bring greater happiness.

In fact, quite the opposite can be true. I remember Paul Brown and his wife, Jill (not their real names), who came to my office, separated and hurting. "We've got it all," Paul said, "and now all of it means nothing. We left God out of our lives; we didn't have time for friends. I worked two jobs. We've got our 4,500-square-foot house; we've got the cars; we've got money in the bank; but in the midst of it all, we've lost each other. I'd give it all away today if we could go back and start over in the little apartment where we lived when we first got married. In those days we had nothing, but we were happy. Today, we have everything, and we're miserable." With a great deal of counseling, Paul and Jill rediscovered each other. They did, in fact, lower their standard of living and raise their level of happiness. However, they could have saved themselves twelve years of miserable affluent living if they had found a proper perspective on money earlier in life.

The desire to have more material possessions is not necessarily an evil desire. The problem comes when we allow money to become the focus of our lives. The Scriptures say, "The love of money is a root of all kinds of evil. Some people, eager for money, have wandered from the faith and pierced themselves with many griefs."[2] Such sorrows are not the result of having money or not having money, but of *loving* money. When obtaining money becomes the motivating force of our lives, we set ourselves up for "many griefs," such as the loss of marital intimacy. When, on the other hand, we keep money in its proper place, it becomes an asset to the marriage.

Joint Ownership

The second aspect of money about which many couples need a change of attitude is the area of ownership. In marriage, it is no longer "my money" and "your money" but rather "our money." In the same manner, it is no longer "my debts" or "your debts" but rather "our debts." If, before you marry, one of you owes $5,000 on an educational loan and the other owes $50 to a local department store, after the wedding you are collectively in debt $5,050. When you accept each other as partners, you accept each other's liabilities as well as each other's assets.

That is the reason full disclosure of assets and liabilities should be made by both partners before marriage. It is not wrong to enter marriage with debts, but you ought to discuss those debts beforehand and agree upon a plan and schedule of repayment. Most couples have some debts when they come to marriage, and a full disclosure by each partner will help them to face marriage realistically.

I have known couples who failed to discuss this area sufficiently before marriage and realize after the wedding that together they have a debt so large that they already feel a financial noose around their necks. What a tragedy to begin marriage with such a handicap. In my opinion, a large debt without a realistic means of repayment is sufficient cause to postpone the wedding.

In the same way, your assets are now joint assets. She may have $6,000 in a savings account and he may have only $90, but when they marry, *they* have $6,090. If you do not feel comfortable with this oneness, then you are not ready for marriage. The very motif of marriage is unity, oneness, togetherness. When it comes to finances, you must move toward unity.

There may be cases in which, because of very large estates or children from a previous marriage, the couple would be wise to retain individual ownership of certain properties or assets. But for most of us, the principle of unity implies joint savings accounts, checking accounts, property ownership, and so on. We are now a team, and we want to express our unity in finances as well as in other areas of life. Since it is *our* money, it means that neither of us will try to control the finances. Instead, we will manage our finances together as a team, using the best of our past experience and wisdom.

Certainly, one spouse may regularly write the checks for the monthly bills and balance the checkbook, but the other partner needs to have full access to all financial matters and freedom to express opinions and negotiate decisions. When one partner tries to control the finances to the exclusion of the other, that person becomes a parent, and the partner, a child. One wife said, "I am ashamed to say this, but it illustrates the problem: Every time I need a pair of hose, I have to go to my husband and say, 'May I have $5 to buy a pair of hose?' It's horrible. I feel like a child." Such an arrangement does not strengthen the marital relationship and will inevitably result in numerous conflicts.

If you and your spouse embrace the two realities discussed in this chapter—(1) our relationship is more important than the amount of money we have, and (2) whatever we possess belongs to us jointly—then you will have laid the foundation for making money an asset in your marriage.

• • •

Putting the Principles into Practice
1. In the past, what has been your attitude toward money? What changes do you need to make in your attitude?

2. Are you willing to embrace the concept that your marriage is more important than the accumulation of money and material possessions? Would you be willing to verbalize this to your spouse?

3. Are you willing to embrace the idea that all your money and possessions now belong to both of you equally and that all your debts are now "our debts"? Would you be willing to verbalize this to your spouse?

4. As an act of affirming these attitudes, perhaps the two of you would like to sign and date the following statement:

We recognize that money will never bring us happiness, that our relationship to each other is more important than what we possess. We further agree that all our possessions belong to us jointly and that all our debts are shared. We will work as a team to manage our finances in such a way as to enhance our relationship.

_____

HUSBAND

_____

DATE

_____

WIFE

_____

DATE

2

WORK IS A NOBLE ENDEAVOR

Work is introduced in the first chapter of the Bible. God said to Adam and Eve, "Be fruitful and increase in number; fill the earth and subdue it. Rule over the fish of the sea and the birds of the air and over every living creature that moves on the ground."[1] Not only were they to have children, but they were to work in order to provide for those children. In the second chapter of the book of Genesis, we get a clearer picture of what that work involved: "The Lord God took the man and put him in the Garden of Eden to work it and take care of it."[2]

Please note that working preceded the Fall. Some have implied that work was a part of the Curse after Adam and Eve sinned. This was not the case; God instituted work before man sinned. Work is a gift of God. When we work, we are cooperating with the divine plan.

God created humans with a mind that had great capacity for learning. But they did not start out knowing all the secrets of the universe. God commanded Adam to *subdue;* that is, to acquire a knowledge and mastery over his material environment and to bring its elements into the service of humankind. Every time I fly in an airplane, I thank God for that mandate. Every time I ride in an automobile, I'm glad someone obeyed God. Every time I turn on a light, I'm glad for someone's work.

To find our work is to find our place in the world. Work is applied effort. It is expending our energy for the sake of accomplishing or achieving something. The opposite of work is not leisure or play, but idleness—not investing ourselves in anything.

Work is normal. When God gave the Ten Commandments, he included the concept of work. "Remember the Sabbath day by keeping it holy. Six days you shall labor and do all your work, but the seventh day is a Sabbath to the LORD your God."[3] The emphasis of the command is on the seventh day for rest and worship, but we must not overlook its relationship to working.

Some of our work results in a paycheck, but some of our work has other rewards. The housework of parents is real work, though it brings in no revenue. The homework of children is real work, though the payoff is not in money.

William Bennett, in *The Book of Virtues,* lists work as one of the ten great virtues. He says, "Those who have missed the joy of work, of a job well done, have missed something very important."[4] Recently I talked to a man who had lost his job. He said, "I enjoy the freedom, but I miss the satisfaction of accomplishment." He was echoing the ancient Hebrew proverb "A longing fulfilled is sweet to the soul."[5] Theologian Carl Henry once said, "When man loses the sacred significance of work, he soon loses the sacred meaning of time and life."[6]

A Sacred Calling

For the Christian, work is indeed seen as a sacred calling. The word *vocation* means "calling." Each of us has certain interests and abilities. God expects us to use these for the good of humankind and for his ultimate glory. All good work is seen as service to God and, thus, sacred. It is through work that parents provide for the physical needs of their children. Once this is done, they have the opportunity to meet their emotional and spiritual needs. The apostle Paul said, "If anyone does not provide for his relatives, and especially for his immediate family, he has denied the faith and is worse than an unbeliever."[7] The idea is that those who are walking in fellowship with God will see their work as a sacred responsibility.

We typically say of a person who is unwilling to work that he or she is lazy. Laziness in the Bible is always seen as sinful. In the book of Proverbs, we read, "Go to the ant, you sluggard; consider its ways and be wise! It has no commander, no overseer or ruler, yet it stores its provisions in summer and gathers its food at harvest. How long will you lie there, you sluggard? When will you get up from your sleep? A little sleep, a little slumber, a little folding of the hands to rest—and poverty will come on you like a bandit and scarcity like an armed man."[8]

Another proverb reads, "The sluggard craves and gets nothing, but the desires of the diligent are fully satisfied."[9] In the writings of the apostle Paul, we find an antidote for laziness. He said to the Christians who lived in the city of Thessalonica, "Even when we were with you, we gave you this rule: 'If a man will not work, he shall not eat.' We hear that some among you are idle. They are not busy; they are busybodies. Such people we command and urge in the Lord Jesus Christ to settle down and earn the bread they eat."[10]

A Normal Part of Life
If we wish to prepare children for adulthood, then we must teach them this truth: Work is a normal part of life. If we do not work, we do not eat. As children get older, we assign them work responsibilities in keeping with their abilities. We let them know that just as Dad works and Mom works, so children also work. Because we work, we get to eat. If we fail to work, we forfeit the privilege of eating.

There is a simple, yet dramatic, way to teach this lesson: You merely assign your children a job and let them know that if they complete the job, they have the privilege of eating dinner that night. If they do not complete the job, they must miss the meal. You need not coax, scold, or intimidate them to complete the job. You simply assign it and explain the consequences. I have yet to meet a child who will miss more than one meal before learning to work. Of course, you must first of all teach the children how to do whatever you expect them to do. Habits of personal hygiene, helping with the laundry, caring for pets, making beds, helping with meals, and other household chores all require learning.

Parents can show their children how to enjoy doing things that have to be done by working with them, by encouraging and expressing appreciation for their efforts, and by modeling for them their own cheerful example. Tasks can be done cheerfully and with pride—or grudgingly and with rebellion. The manner in which we do them is really up to us. It is a matter of choice. There are no menial jobs, only menial attitudes. If children learn to work cheerfully in the home, parents have taught them one of the major ingredients for being successful adults.

The Financial Impact of Nonpaying Jobs

As adults, it is typically our work that brings us income. But do not underestimate the financial impact of nonpaying jobs. The husband or wife who mows the lawn has contributed $30 or more (depending on the size of the lawn) to the family assets. The person who cooks meals, washes clothes, vacuums floors, and cleans commodes is also making a positive impact on the financial well-being of the family. Whether or not we receive a paycheck for it, our work impacts positively the financial assets of the marriage.

The Christian couple who are committed to the work ethic revealed in Scripture understand that they are working not only for the benefit of their marriage and family, but also for God. Paul said, "Whatever you do, work at it with all your heart, as working for the Lord, not for men, since you know that you will receive an inheritance from the Lord as a reward. It is the Lord Christ you are serving."[11]

It is by means of work that we obtain money to provide for our needs and to enrich the lives of others. Whether you and your spouse both work for pay or only one gets paid, you both work for the benefit of the family.

• • •

Putting the Principles into Practice

1. If you are employed for pay, do you sense that the manner in which you are investing your energy is making a contribution to the well-being of others and thus bringing glory to God? If not, would you consider exploring the possibility of changing vocations?

2. If your work does not involve a paycheck, do you recognize the intangible value of what you are doing—the contribution you are making to your family and to others? Is there anything you would like to change about the way you are investing your life?

3. Do you and your spouse agree that providing for the physical, emotional, and spiritual well-being of your family (which includes the two of you) is a sacred responsibility? If so, are you daily asking for God's wisdom?

4. Does either of you feel that it is time to explore the possibility of changes in your work—who works for pay, how many hours that person will work outside the home each week, who takes care of various nonpaying jobs, etc.? If so, discuss this idea and find a strategy to execute these changes.

3

IN GOD WE TRUST

WHEN I WROTE THE TITLE OF THIS CHAPTER, I instinctively reached for my wallet and took out my cash. On the back of the one-dollar bill, I read "In God We Trust." I looked at the five-dollar bill and read "In God We Trust." The same was true of the ten- and twenty-dollar bills. And if I'd had a fifty- and a hundred-dollar bill, they would read the same—"In God We Trust."

No matter how much money we have, it is still "in *God* we trust." To trust in money to give life meaning is to trust in an idol. The Scriptures declare, "Every good and perfect gift is from above, coming down from the Father of the heavenly lights, who does not change like shifting shadows."[1] All that we have or ever expect to obtain is a gift from God. There are no "self-made" men.

C. S. Lewis writes, "One of the dangers of having a lot of money is that you may be quite satisfied with the kinds of happiness money can give and so fail to realise your need for God. If everything seems to come simply by signing checks, you may forget that you are at every moment totally dependent on God."[2]

There are individuals who pride themselves on having accumulated great wealth. They may look at themselves as "self-made," but one small germ or virus can quickly change their perspective. We could accomplish nothing without the help of God. Life itself is a gift from God. It is true that we can take steps to preserve our health, and we can develop the mind that God has given us. And through these efforts we can accomplish much in life, as we discussed in the previous chapter. But both our bodies and minds are gifts from God.

Make God Your Business Partner

Why am I talking about God in a topic about money and marriage? It's because we were created to live in union with God. We are at our best when we cooperate with God. Many couples have made foolish financial decisions because they left God out of the process. Those who seek God's wisdom and make financial decisions based on the principles revealed in Scripture will save themselves much heartache.

We accept the challenge of work, but we do not depend on ourselves. We look to God for wisdom as to how to use our abilities in the most productive manner. I remember a young man who said to me, "I had wrestled for weeks with an engineering problem and was unable to come up with a workable solution. Finally, a friend of mine suggested that I pray and ask God to give me an answer. I did, and within thirty minutes, it came to me. I had the solution. So I have decided that God and I make a pretty good team." This young man was reaping the benefits of God's offer: "If any of you lacks wisdom, he should ask God, who gives generously to all without finding fault, and it will be given to him."[3]

R. G. LeTourneau, one of the industrial giants of the last generation, often spoke of the day he made God his business partner. He was floundering and deeply in debt when he realized that he was trying to build a business by his own ingenuity. After making God his partner, he built some of the most effective earthmoving equipment ever built. During World War II, his earthmoving machines became the "secret weapons" of the war. After the war, he received the 10th Annual Award of the National Defense Transportation Association as the person whose "achievement contributed most to the effectiveness of the transportation industry in support of national security."[4]

One of the benefits of trusting in God is that we don't have to worry about money. Jesus made this abundantly clear when he said,

I tell you, do not worry about your life, what you will eat or drink; or about your body, what you will wear. Is not life more important than food, and the body more important than clothes? Look at the birds of the air; they do not sow or reap or store away in barns, and yet your heavenly Father feeds them. Are you not much more valuable than they? Who of you by worrying can add a single hour to his life? And why do you worry about clothes? See how the lilies of the field grow. They do not labor or spin. Yet I tell you that not even Solomon in all his splendor was dressed like one of these. If that is how God clothes the grass of the field, which is here today and tomorrow is thrown into the fire, will he not much more clothe you, O you of little faith? So do not worry, saying, "What shall we eat?" or "What shall we drink?" or "What shall we wear?" For the pagans run after all these things, and your heavenly Father knows that you need them. But seek first his kingdom and his righteousness, and all these things will be given to you as well.[5]

God is committed to caring for his children. This does not mean that we are to sit back and expect God to do everything. There is an old German proverb that says, "God gives the birds their food, but he does not throw it into their nests." We are to use the mind and body he has given us, but we are to do it in cooperation with him, looking to him for wisdom so that we can complete what he desires us to accomplish in life. Trusting in God means that we no longer need to live under the burden of self-effort.

With God, we have a partner in business who is committed to our well-being. The apostle Paul made this practical when he said, "Do not be anxious about anything, but in everything, by prayer and petition, with thanksgiving, present your requests to God. And the peace of God, which transcends all understanding, will guard your hearts and your minds in Christ Jesus."[6] It is daily talking with God, seeking his wisdom and guidance, that makes us most productive financially as well as in all other areas of life.

Make Money Your Servant, Not Your Security Blanket

In contrast to God-centered living, there are those who place their trust in money. Money becomes their security blanket. Money, for them, is a sign of success. All their decisions are made in response to the question "What offers the greatest financial advantage?" I remember the husband who said to me, "I moved my family across the country, against the advice of my wife and my friends, in order to make $50,000 more per year. In the new location my teenage daughter got involved in drugs and my college-age son got involved in a cult. I have spent far more than I gained, trying to rescue them. I wish I had listened to my wife."

When we trust in God, we realize that some things are more important than money. For the person who trusts in God, the question is, "How will this decision affect my marriage and family?" (In case you hadn't noticed, we are applying the principle we discussed starting on page 118, where we say that relationships are more important than things.)

The wise couple will make money their servant. They will seek to use money for the good of their family and to help others. They will never allow money to be their master, dictating their decisions. Jesus addressed this issue when he said, "No one can serve two masters. Either he will hate the one and love the other, or he will be devoted to the one and despise the other. You cannot serve both God and Money."[7]

Too many couples have followed the wrong god and lived to regret it. I remember the middle-aged, female attorney who said with tears in her eyes, "I recently quit my job. For eighteen years, I invested my life in climbing the corporate ladder. Betty Friedan [one of the founders of the modern feminist movement] told us we could have it all. But she didn't tell us how much it would cost. It cost me my first marriage. Now that I have found another husband who loves me, I will not make the same mistake twice. I have realized that, for me, marriage and family are far more important than position and money."

I am not suggesting that wives who trust in God cannot have jobs outside the home. Many wives have been able to pursue a vocation and maintain a healthy marriage and be a responsible parent. It all depends on the nature of the job, the personality of the individuals involved, and the dynamics of the family relationships. What I am saying is that the decision needs to be based on how the job affects the marriage, the children, and one's relationship and service to God—not merely on the desire for money or prestige.

Promote the Kingdom of God with Your Work

Another way in which trusting in God affects our financial decisions is in the type of job we pursue. For the Christian, all of life comes under the lordship of Christ. Everything we do should be beneficial to others and promote the Kingdom of God. Some jobs do not meet these criteria. The selling of illegal drugs, the promotion of prostitution, and the whole pornography industry are obvious examples. But there are also other jobs that may not be worthy of your pursuit. Ask yourself these two questions:

• Is what I am doing in my vocation making a positive impact on people?
• Do I sense when I am at work that I am pleasing God?

If you are trusting in God, you will want to be investing your vocational energy in something more than simply "making money."

There are also couples who hear the call of God to invest their lives in Christian ministry. This calling may lead them to work within the church or other Christian organizations. Almost all these people make the conscious choice to live on less money in order to invest their energies in vocational Christian service. The choice to trust in God rather than money as the source of life's meaning will have huge implications for their marriages.

Other couples who trust in God have been given the privilege of accumulating great wealth. They seek to use it for the benefit of their family and the larger community under the direction of God. Still other couples who trust in God live with meager financial income but sense no lack of satisfaction because they are investing their lives in a manner consistent with God's principles. It is not a matter of how much money we have; it is a matter of where we place our trust.

Joshua, the successor to Moses, gave the people of Israel these instructions as he prepared to lead them into the Promised Land:

> Do not let this Book of the Law depart from your mouth;
> meditate on it day and night, so that you may be careful
> to do everything written in it. Then you will be prosperous
> and successful. Have I not commanded you? Be strong
> and courageous. Do not be terrified; do not be discouraged,
> for the LORD your God will be with you wherever
> you go.[8]

Later, Joshua gave this challenge to the Israelites:

> Choose for yourselves this day whom you will serve, whether
> the gods your forefathers served beyond the River, or the gods
> of the Amorites, in whose land you are living. But as for me
> and my household, we will serve the LORD.[9]

I have never met a couple who regretted trusting in God. But I have met hundreds who have trusted in money—some who are wealthy and some who are not—none of whom found ultimate satisfaction in money. When our trust is in God, we will see money as an instrument to be used for good under his direction. Our greatest desire will be to please God as a good manager of the resources he gives us.

•   •   •

Putting the Principles into Practice
1. Can you sincerely say, "My greatest satisfaction is in pursuing God, not in pursuing money"? If not, would you be willing to change the direction of your pursuits? If so, why not express that decision in a prayer to God?
2. Do you think your spouse would sincerely agree with the statement "My greatest satisfaction is in pursuing God, not in pursuing money"? If not, perhaps the two of you could read this chapter together and discuss the possibility of redirecting the focus of your life.

3. As you read this chapter, did you discover areas of your life where you need the wisdom of God? If so, perhaps you would like to make the words of James 1:5 your prayer:

> If any of you lacks wisdom, he should ask God, who gives generously to all without finding fault, and it will be given to him.

4
GIVING IS AN
EXPRESSION OF GRATITUDE

THERE ARE ONLY THREE THINGS we can do with money: We can give it away, we can save it, or we can spend it. All three are valid ways of using money. In this chapter, we will look at giving it away. Obviously, we cannot and should not give all our money away. Some must be used to meet the physical needs of our families. But if we give none of it away, we are failing to be grateful for what God has given us.

It is interesting that when God laid down concepts by which ancient Israel was to live, he included the area of giving:

> A tithe of everything from the land, whether grain from the soil or fruit from the trees, belongs to the LORD; it is holy to the LORD. . . . The entire tithe of the herd and flock—every tenth animal that passes under the shepherd's rod—will be holy to the LORD. . . . These are the commands the LORD gave Moses on Mount Sinai for the Israelites.[1]

God did not simply refer to "giving" as a vague concept. No, he specified that his people were to give a tenth of their income. The word *holy* means "separated." They were to separate one tenth of their possessions and designate them specifically for the work of God. This gift was to be channeled through the Levites, the spiritual leaders of Israel, and used to meet their needs as well as the needs of the poor. In addition to the tithe, Israel was also encouraged to give offerings.

Years later, we discover that God has not changed his mind about this pattern of giving. In the last book of the Old Testament, we read,

> "Will a man rob God? Yet you rob me. But you ask, 'How do
> we rob you?' In tithes and offerings. You are under a curse—the
> whole nation of you—because you are robbing me. Bring the
> whole tithe into the storehouse, that there may be food in my
> house. Test me in this," says the LORD Almighty, "and see if
> I will not throw open the floodgates of heaven and pour out
> so much blessing that you will not have room enough for it.
> I will prevent pests from devouring your crops, and the vines
> in your fields will not cast their fruit," says the LORD Almighty.
> "Then all the nations will call you blessed, for yours will be a
> delightful land," says the LORD Almighty.[2]

In this passage, the blessing of God is tied to the faithfulness of Israel in giving a tenth of their income back to God. And the curse of God, the removal of God's blessing, is tied to their failure to give.

Are We Required to Give?

In the New Testament, Jesus endorsed the idea of giving a tenth of one's income, while at the same time pointing out to the religious leaders of his day that such giving is to be accompanied by godly living. Jesus said,

> Woe to you, teachers of the law and Pharisees, you hypocrites!
> You give a tenth of your spices—mint, dill and cummin. But
> you have neglected the more important matters of the law—
> justice, mercy and faithfulness. You should have practiced the
> latter, without neglecting the former.[3]

Jesus emphasized that giving 10 percent of one's income is to be done not as a religious duty but as an expression of gratitude from one's heart;

and along with the gift one should exhibit a concern for justice, mercy, and faithfulness to God.

While the New Testament does not require Christians to give 10 percent of their income, it does stress the concept of giving back to God out of what he has given us. Jesus clearly taught that the blessing of God upon our lives is tied to our spirit of gratitude, expressed in giving. Jesus said, "Give, and it will be given to you. A good measure, pressed down, shaken together and running over, will be poured into your lap. For with the measure you use, it will be measured to you."[4] When we express our gratitude to God by giving back to him out of what he has given to us, Jesus promises that God will give us more. One cannot outgive God.

The apostle Paul reiterates this concept when he says,

Remember this: Whoever sows sparingly will also reap sparingly, and whoever sows generously will also reap generously. Each man should give what he has decided in his heart to give, not reluctantly or under compulsion, for God loves a cheerful giver. And God is able to make all grace abound to you, so that in all things at all times, having all that you need, you will abound in every good work.[5]

Paul clearly states that we are to give out of a heart of gratitude, not out of a sense of compulsion. He also affirms that, in giving, we do not diminish our resources because God will abundantly supply all that we need.

An ancient Hebrew proverb says, "Honor the LORD with your wealth, with the firstfruits of all your crops; then your barns will be filled to overflowing, and your vats will brim over with new wine."[6] The New Testament affirms this concept. Paul said to the Christians living in Philippi who had sent him money for his ministry, "The gifts you sent . . . are a fragrant offering, an acceptable sacrifice, pleasing to God. And my God will meet all your needs according to his glorious riches in Christ Jesus."[7]

Clearly our giving is important to God. I think that's because it is a true reflection of our gratitude to God and our love for people. The question is not whether we will give. The questions are how much shall we give and to whom shall we give it?

How Much Shall We Give?

I have always felt strongly that if God required 10 percent of ancient Israel, then those of us who have experienced his forgiveness and the gift of eternal life through Christ our Lord should give even more than that. I believe that 10 percent of one's income is a good starting point and that this should be given off the top of our regular income. Then as we become aware of special opportunities and needs, we may give additional gifts. In the Old Testament, God expected Israel to give 10 percent and even indicated that it already belonged to him. Why should we think that he would expect less of us?

My challenge to Christian couples has always been to give 10 percent of their income to God and adjust their budget to live on the remaining 90 percent. It may require lowering your standard of living, but in the long run, it will raise the quality of your life. Obviously this means that not every couple give the same amount. We give in proportion to what we receive. If we earn $200 a week, then we give $20. If we earn $500, we give $50. If we earn $5,000, we give $500. Whatever our level of income, such giving is a realistic way to start.

R. G. LeTourneau, whom I mentioned in the last chapter, was so greatly blessed by God that in the latter years of his life he gave 90 percent of his income to God and lived on the remaining 10 percent. He once said, "The question is not how much of my money I give to God, but rather how much of God's money I keep for myself."[8] He had learned the joy of giving.

To Whom Should We Give?

In Old Testament days, giving was fairly simple. The gifts were to be brought to the Tabernacle (and later, the Temple) where they would be administered by the Levites and priests.

As Christians, we can follow this precedent by giving our tithes to our church. My personal pattern has always been to give 10 percent to the church I attend and to give additional offerings to other organizations as I am able and feel prompted by God.

Many Christian organizations have been created, some by the church and others by individuals and groups of Christians, to meet a particular need or to explore a particular possibility for the expansion of the Kingdom of God. All these kinds of organizations are worthy of support. The churches with whom I have been associated through the years also give some of the funds they receive to other Christian organizations.

It has always been important for me to remember that I do not give *to* the church, but rather I give *to God through* the church. I do not give *to* Christian organizations, but rather I give *to God through* Christian organizations.

There is also a time to give to individuals who are in need. The apostle John speaks of that when he says, "If anyone has material possessions and sees his brother in need but has no pity on him, how can the love of God be in him? Dear children, let us not love with words or tongue but with actions and in truth."[9] Obviously, one should be conscientious about establishing need and not be taken in by scams. It's also important to determine how best to help an individual in need. Often, it's best not to give cash but to provide food or to pay a utility bill. This is especially true if the person who is in need is addicted to alcohol or drugs. Cash gifts to such a person simply help perpetuate a problem.

Christians who recognize that everything we have is a gift from God express this reality by giving out of what we have received. Such giving is an expression of gratitude. The amount we give and the channels through which we direct our giving will vary, but the attitude is always the same: "Thank you, Father, for your goodness to us."

●　●　●

Putting the Principles into Practice
1. On a scale of 1–10, how grateful are you for what God has given you? Does the level of your giving reflect the level of your gratitude?
2. Are you satisfied with your present pattern of giving? If not, what would you like to see changed?
3. Discuss with your spouse the changes the two of you would like to make in your pattern of giving. (Perhaps your spouse would be willing to read this chapter before you talk about it together.)

5

SAVING IS A SIGN OF WISDOM

THE COUPLE WHO SAVE A PERCENTAGE OF THEIR INCOME REGULARLY will not only have the reserve funds they need for emergencies but will also have the satisfaction that comes from being good managers of their money. Regular savings ought to be a part of your financial plan.

Some feel that Christians should not save, that saving money is a sign they are not trusting God to provide for the future. However, this is not the perspective found in Scripture, which indicates that we are to be good managers of our money. The wise manager faces the future realistically. A Hebrew proverb says, "A prudent man foresees the difficulties ahead and prepares for them; the simpleton goes blindly on and suffers the consequences."[1] It is wise to plan ahead to meet the needs of your family, business, or other endeavors.

There are many reasons for saving money. One is illustrated by this story that Jesus told: "Suppose one of you wants to build a tower. Will he not first sit down and estimate the cost to see if he has enough money to complete it? For if he lays the foundation and is not able to finish it, everyone who sees it will ridicule him, saying, 'This fellow began to build and was not able to finish.'"[2] Many couples have plans to build or buy a house in the future. Others have plans for starting a business. Saving money in order to accomplish these objectives is clearly a wise use of money.

You and your spouse will need to agree on the percentage you would like to save, but you should save something on a regular basis. Many financial advisors suggest allotting 10 percent of your net income to savings. You may choose more or less; the choice is yours. However, if you save only what is left over at the end of the week or the month, you will not save. Being *regular* and *consistent* in what you save is more important than the amount you save.

Preparing for the Future
One of the best reasons to save is the very real possibility of difficult times in the future. Saving is a way of preparing for those difficult times. In the history of Israel, this is illustrated by Joseph, who was called from prison to interpret the dreams of Pharaoh, king of Egypt. The dreams, which God enabled Joseph to interpret, meant that there would be seven years of plenty, followed by seven years of famine. Joseph's financial plan, obviously guided by God, was "to take a fifth of the harvest of Egypt during the seven years of abundance. They should collect all the food of these good years that are coming and store up the grain under the authority of Pharaoh, to be kept in the cities for food. This food should be held in reserve for the country, to be used during the seven years of famine that will come upon Egypt, so that the country may not be ruined by the famine."[3] Pharaoh liked the plan and appointed Joseph to administer it. As a result, Joseph was used of God both to preserve the lives of the citizens of Egypt and also to care for his own family.

Most of us do not have dreams about future difficulties, but we have lived long enough to know that life is not a smooth journey. Difficulties are a part of most of our lives. People lose jobs, get sick, and have disabling accidents. Setting aside some money to prepare for these realities is wise. Again, the wisdom literature says, "In the house of the wise are stores of choice food and oil, but a foolish man devours all he has."[4] In an agricultural economy, people store food and oil. In an industrial economy, people save money so they can buy food and oil.

The Hebrew proverbs offer an illustration from nature: "Go to the ant, you sluggard; consider its ways and be wise! It has no commander, no overseer or ruler, yet it stores its provisions in summer and gathers its food at harvest."[5] There is an old adage that says, "The time to save money is when you have some."

Unfortunately, ours is a consumer society. Many of us have not been taught to save. For every television ad encouraging us to save for the future, there are fifty encouraging us to spend. One young student was asked by his math teacher, "If your father saved $10 a week for a whole year, what would he have?" The student replied, "An iPod, a new suit, and a lot of furniture." This was not the answer the teacher was expecting, but it clearly was the mind-set of the student and his father.

Saving and Investing

There is a difference between saving and investing. The difference lies not only in the level of risk and return on one's money but also in the purpose. Typically, we *save* for an anticipated purpose. We may save for the college education of our children, for the purchase of a new car or house, for Christmas spending, or scores of other anticipated expenditures. We may even save in order to have money to invest. On the other hand, *investing* typically involves funds that are not presently needed or are not designated for a particular purchase in the future. They are set aside, perhaps for retirement or for the purpose of letting the money earn dividends and potentially increase in value.

The typical venues used for savings are bank savings accounts, which have a rather low rate of interest return, and certificates of deposit, which have a somewhat higher rate of return. Investments typically involve the purchase of stocks and bonds, often in the form of mutual funds, which have the potential of bringing in a much higher rate of return but also run the risk of decreasing in value.

Most couples should have considerable money in savings before they begin investing. In today's climate, which encourages not only traditional investing but online investing, many young couples jump into the investment world knowing little about the risks and end up losing far more money than they make. Often they lose money that in their minds was designated for savings. Thus, they undermine their original purpose by the allurement of higher returns.

Establishing a regular pattern of saving is the first step in getting ready to invest. While you are saving, you can educate yourself on the potential and the risks of investing.

If you give 10 percent to God and save 10 percent, that leaves 80 percent to be divided among mortgage payments (or rent), electricity, telephone, heat, water, insurance, furniture, food, medicines, clothes, transportation, education, recreation, and so forth. In the next chapter, we will look at some creative ways of spending that have the potential of freeing up additional funds for saving or giving.

● ● ●

Putting the Principles into Practice

1. What percentage of your present income are you putting into savings or investments? Are you pleased with this percentage? What changes would you like to make?
2. Would your spouse be willing to join you in a discussion about your present saving and investment plans? Would the two of you profit from reading a basic book on the fundamentals of saving and investing? If so, see the Suggested Resources section, pages 365–367, for suggestions.
3. Starting where you are, can the two of you agree on the next step you want to take to strengthen your program of saving and/or investing?

6

CREATIVE SPENDING ENHANCES PROFIT SHARING

A NUMBER OF YEARS AGO, I took a group of college students to Chiapas, the southernmost state of Mexico, for a visit to the Wycliffe Bible Translators "jungle camp." Here we observed missionaries being trained in the technique of living in primitive conditions. They learned how to build houses, ovens, chairs, beds—all out of materials available in the jungle. I have reflected on that experience many times. If that same creativity could be used by the average couple in America, what could be accomplished?

People are instinctively creators. The museums of art and industry located across the world bear visual witness to human creativity. We are made in the image of a God who creates, and we who bear his image have tremendous creative potential. The couple who will exercise this creativity in financial matters will find significant assets. Sewing, refinishing used furniture, recycling others' discards, and painting your own house can do wonders for your budget.

In this chapter, I want to challenge you to apply your creativity to the manner in which you spend your money. When I was growing up, my father often said, "A dollar saved is a dollar earned." He was not using that adage to encourage me to put a dollar in the bank; he was encouraging me to compare prices before I bought something. If I could buy the same item for a dollar less in the store next door, I had saved a dollar, which was just as significant as working to earn a dollar. Dad was teaching me to *shop*, not simply *buy*.

Taking the time to compare prices goes against the grain of many men. "I don't want to spend half a day shopping. I want to go into a store, buy what I want, and get out" is their philosophy. If a man has unlimited resources, then that philosophy is feasible. But if finances are tight, that philosophy is irresponsible, is a disservice to his wife, and will likely lead to conflicts in the marriage.

I believe that creative spending could radically change the climate of your marriage. I present the following ideas in an effort to stimulate your creativity about how to get more for your dollar.

This chapter is not written for the wealthy. In fact, the person who has unlimited resources is probably not reading this part of the book. This chapter is for the couple who have average or modest income but who constantly struggle with having enough money to meet the needs of the family.

Discount Shopping

In most towns, there is a good store that sells items cheaper than all the rest. Why not buy your groceries there? Typically, these discount stores, whether they are called that or not, will save you money. If you regularly buy at these stores, you will save several hundred dollars per year on regular household purchases. This is especially true for food and household items. And if you want to save even more, look for the weekly discounts in these discount stores. Stock up on items when they are super discounted.

A second level of discount shopping is using manufacturers' coupons. These are often received in the mail, available in the local newspapers, and sometimes available at the coupon desk or bulletin board in the local store. These coupons can reduce the price of your purchases by several dollars. One lady shared, "I got $60 worth of groceries for $35 after cashing in my coupons." I could tell she was excited about the way her creative spending was impacting the family budget.

Buying at the cheapest store, using coupons, and stocking up on the special sale items can save literally hundreds of dollars on your food and household budget.

Recycle Shopping

Most communities have a Goodwill store, a thrift store, and/or a Salvation Army store. These stores serve a valuable purpose in the community. They take discarded items from individuals and then sort and keep only those that are truly usable. They display and sell these items at greatly reduced prices and use the proceeds to minister to those in need.

One customer said, "I started buying clothes for my children here but soon realized that the store had really nice clothes for ladies. I can't believe the money I've saved on my clothes since I started shopping at Goodwill." The added value of shopping at resale stores run by charitable organizations is that you are also helping them fulfill their mission. If you think it is below your dignity to shop at such stores, you probably haven't visited one in a few years. Most of them are well-managed; the clothes and products are clean and in excellent condition.

At one of my marriage seminars, a couple told me that they had saved thousands of dollars by recycle shopping. It all started with an experiment. They agreed that for six months they would seek to buy all their household items, all their clothes, and all the children's toys and school supplies at resale or consignment shops. After the six-month trial period, they were hooked.

Free Shopping

A couple who live in Florida told me they had found something even better than shopping at Goodwill. "We call it *free shopping*," the husband said.

"How does that work?" I asked.

"Three ways," he said. "First, we drive through affluent neighborhoods the night before the discards are to be collected. It's amazing the things you find sitting beside a garbage can. Recently, we found a perfectly good basketball goal. We brought it home, and our kids love it. At first, we felt guilty that maybe we were stealing. So now, we ring the doorbell and ask the family if they would mind our having whatever is sitting beside their garbage can. We've never had anyone refuse to give it to us.

"The second approach is that we have let all our friends know that we are open to receiving hand-me-downs, especially children's clothing and toys. We get more than we need, so we pass the extra items along to others.

"The third approach is to inform our parents of specific toys that our children have requested. We know that they are going to give the children presents on their birthdays, Christmas, and other occasions, so why not have them purchase things that the children really want?

"With these three approaches, about the only thing we have to buy our children is food. And now that the children are older, next summer we are going to start a garden," he said with a smile.

Seasonal Shopping

Another approach to saving money is seasonal shopping. My wife is an expert in this kind of shopping, which is especially helpful when buying clothing. Karolyn likes to wear nice clothes, and I like to see her in nice clothes. But she never pays full price for anything. She always shops at the seasonal sales. I don't mean the first day of the sale; I mean after it has been reduced one, two, or three times. The other day she came home with a $399 outfit that she had bought for $59. I love the woman, and I love her skills. I told her, "We could not afford for you to work outside the home because you wouldn't have time to save us all this money." I was teasing, but actually, the money she saves by seasonal shopping provides a rather good income.

Even those couples who are not financially strapped have found that seasonal shopping is wise stewardship. All stores have seasonal sales in which products are greatly reduced. The stores want to get rid of their stock so they can bring in the next season's wares. In order to do this, they sell at greatly reduced prices. This is true for large items like cars as well as smaller items like clothes. Seasonal shopping is creative spending, and the profit sharing is great.

Creative spending can become an exciting part of life for the couple who are trying to take hold of their finances, utilize their assets in the best possible manner, and create money that can be used in other ways to enrich their marriage. Another way to use your creativity in helping the family budget is in developing your skills in such crafts as sewing, refinishing furniture, making dolls and stuffed animals. Whatever you make or refurbish almost always costs considerably less than purchasing those items made by someone else. When you allow your children to join you in these creative arts, you have the added advantage of teaching your children the joy of creativity.

I remember the couple who said, "When we got serious about our finances, we set aside a weekly amount to be used to purchase our food. Whatever we didn't spend in a given week we put in a fund to be used for our vacation. We kicked in the creative juices on how to get more for our dollar when purchasing food. I will never forget how exciting it was when we ended up with $2,000 laid aside to use for fun when we went on our vacation." One of the purposes of money is to deepen the marital relationship and enrich the lives of our children. This couple had found that creative spending helped them do that.

• • •

Putting the Principles into Practice

1. Would you be willing to sit down with your spouse, look at each of the ideas suggested in this chapter, and ask the question "Is this for us?" Here are the creative spending ideas covered in the chapter:

   • Discount shopping
   • Recycle shopping
   • Free shopping
   • Seasonal shopping

2. Does either of you have a skill, such as sewing or refinishing furniture, that could be used to improve your family finances?
3. What additional creative ideas can you come up with related to spending or making things for yourselves that would enhance your family's financial condition?

7
LIVE WITHIN YOUR MEANS

AN OLD ADAGE SAYS, "LIVE WITHIN YOUR MEANS." To put it more pointedly, "Don't spend money that you don't have." It is a lesson that few couples in our society have learned. Consequently, many couples have found money to be a drain on their relationship.

The necessities are relatively few. I am certain they can be met on your present income. (If you are unemployed, then our government has help for you. The poorest in this country can have the necessities.) I am not opposed to aspiring for more than the necessities, but I am suggesting that you live in the present rather than the future. Leave the future joys for future accomplishments. Enjoy today what you have today.

Previously, I suggested setting the goal of giving away 10 percent of your income, saving 10 percent, and living on the remaining 80 percent. I suggested that goal because I believe it is a wise pattern of financial management. I suggested it also because I know it works. When my wife and I were first married, I was in graduate school. She was working part time, and I was working part time. Our income was meager, but our plan worked. During those years, we began to play a little game that we came to enjoy very much. It is called Let's See How Many Things

We Can Do Without That Everyone Else Must Have. I don't remember where we got the idea, but very soon we were hooked on the game and continued to play it long after it was necessary.

The game works like this: On Friday night or Saturday, you go together to a department store and walk down the aisles, looking at whatever catches your eye. Read the labels, talk about how fascinating each item is, and then turn to each other and say, "Isn't it great that we don't have to have that?" Then while others walk out with arms loaded and names duly signed on charge slips, you walk out hand in hand, excited that you do not need "things" to be happy. I highly recommend this game for all young married couples.

Using Credit Cards

I must admit it was much easier to play that game in those years than it is today because credit cards were not given as freely as they are now. I remember when we were getting ready for the arrival of our baby. We both agreed that we needed a crib, so we went to the local Sears store and applied for a credit card in order to buy one. However, our application was refused because of our low income. Had we received the card, we may well have been on our way to spending money that we did not have. Instead, because we were refused, we asked around and found a couple who were happy to loan us a crib that they were no longer using. Looking back, I've always been grateful to Sears for helping us live within our means.

Unfortunately, the department stores and credit-card companies in today's world have removed those standards, and anyone can get a credit card. In fact, the media screams from every corner: "Buy now! Pay later!" What is not stated is that if you buy now without cash, you will pay *much more* later. Interest rates on charge accounts are usually 18 to 21 percent, or even higher. Couples need to read the small print . . . and then read it again.

I am not opposed to having a credit card. In fact, in today's world, it is difficult to travel without one. You cannot rent a car with cash, and few people use cash to purchase airline tickets. The problem is not having the card; the problem is using the card to purchase what you cannot afford. For many couples, the credit card has been a membership card to "the society of the financially frustrated." It encourages impulse buying when most of us have more impulses than we can afford to follow. I know that credit cards can aid in keeping records and that, if payments are made promptly, charges are minimal. Most couples, however, will spend more and stretch out payments longer if they have credit cards. The business community's eagerness to issue credit cards is evidence of this fact.

Why do we use credit? Because we want now what we cannot pay for now. In the purchase of a house, using credit may be a wise financial move. We would have to pay rent anyway. If a house is well selected, it will appreciate in value. If we have money for the down payment and can afford the monthly payments, such a purchase is wise.

But the sad fact is that most of our purchases do not appreciate in value. On the contrary, their value begins to decrease the day we buy them. We buy them before we can afford them. Then, over a period of time, we pay the purchase price plus the interest charges while the articles themselves continue to depreciate in value. Why? For the momentary pleasure that the items bring. I ask, Is this a sign of responsible money management?

Waiting until You Have the Funds

Living within your means will require waiting. Rather than purchasing now and paying more later, we make a choice to wait until we have the money to make the purchase. Many times when we follow this guideline, by the time we have the money, we realize that we no longer want the product. So we can use the money we have saved to purchase something that will benefit our relationship.

For most young couples, there is probably enough unused stuff in their parents' garages and grandmothers' attics that they would not need to purchase anything for the first two years of marriage. And chances are, parents and grandparents would be glad for it to be used—in fact, would probably make a gift of it.

Waiting builds character. Patience is a virtue that is developed by waiting. In the process of waiting, we have an opportunity to evaluate the importance of a purchase and are far more likely to make wise purchases. Children also need to learn the virtue of waiting. When we fulfill every desire of children instantly, we set them up for failure as adults. Life is a process. We aspire to accomplish certain things in life, and we take the necessary steps to get there. Waiting to make purchases teaches us the art of responsible living.

Waiting stimulates our creativity. If we greatly desire something, we tend to be creative about ways to get the money to purchase it. One couple, who agreed that they really wanted to have a weekend away but knew that they could not afford it, sat down to think about what they might do to earn some extra money. The wife was an excellent cook and baked especially delicious pound cakes. They selected a restaurant that they knew did not have very good desserts. She donated one of her cakes to the restaurant as a "trial run." The restaurant had so many compliments that the owners agreed to start buying cakes from her. Before long, they also wanted pies. Within six months, the woman had to recruit one of her friends to help her make the desserts. Their homemade desserts developed into a very profitable part-time job for both of them. Not only did this couple's creative thinking provide them the funds for a weekend away, it also provided an ongoing stream of income they had not anticipated.

Waiting provides time for you to analyze what funds you are presently spending for activities or products that are not beneficial to your marriage or to your health. Upon reflection, one couple decided to stop drinking colas for three months. Another husband decided to give up cigarettes. Another couple decided to live without desserts for six months. Choosing to eliminate something from your normal list of purchases creates funds that can be applied to those things you deem to be valuable.

For many of us, living within our means will require that we lower our standard of living. It may mean returning to a smaller house and driving a pre-owned vehicle. It may mean purchasing used furniture rather than new. It may mean borrowing a crib rather than purchasing one. Our society has not trained us in the art of scaling back. Everyone encourages us to aspire for more, but the evidence is overwhelming that more does not always mean a better relationship. Most couples in this country could live on far less and would be far happier. Most of us are trying to "keep up with the Joneses," rather than demonstrating to the Joneses that a simpler life may well be a happier life.

Far too many couples get married and try to have in the first year of marriage what it took their parents thirty years to accumulate. Why must you have the biggest and best now? With such a philosophy, you destroy the joy of aspiration and attainment. When you acquire immediately, the joy is short lived and you spend months trying to pay for things. Why saddle yourself with such unnecessary pain?

Couples who live within their means create for themselves a world relatively free of financial stress and also teach their children many valuable lessons. They do not fear the creditor because they do not have a creditor. They are enjoying the profit-sharing plan of never spending money they don't have.

● ● ●

Putting the Principles into Practice
1. Have you ever seriously considered giving 10 percent, saving 10 percent, and living on 80 percent of your income? Would this be a good time for the two of you to discuss this possibility?
2. Do you feel financially strapped? Do you have more bills than you can pay each month? If so, would you be willing to consider some of the options discussed in this chapter, such as lowering your standard of living? What practical steps could you take to make this a reality?
3. Try playing the game Let's See How Many Things We Can Do Without That Everyone Else Must Have. This Friday or Saturday would be a good time to start.
4. Talk with your spouse about initiating the concept of waiting to make future purchases until you have the money in hand.
5. Are there creative things that either of you could do that might increase the flow of income for your budget?

8

WHO WILL KEEP THE BOOKS?

TOGETHER, A HUSBAND AND WIFE MUST DEVELOP A PLAN for handling their finances. The fact is, all couples need a budget. Some couples, when they hear the word *budget*, go into trauma. One husband said, "Oh no. I don't want to get on one of those things. You can never be spontaneous, and you will always be counting every penny."

The fact is, you are already on a budget. A budget is simply a plan for handling your finances. You may never have written your plan on paper, but you have a plan. Some couples' plan is to spend all their money the day they get it. The stores stay open late now, and you can do that. Not a very good plan, but it is a plan. Other couples' plan is to spend all their money *before* they get it. So everything is purchased on credit cards, and they make the monthly payments according to what they have left over. These couples are headed for disaster. Other couples seek to be more responsible.

Putting Your Budget on Paper
If you have never put your budget on paper, it's a good idea to do so. But don't try to do it today. Instead, I suggest that you start by keeping

records for two months. Record all the money that comes in, all the money you give away and what you give it to, the money you save, and the money you spend and what you spend it for. After two months, you will have your present budget. This is the plan you have been following without thinking. Now it's time to think.

Look at your budget and ask yourselves, "Is this the way we want to be handling our money? Do we want to give more? save more? Do we want to spend our money in a better way? How could we apply the principles in this part of the book to either increase our income or become better managers of the money we spend?" Together, work out a budget that you both feel comfortable with, one that will alleviate stress if you follow it.

Let me also suggest that you include in your plan some money for each of you to use as you wish without accounting for every penny. This doesn't have to be a large amount, but a husband needs to be able to buy a candy bar without having to ask his wife for a dollar. Likewise, a wife needs to be able to go out to lunch with a friend without asking her husband for a loan. Whatever amount you decide on, it should be an equal amount for the husband and the wife. This is money with which each of you can buy incidentals for yourself and not feel you are violating the family budget.

Choosing a Bookkeeper

Once the two of you have agreed on a plan for allocating your money, then one of you must become the bookkeeper. Since you are a team, why not let the team member best qualified for the task take it on? As a couple discuss financial details, it will usually be obvious which one is more adept at such matters. Why not assign that one the responsibility?

This does not mean that the one chosen to keep the books is in charge of making financial decisions. Such decisions are to be made as a team. The bookkeeper is simply keeping the couple on track with their plan. He or she is paying the monthly bills, balancing the check register monthly, and seeing that the funds are spent according to the plan upon which both have agreed. It is a formidable task. But for one who enjoys working with numbers, it can be satisfying.

The bookkeeper may not necessarily remain the bookkeeper forever.

For various reasons, you may agree that after the first six months, it would be far wiser if the other partner became the bookkeeper. It is your marriage, and you are responsible for making the most of your resources. However, be certain that the one who is not keeping the books knows how to do so and has full knowledge of the various checking and savings accounts. Let's be realistic. As much as we avoid thinking about it, the fact is that one of you will likely die before the other. A good working knowledge of the system you've been using will leave the surviving spouse much better equipped to take over the family finances. It will also be helpful if the spouse who normally does the bookkeeping becomes sick and is unable to fulfill those responsibilities for a time.

And making sure both of you have full knowledge of your financial affairs is also good for your marital relationship. When one spouse keeps the books and the other is uninformed, there can develop a parent-child mentality. When this happens, it is detrimental to the marriage relationship. You are partners; it is your shared money—but while one is keeping the books, the other needs to be fully informed and to feel comfortable with how the money is being used.

● ● ●

Putting the Principles into Practice
1. There are three things we can do with money: Give it away, spend it, and save it. Does your budget include all these areas?
2. If you have never put your budget on paper, will you consider keeping records for two months to find out what your present budget really is?
3. After keeping records, would you be willing to sit down with your spouse to analyze your present plan and discuss changes that need to be made to move you in a more positive direction?
4. Who do you think is best qualified to keep the books in your marriage?
5. Does either of you feel that you are not an equal partner in the financial area of your marriage? If so, what steps need to be taken to change this perception?

* * *

Closing Thoughts on Profit Sharing

In this part of the book, I have shared with you eight key insights on how to make money an asset in your marriage.

1. It all begins with attitude. Your relationship is more important than money. You are a team, and you need to work together in managing your money.
2. Work is a noble endeavor. Work is God's plan, each couple providing for your own needs and the needs of your children.
3. In God we trust. Money is to be your servant, never your master. You tell money what to do. Money does not tell you what to do.
4. Giving is an expression of gratitude. All that you have is a gift from God. Out of gratitude, you may choose to give as you have received.
5. Saving is a sign of wisdom. Saving is a responsible step in money management. Preparing for both a rainy day and a sunny vacation has merit.
6. Creative spending enhances profit sharing. When you buy for less, you are increasing your income.
7. Live within your means. Don't spend money that you don't have.
8. Decide who will keep the books. But remember that the bookkeeper is not the boss. The bookkeeper simply follows the plan upon which both of you have agreed.

Having the right attitude toward your money and handling it as a responsible team will make money an asset to your relationship. Money should be managed in such a way that both of you feel loved, appreciated, and respected. What could be more important than that?

The size of the house, the model of the car, the price tags on the clothes are relatively unimportant. What is important is your relationship with each other and your relationship with God. Life's meaning is found not in money or the accumulation of things but in relationships: first of all, your relationship with God; second, your relationship as husband and wife; and last, your relationship with children, friends, church, and community.

When you use money to enhance relationships, you have found the purpose of money. Money then becomes an asset to your marriage, rather than a battleground upon which you shoot each other.

As husband and wife, you are on the same team. It is your money, and together you must find a way to manage it that allows both of you to be involved. You must decide the sacrifices you will make, the goals you will establish, and the steps you will take to get there. When you work as a team, you are far more likely to accomplish your objectives. In the process, both of you will have opportunities to use your creativity for the benefit of the marriage.

If you remember that you are a team and, therefore, work as a team, seeking practical help where needed and agreeing on financial decisions, you will find money to be your faithful servant. If, however, you disregard the principles we have discussed in this book and simply "do what comes naturally," you will soon find yourself in the same financial crisis that has become a way of life to thousands of couples.

Some couples, because of poor models established by parents or lack of training by parents, have entered into marriage with very few money-management skills. Consequently, they soon find themselves in financial trouble. If you are one of these couples, I urge you to enroll in a class at your church on financial management, read a book on the topic, or go for private personal counseling. Perhaps a combination of all three of these is the answer. Help is readily available. You do not need to continue in a state of financial crisis. The sooner you reach out for help, the sooner you will get on the road to financial stability. It will require honesty, openness, and a willingness to change. But together you can do it. And when you do, you will both participate in the profit-sharing plan and make money an asset to your marriage.

If you are presently feeling the pain of crisis, it is time for a radical change. There is a way out. If you cannot think clearly enough to solve the problem, then it is time to seek the counsel of a trusted friend or financial counselor who can help you take a realistic look at your situation and decide the steps that need to be taken to bring you to a healthier financial position. Do not continue to allow finances to cripple your marriage. Money was designed to be an asset to your relationship, not a divisive factor.

Learning to handle money in a responsible and mutually satisfying manner is a huge step in creating a healthy marriage. I hope that the ideas I have shared in this part of the book will be helpful to you as you seek to grow in the skills of profit sharing. If you find the ideas helpful, I hope you will share them with a friend. If you have stories to share with me, I invite you to select the Contact link at www.garychapman.org.

• • •

Some Ideas Worth Remembering
- Money can be used to provide more creature comforts, but money will not create a successful marriage. It is the pursuit of righteous living, love, patience, gentleness, and compassion that builds meaningful relationships.
- The desire to have more material possessions is not necessarily an evil desire. The problem comes when we allow money to become the focus of our lives.
- Some have implied that work was a part of the Curse after Adam and Eve sinned. This was not the case; God instituted work before man's sin. Work is a gift of God.
- Any task can be done cheerfully and with pride—or grudgingly and with rebellion. The manner in which we do it is really up to us. It is a matter of choice. There are no menial jobs, only menial attitudes.
- It is daily talking with God, seeking his wisdom and guidance, that makes us most productive financially as well as in all other areas of life.
- The wise couple will make money their servant. They will seek to use money for the good of their family and to help others. They will never allow money to be their master, dictating their decisions.
- There are only three things we can do with money: We can give it away, we can save it, or we can spend it. All three are valid ways of using money.

- Obviously, we cannot and should not give all of our money away. Some must be used to meet the physical needs of our families. But if we give none of it away, we are failing to be grateful for what God has given us.
- Some feel that Christians should not save, that saving money is a sign that we are not trusting God to provide for the future. However, this is not the perspective found in Scripture. The Scriptures indicate that we are to be good managers of our money. The wise manager faces the future realistically.
- Many financial advisors suggest allotting 10 percent of your net income to savings. You may choose more or less; the choice is yours. However, if you save only what is left over at the end of the week or the month, you will not save. Being regular and consistent in what you save is more important than the amount you save.
- Creative spending can become an exciting part of life for the couple who are trying to take hold of their finances, utilize their assets in the best possible manner, and create money that can be used in other ways to enrich their marriage.
- Living within your means will require waiting. Rather than purchasing now and paying more later, we choose to wait until we have the money to make the purchase.
- Our society has not trained us in the art of scaling back. Everyone encourages us to aspire for more, but the evidence is overwhelming that more does not always mean a better relationship.
- A budget is simply a plan for handling your finances. You may never have written your plan on paper, but you have a plan.
- Let me suggest that you include in your plan some money for each of you to use as you wish without accounting for every penny. This doesn't have to be a large amount, but a husband needs to be able to buy a candy bar without having to ask his wife for a dollar. Likewise, a wife needs to be able to go out to lunch with a friend without asking her husband for a loan.
- Be certain that the one who is not keeping the books knows how to do so and has full knowledge about various checking and savings accounts.

Part Four

Now What?

Marriage after the Children Arrive

THIS PART OF THE BOOK is not on parenting, though I will share some tips for parents. This is not a treatise on marriage, though I will give some marriage pointers. Rather, it addresses the question "How do we keep our marriage alive now that the children have arrived?"

"Now What?" was born out of a conversation I recently had with a frustrated young father. He said, in a pained voice, "I've lost my wife."

"What do you mean by that?" I inquired.

"I've lost my wife to the baby."

"Tell me about it," I said.

"We've been married for three years and started out with a really good relationship. We both wanted to have a baby and agreed it was time. But if I had known that the baby was going to destroy our marriage, I never would have agreed."

"What do you mean by 'destroy our marriage'?" I asked.

"We just don't have a marriage anymore," he said. "Her life is focused on the baby; my life is focused on the baby. It's like the two of us do not exist anymore. It's like we became parents and lost our marriage."

"How about your sexual relationship?" I asked.

"It's nonexistent. Maybe two or three times since the baby came."

"How old is the baby?" I inquired.

"He turned two last week."

"Have you talked to your wife about your feelings?" I asked.

"I've tried," he said, "but it's hard to talk with her. She says that I don't understand how hard it is to rear a child and work. I told her she could quit work, but she says we can't live on just my salary. I think we could . . . but there's no need to argue with her. I know it sounds selfish, but I just wish I could have my wife back and it could be like it was before the baby came."

I came away from that conversation knowing I had to write this section. I knew this problem was not an isolated phenomenon. I've heard similar stories many times during the last thirty years as I have counseled couples about their marriages. I knew also that this young man's wife was as frustrated as he, that she too struggled with the pressures of being both a parent and a spouse. I believe that thousands of couples can identify with this young couple's pain.

In another recent encounter, a young woman approached me with her Bible open. I could tell that she was serious. "When are you going to talk about how children affect a marriage?" she asked.

I had the idea that her question was simply a bridge to something far more personal, so I responded, "Why do you ask?"

"I'm confused," she replied. "It says in the Bible—" she pointed to Psalm 127 "—that 'Sons are a heritage from the LORD. . . . Blessed is the man whose quiver is full of them.' It may be happy for the man," she said, "but not for the woman. I thought having a baby would pull us together and we would both be happy. The exact opposite is true for us. Since the baby came, our marriage has fallen apart."

I assured her that she was not alone in her frustration, that many couples acknowledge that the first eighteen months after the birth of a child is the most trying time they have ever experienced in their marriage. Mothers of small children often feel isolated and overwhelmed. They feel unwanted or unappreciated by their husbands. They often feel unattractive. "My husband doesn't understand why I am so tired. He complains that I don't bake cherry pies anymore. I'm up to my ears in diapers and vomit, and he's complaining about cherry pies."

Many fathers of young children feel taken for granted by their spouses, unappreciated, and unimportant. They feel that they are no longer number one; the baby has taken their place. They become resentful—not necessarily of the baby, but of the wife's attention to the baby. "She never has time for me. It's always the baby. Even when I ask her to go out, she's afraid to leave the baby. When I want to rent a video, she says she doesn't have the energy to watch it. I don't know what else to do."

Why is this marital pressure such a common experience? Because a whole new world of potential conflicts arise when a child enters a marriage.

A child means more work. Who does the work? Mom or Dad?

More work means more time. Whose time? Mom's or Dad's?

More work means more energy. Whose energy?

A child means more money. What money—the money that we previously set aside for restaurants and entertainment?

Research has shown that a mother feels the impact of a child upon the marriage most acutely in the first six months of a child's life, when she is trying to adjust to the expanded demands on her time and energy, whereas the father recognizes the impact of the child upon the marriage most acutely during the time the child is six to eighteen months of age. During this time, the husband perceives his wife to be more critical, less supportive, and withdrawing from him sexually.[1]

And unfortunately, the impact of children upon a marriage does not end when the baby is eighteen months old. Jim and Evelyn were in my office seeking help for their fourteen-year-old daughter. After briefly discussing the problems they were having with her at school, they admitted that the main reason they had come to see me was that their marriage was in trouble. "It seems that when it comes to Julie, we disagree on almost everything. Our disagreements on how to rear her have brought us to the point of fighting all the time. Neither of us likes it, but we don't know what to do. It seems we disagree every day on something related to Julie."

I sometimes ask couples, "What was your marriage like before the children came?" I will receive answers like "Well, we were struggling, but we thought a baby would draw us together." Don't expect a baby to create a good marriage; that is not the responsibility of a child. Children do not create a good marriage, nor do they create problems in a marriage; they only reveal problems that were already there. A ten-year study by Carolyn and Philip Cowan revealed that "the most important piece of information to forecast how men and women will fare as parents is how they are doing before they begin their journey to parenthood."[2]

The fact is, rearing children is a joint venture that requires communication, understanding, love, and willingness to compromise. Couples who have not developed these attitudes and skills before a baby arrives will not find them automatically emerging upon the arrival of the child.

Some couples have good marriages before the children come but five years later realize they have spent so much time being "good parents" that they have let their own relationship grow stale. This kind of staleness does not happen overnight, nor is it the result of open conflict. Rather, it is a slow erosion of intimacy caused by the lack of quality time, expressions of love, and communication. In these marriages, the road to restoration is fairly short because these couples basically have a good relationship that has diminished by default. When one spouse shares a concern with the other, the two of them will likely make a course correction, and their marriage will get back on track.

On the other hand, for couples who have developed unhealthy patterns of relating before the children came, the road to restoration will be much longer. The changes needed—effective conflict resolution, meaningful communication, tolerance of differences, looking for compromises rather than conquests, and expressions of love in a language one's spouse will feel—require skills that take time to develop. I must add, however, it is never too late to begin. Any couple can learn these skills if they are motivated to do so.

You, too, may be seeking answers to the question, "How do we keep our marriage alive now that the children have arrived?" I believe there are answers to that question, and in part four I will seek to share them.

You can probably read this part, "Now What?" in less than two hours. And if you do, you will discover how to make time to read books and make time for your marriage. You will also learn how to take control of your finances so that you can accomplish what is of value to you in life. Most important, you will learn how to rekindle marital intimacy and keep it alive while at the same time being good parents. You will find that you are not the only couple who have walked this road. Others have learned how to maintain a healthy marriage while successfully rearing children. You can profit from their discoveries. At the end of each of the five chapters in this part, you will find practical suggestions on how to weave these ideas into the fabric of your own marriage.

I assure you that you *can* be happily married and be successful parents at the same time.

1

MAKING MARRIAGE A PRIORITY

There comes a time in most marriages when two become three. Sometimes, two become four or five or six or more! This is the design initiated by God in the Garden of Eden when he said to Adam and Eve, "Be fruitful and increase in number; fill the earth and subdue it."[1] Both Scripture and modern sociological research indicate that the best environment for children is the environment created by a loving father and mother who are committed to each other for a lifetime. The Scriptures also indicate that in marriage the husband and wife are to become "one flesh."[2] The term *one flesh* speaks of deep intimacy. Modern research also affirms this concept: Most couples who get married do so because they want to have an intimate, exclusive relationship with each other. If an intimate marriage and parenting are both a part of God's design, then surely there is a way to do both successfully.

Let's freely admit that when children arrive, they greatly affect the marital relationship. There is a new person in the house, and he or she will be there for a long time. That first child may be joined by siblings over the next few years. Each child creates a new dynamic in the household. Someone has said, "The decision to have a child—it's momentous.

It is to decide forever to have your heart go walking around outside your body."[3] Parents can identify with that statement. The child is a part of them, and their hearts are linked to the child's well-being. However, in their love for the child, they must never forget that the child is the offspring of their love for each other. Therefore, they must continue to cultivate that love relationship, not only for their own well-being but for the well-being of the child as well.

When a couple neglect their own love relationship, either intentionally or unintentionally, they do so to the detriment of their children. Research clearly shows that the effect of divorce upon a child is devastating. Divorces typically do not occur on the spur of the moment. They are preceded by months and sometimes years of neglecting the marital relationship. Therefore, for the conscientious parent, there is nothing more important than rekindling or keeping alive an intimate relationship with his or her spouse. The antidote to divorce is to stop the process of drifting apart. Choose to paddle your canoes toward each other rather than away from each other. In the last chapter of this part of the book, starting on page 205, I will tell you how to do that. But first you must commit yourselves to the process by *making marriage a priority*.

What does it mean to make marriage a priority? It means, first, that we pause long enough to assess the quality of our marriage. Then we must make a conscious choice that—for the benefit of our children, for ourselves, and (if we are Christians) for the glory of God—we will commit ourselves to each other and acknowledge that our marriage is important to us. Finally, we must agree that with God's help we will find a way to strengthen our intimacy. Making marriage a priority is a conscious choice to make things better.

There is a song that says, "Love and marriage go together like a horse and carriage."[4] I would like to change part of that analogy and say that *marriage and parenting* go together like a horse and carriage. The horse and the carriage exist as separate entities; they can be separated from each other. When the horse is separated from the carriage, it is free to roam and frolic as it likes. In a similar manner, marriage and parenting are separate endeavors, but parenting is at its best only when it is linked with marriage.

When the horse is harnessed to the carriage, its freedom is limited, but its energy can be used for positive purposes. The carriage cannot fulfill its created function without the horse. Before children, a husband and wife are able to roam and frolic as they choose. Once children come, parents' freedom is limited. But their choice to be connected with their children is for the good of both parents and the children.

However, limited freedom does not equal no freedom. The horse is often uncoupled from the carriage and returns to the pasture—a horse that stayed harnessed to the carriage day and night would soon become a frustrated horse. Nor would this be good for the carriage and its passengers. Similarly, a couple who are so attached to their child or children that they have no time for themselves will become a frustrated couple. This is not good for the children or the parents.

Like the horse apart from its carriage, parents have an existence apart from their children. This existence is called marriage, which at its best provides parents time to frolic and enjoy each other so that they are renewed for their task of parenting.

Please note that the title of this chapter is "Making Marriage a Priority." Notice I say *a* priority. I often encounter couples who argue over whether the child should be their priority or marriage should be their priority. That's like arguing over whether water or food should be *the* priority for the human body. The truth is they are both priorities. Parents who do not seek to be good parents are delinquent in their responsibilities. On the other hand, couples who do not give priority to their marriage are also delinquent.

A couple who neglect their children in pursuit of their own happiness will live to regret their decision. On the other hand, a couple who neglect their marriage while focusing all their energy on their children will also live to regret their choice.

Keeping your marriage vibrant and alive is one of the best things you can do for the health of your children, who will also likely one day be married. They desperately need a model of what a healthy marriage looks like. If you neglect your marital relationship, you may meet the children's physical needs but realize in time that you have failed to teach them relational skills. Marriage is a priority; parenting is a priority—the choice is not either/or. To neglect either is detrimental to the other.

In my book *The Four Seasons of Marriage*,[5] I used the seasons to describe the various stages of a marriage:

- **Springtime** in marriage is a time of new beginnings, new patterns of life, new ways of listening, and new ways of loving. Feelings we experience during this season include excitement, love, trust, hope, and joy.
- **Summer** couples share deep commitment, satisfaction, and security in each other's love. They are connected and supportive of each other.
- **Fall** brings a sense of unwanted change, and nagging emptiness appears. We might feel apprehensive, concerned, sad, discouraged, and uncertain.
- **Winter** means difficulty. Marriage is harder in this season of cold silence and bitter winds. Couples experiencing a winter season in their marriage will act and feel harsh, angry, disappointed, and detached.

You may want to ask, "What season was our marriage in before the children came? What season is our marriage in now?" If you are not happy with your present season, "Now What?" is definitely for you. In the next four chapters, I will share practical ways of restoring and maintaining a healthy marriage while at the same time being successful parents.

• • •

Putting the Principles into Practice

1. Using the idea of the four seasons, assess the quality of your marriage by underlining the words in each description that best describe your current feelings about your marriage. Then ask your spouse to read this chapter and make an assessment as well.
2. If you discover that your marriage is in the unsettledness of fall or the coldness of winter, you need not remain there. You and your

spouse can return to the spring or summer seasons of marriage by confessing your failures to each other and asking forgiveness.

3. Can you both agree to make your marriage a priority? Your motivation may be for the children, for yourselves, or for God. But whatever your motivation, when you make marriage a priority, you are moving in the right direction.

2

TAKING CONTROL
OF YOUR SCHEDULES

IN MY EXPERIENCE, the issues that are most likely to lead to conflict between a husband and wife in any stage of parenting are the division of the workload in the family, the amount of time spent together as a couple, frustration about their sexual relationship, management of family money, the need for time alone, differing ideas about rearing children, communication with each other, and a willingness to work on improving their relationship. It's obvious that processing all these issues will take time. But where does this time come from? We already sense that there is not enough time available to do what needs to be done. I believe that the answer to finding time to build a strong marriage, while at the same time being good parents, lies in *taking control of our schedules*.

Taking control of our schedules means that we consciously examine who is doing what and when it is being done, looking for a better solution. Marital schedules involve two factors: Who will do what? and When will it be done? Many couples have never thought seriously about their marital schedules. They have simply drifted into a pattern of operation largely dictated by what they saw their parents do. This pattern may be effective or ineffective. If their marriage is suffering, their pattern is likely highly ineffective.

Get the Right Person Doing the Right Job

In family life, certain tasks must be done, and done regularly—some daily and some weekly. The first step in getting control of your schedule is to make a list of these daily and weekly tasks. Once the list is made, the two of you can evaluate which of you is best equipped to do each task. (When children are small, there are only two people to do these tasks: the husband and the wife. As the children grow, they can be brought into the work team and learn experientially what it means to be a member of the family.)

The key is getting the right person doing the right thing so that both partners are maximizing their abilities for the benefit of the team. For example, he may be a great cook but is not adept in operating a lawn mower, whereas she may find mowing the lawn relaxing and even enjoyable. If he has been mowing the grass for the first three years of their marriage (because his father did), and she has been cooking during those years (because women are "supposed" to do the cooking), they have both likely found their tasks burdensome and drudgery. However, if they shift their responsibilities, letting him do what he enjoys most and letting her do what she enjoys most, they can intensify their emotional energy and their sense of well-being.

Decide When Tasks Will Be Done

Once they have agreed on who will do what, based on their interests and abilities, the second step is to decide when they will do these tasks. Again this requires teamwork. While she is mowing the grass, he agrees to stay inside and take care of the children. If the children are young, perhaps he can balance the checkbook and pay the monthly bills while keeping an eye on the children. If they are older, he may be helping them with homework or playing with them. If his vocational commitment makes this impossible, then perhaps they could afford to pay a sitter to watch the children while she mows the grass. If finances are limited, perhaps she could work out an exchange program with a friend where they agree to keep each other's children for a few hours while the other completes a task. If he is going to cook the evening meal three nights a week, it may require her helping the children with homework while he does his task. If his work schedule gets him home later, then dinner may have to be later on those evenings.

Eliminate Unnecessary Tasks

Taking control of our schedules also involves asking the question, "What are we doing or trying to do that may not be necessary?" I remember the wife who was frustrated because, before the baby came, she dusted the house every other day (because her mother had done so). After the baby came, she found this to be extremely stressful. When she was not able to accomplish the task, she felt she was failing in her responsibilities. Once we examined the issue, we discovered that her mother dusted every other day because she lived on a dirt road and kept the windows open during the summer. The daughter's house was on a paved street, and it had air-conditioning. What made sense for her mother made little sense for her. Upon discussing it with her husband, together they agreed that dusting once a week was acceptable to both of them. Eliminating unnecessary tasks creates time that can be set aside for marital enrichment.

I remember the husband whose wife complained about his playing golf every Saturday. His viewpoint was, "This is my only day for relaxation. I find golf relaxing." As we examined the situation, we discovered that his father had played golf every Saturday and had taught his son to do the same thing. Her complaint was that on Saturday there were household tasks that needed to be done, since both of them worked during the week. So on Saturdays, she worked while he played. Then he came home and wanted to have sex. She resented this arrangement.

It took a few counseling sessions, but eventually the husband discovered that he much preferred sex over golf. He started spending Saturday mornings doing some of the weekly tasks with his wife. In the afternoon they sent the children to the YMCA for swimming lessons, and every Saturday, they experienced an afternoon delight. Getting control of our schedules may mean that we cannot continue doing all the things we have been doing.

Get Your Children on a Schedule

Schedule control also involves getting your children on a routine that interfaces positively with your schedule. You are not stifling their creativity when you help children establish scheduled living. Children actually thrive best when their lives have boundaries. A child who grows up without boundaries will be an undisciplined teenager and an irresponsible adult.

Establishing consistent times to go to bed and to get up in the morning is a good place to start setting boundaries for your children. I am always amazed when I see four-year-olds in the local Wal-Mart at 10 p.m. Little wonder that parents complain they don't have time for each other. Four-year-olds should be in bed long before ten o'clock. Then Mom and Dad will have time for some of the important things we've been discussing. They might read and discuss a book on marriage in order to learn to communicate with each other positively. They can learn to respect each other's ideas and find resolutions to their differences. And they will have time to enjoy sexual intimacy.

You must decide what you think is realistic, but I suggest a bedtime of seven o'clock for children up to the age of eight. After that, you might begin to extend their bedtime, but never more than fifteen minutes per year. That means that at age twelve, a child's bedtime would be eight o'clock. Whatever you decide, remember that a consistent bedtime for the children is good for them and for your marriage.

It is not just bedtimes that need to be scheduled. Children need a schedule for the day as well. During the preschool years, there should be a time for art; a time for listening to parents read a book to them; a time to help parents with cooking, setting the table, sweeping, and folding the clothes; and a daily period of time in which the child is alone in his or her room playing with toys and learning to be creative. There should also be regular nap times. Children should not be forced to go to sleep, but simply to lie down and rest. If they sleep, fine; if they don't sleep, fine—but everybody takes a daily rest. It is the room times and the rest times that give parents time to read books, to rest, or to do anything that they find meaningful. As the children get older, there is also time scheduled for homework and chores. Putting your children on a schedule is not only good for the children but enhances your own physical, emotional, and spiritual well-being.

If you have parents who live nearby and they want to be involved in the lives of your children, this also should be scheduled. When relatives pop in whenever and wherever, their presence can be annoying because it interrupts your planned program for the afternoon or evening. But when you schedule time for your children to be with their grandparents, then it allows you and your spouse to do something that enhances your marriage.

Make Time for Yourself

Scheduling also provides time for each of you to be alone. All of us need some time apart from the pressures of family life. Spending time alone is not selfish. No one can be "on duty" twenty-four hours a day for an extended period of time without becoming emotionally and physically depleted. This is never good for a marriage. You need time alone to breathe deeply, enjoy the beauty of nature, and commune with God. This time should be spent in doing something that you find invigorating or relaxing. It can be playing golf, reading a book, watching television, taking a walk, or working out at the local gym—anything that invigorates your mind or your spirit. Organizing everybody's schedules in such a way that each of you can have time alone is an essential ingredient to building your marriage.

In summary, getting control of your schedule means getting the right person doing the right task and deciding when it will be done, eliminating any unnecessary tasks that you are presently doing, getting your children on a schedule that interfaces positively with your schedule, and making time for yourself.

All this will help enable the two of you to engage in marital enrichment times in which you can learn to process your differences and give loving support to each other, thus building intimacy.

●   ●   ●

Putting the Principles into Practice
1. Make a list of all the tasks that must be done regularly (either daily or weekly). Ask your spouse to make a similar list. Then bring

your two lists together and make a composite list. Now each of you take a copy of the comprehensive list of tasks and put your initials by the ones you think you are best equipped to do or would most enjoy. If there is something you think the two of you should share, then put both of your initials, but underline the person you think should take the basic responsibility for that task. Then come together and discuss your lists. See where you have agreed and where you have disagreed. Where you disagree, negotiate. You need not keep these assignments forever, but for the next few weeks, try this plan. You may find that getting the right person doing the right task will radically change your perspective on household chores.

2. Agree on the day of the week and/or the approximate time each day that each task will be performed. For example, if the husband is going to take the responsibility for taking the garbage outside, will he do this at the end of each day or at the beginning of each day? Getting on the same page can eliminate a lot of tension between the two of you. Knowing that he is going to cook the evening meal on Tuesday and Thursday can help both of you plan your schedules in a supportive manner.

3. What is the first step you need to take in getting the lives of your children scheduled? If your children are older, expect some opposition. But once they see that you are kind but firm, they will "get with the program."

4. What changes would you like to see in your time alone? What steps will you take to make these changes?

5. If you had more time to be with your spouse, what would you like to do? Compare your answer with your spouse's answer, and negotiate a way to make it happen.

3
TAKING CONTROL
OF YOUR MONEY

THEY WERE IN MY OFFICE. She was weeping uncontrollably. He was out-wardly stoic, but I could tell he was deeply frustrated. Seven years and two children into their marriage, it was in shambles.

From her perspective, before they were married, he was romantic, loving, and caring. After the wedding, he became cold, withdrawn, and self-centered. With tears flowing freely, she said, "All I've ever wanted is a husband who will love me, who enjoys being with me—someone with whom I can share life. Is that too much to ask? I thought we had this before we got married. I don't know what happened, but after the wedding, he was like a different man. Two years later, we had our first child. I thought that would bring us together, but I was wrong. Then came the second child. He started helping more around the house, but there was never any time for *us*. I felt like we were roommates taking care of two children. I love my children, but I also want a husband who will talk with me. I want us to have a life apart from raising children."

When I looked at her husband, he said, "I'm sorry I haven't been able to meet her needs. Finances have been tight. I have a good job, but I'm not a rich man. She works only part time. She likes gifts; she wants to go places and do things. All of that costs money, money that we don't have. I've been trying to save money so we can buy a house. I know that she doesn't like where we are living. There's just not enough money to do everything."

Later, when we looked at their financial situation, we discovered that they were an average family with an average income. The problem was they had never integrated their marriage and their money. He had been saving every penny to make a down payment on a house. In addition to his full-time job, he had worked a part-time job three evenings a week, and every extra dollar had gone into the housing fund. While she, too, wanted to buy a house, she would have preferred an intimate marriage. When he was at home, he spent time with the children and time watching sports events on television, but little or no time with his wife. Consequently, she was at a point of desperation. They were now living in their new house, and they were miserable. Upon reflection, he also agreed that the marriage was more important than the house, but this had not been reflected in his actions.

Put Your Money Where Your Priorities Are

There is a simple principle that, when applied, will keep a marriage alive regardless of a couple's income. The principle is this: Put your money where your priorities are. If the marriage relationship is a priority—and if special gifts, a weekly date night, and occasional weekend getaways will enhance the marriage—then invest money in making these a reality. The house may come two or three years later than anticipated, but at least you will have a marriage to place in the house. The house will be a home rather than a boarding place.

Without question, children are expensive. One recent report indicated that to rear a child from birth to college will cost approximately $250,000.[1] To the average couple, such figures may seem overwhelming. The good news is that, especially in the United States, the opportunities for successfully financing a family are unlimited. There are numerous ways to cut corners, save, and invest that make it possible to have a successful marriage and rear healthy children on almost any level of income. The key is in utilizing these opportunities. Far too often couples get caught up in mimicking their neighbors' lifestyle rather than thinking creatively about how to accomplish their own priorities.

If our priorities are a healthy marriage and creating a positive learning environment for our children, then our money should be channeled toward reaching these objectives rather than following the materialistic lifestyle of our neighbors. If you are feeling that you do not have enough financial resources to do the things that enrich your marriage, then it is time for you to *take control of your money.*

There are only two basic methods to increase funds to invest in your marriage. They are simple to state but require effort to implement. One is lowering your expenditures, and the other is increasing your income. In my opinion, the easiest place to start is in lowering your expenses. In the next few paragraphs, we have reviewed some practical suggestions for doing this. Some of these will require a change of attitude, but it will be a change that will greatly enhance your marriage relationship.

Spending Less and Enjoying It More
There are numerous ways to increase a couple's marital-enrichment fund by spending less. Bob and Jean live in southern Illinois. At one of my marriage seminars, they shared with me that they had saved thousands of dollars by *recycle shopping.* It all started with an experiment. They agreed that for six months they would buy all their household items, all their clothes, and all the children's toys and school supplies at one of three places—the local Goodwill store, Salvation Army store, or consignment shop. After six months, they were hooked.

"We love it," said Jean. "The things we buy are high quality, and we get them at really good prices."

Another couple who live in Florida described something even better than shopping at Goodwill—*free shopping,* which is discussed more fully in chapter 6 of "Profit Sharing," starting on page 149. The couple drive through affluent neighborhoods the night before the discards are to be collected, they let their friends know they are open to receiving hand-me-downs, and they request specific toys as gifts for their children from their parents.

Another way to save money by spending less is *seasonal shopping.* My wife is an expert in this kind of shopping, which is especially helpful when buying clothing. Karolyn likes to wear nice clothes, and I like to see her in nice clothes. But she never pays full price for anything. She always shops at the end-of-season sales. I don't mean the first day of the sale; I mean after items have been reduced one, two, or three times. The money she saves by seasonal shopping provides a rather good "income."

When it comes to food and household items, there is also *discount shopping*. In most towns, there is a good store that sells products cheaper than all the rest. Why not buy your groceries there? Their bananas came off the same boat as the bananas at the more expensive store. And by using manufacturers' coupons, you can save even more. Buying at the cheapest store, using coupons, and stocking up on the special-sale items can save literally hundreds of dollars in your food and household budget.

With all these additional funds, you can pay for that weekend getaway, start a savings fund for your children's college education, and save money for the new house. These savings can be channeled toward your priorities—an enriched marriage and healthy, responsible children.

Increasing Your Income

The second basic method of having more money for your marital-enrichment fund and family-fun fund is to increase your income. One way to do this is by saving and investing. Typically, a savings account is established to accomplish a particular objective such as taking a family vacation, buying a new car, or preparing for your child's education. On the other hand, investing involves putting discretionary funds to work for you. The yield on investments is usually higher over the long haul than the yield on savings accounts. But realize also that there are greater risks with investing. Never invest money that you really need for something else. Invest only money that you could afford to lose. Many couples have failed to follow this principle and have created severe financial pressure.

A second way to increase your income is for one of you to take on additional work. This may be a part-time job in the home or outside the home. Two guidelines should be followed when exploring this possibility: First, make sure that you understand the requirements of the job before you take the plunge. Second, assess with your spouse the impact this additional job will have on your marriage relationship. Remember, your ultimate priority is a better marriage, not more income. If the income will enhance your marriage and the job will not detract from your intimacy, then perhaps it is a good move.

Let me conclude this chapter by saying that the best things in life are free—or at least inexpensive. Taking time to enjoy a sunset, picking a wildflower and giving it to your spouse, enjoying the colors of fall leaves, going to church, taking a walk together, or sitting together on the porch while the crickets serenade you costs nothing! Sharing ice-cream cones, eating your favorite pizza, taking a swim, or attending a movie together are all relatively inexpensive.

The challenge of this chapter is for you to take control of your money so that you will have the necessary funds to enrich your marriage on a regular basis as well as provide for the material needs of your family.

• • •

Putting the Principles into Practice

1. At the present time, is the way you handle finances working *for* your marriage or *against* your marriage? Is decreasing your expenditures to increase funds for enriching your marriage an option you are willing to consider? If so, review the creative shopping ideas (recycle, free, seasonal, and discount) and determine which ones seem to be most feasible to you.

2. Discuss these with your spouse and agree on a spending plan for the next six months.

3. Are you pleased with your present pattern of saving and investing? If not, what would you like to change? Discuss these changes with your spouse and see if you can agree on a more productive plan.

4. Is there a realistic possibility that one of you could accept additional work for the purpose of producing additional income? How would this impact your marriage relationship? Explore this possibility with your spouse.

4

LEARNING TO EFFECTIVELY DISCIPLINE CHILDREN

ONE OF THE MOST COMMON AREAS OF CONFLICT between husbands and wives is how to discipline the children. "He's too harsh," the wife says. "She lets them get away with murder," the husband responds. The conversation goes downhill from there, each accusing the other of being too lenient or too hard on the children. When a couple are continually having these kinds of arguments, it obviously has a detrimental effect on their marital relationship. Each parent has a genuine concern for the well-being of the children. However, their arguments leave them wounded and resentful.

If that sounds familiar, this chapter will help you and your spouse get on the same page with regard to effective discipline. The word *discipline* is not a negative word, nor is it to be equated with spanking or yelling at children. The word *discipline* means literally "to train." Most parents recognize that children need training. Without positive discipline, children will self-destruct; they cannot train themselves.

The problem is that most parents have had little or no instruction in how to effectively train children. Therefore, they come to parenting with only the example of their own parents. If they perceive their parents as good parents, they will try to follow those models. If they perceive their parents as poor parents, they will try to do the opposite.

At any rate, their views of proper discipline will often bring them into conflict. For the sake of their marriage, they desperately need to get on the same page. For the sake of their child, they need to make sure they are on the *right* page. Children are greatly influenced by their parents. We want to make sure that the influence is positive.

To be good parents, we must understand the fundamentals of rearing children. The basics of child rearing are not difficult to understand, although they require the willingness to change negative patterns and consistently establish positive patterns.

Children Need to Feel Loved

The first fundamental in rearing children is that children need to feel loved by their mother and father. Children who do not feel loved and respected by their parents will grow up with many emotional struggles, and their behavior will reflect these emotional struggles. Most parents sincerely love their children, but thousands of children do not feel loved. The problem is that parents are not communicating love in a language that children can understand.

In my research, I have discovered there are five fundamental ways of expressing love. I call them the five love languages, which I discussed in part two, "Home Improvements." Let me summarize them briefly in relation to parenting.

The first is Words of Affirmation—using words to communicate to a child how much you love him or her, expressing appreciation to the child when he/she does something worthy of commendation, and using words of encouragement when the child is fearful. Here are examples of Words of Affirmation: "I love you sooo much." "I like your art. The way you blended the colors together makes it look exciting." "Thanks for helping Mommy set the table." "I appreciate your taking the trash outside for me." "I think you can make the team because you have a lot of drive, but you will never know until you try. If you really want to do it, I would encourage you to try. If you don't make it, you can try again next year."

NOW WHAT? || 195

The second love language is Acts of Service—doing something for your children that you know they would like for you to do: mending a doll's dress, repairing a bicycle, pumping up a football, baking their favorite cake, or teaching them to swim. All these are acts of service. The emphasis is on doing things for your children that they cannot yet do for themselves. Later, you serve them by teaching them how to pump up footballs and repair bicycles.

The third love language is Gifts. The giving and receiving of gifts is a universal expression of love. I would be quick to emphasize that the gifts need not be expensive and that we need not give our children everything they desire. To do so would be poor parenting indeed. But if gifts express love, then even simple gifts like stones you pick up from a public parking lot or a flower from the yard will communicate that they are loved.

The fourth love language is Quality Time—giving your child your undivided attention. Perhaps you are playing a game or reading a book; perhaps you are having a conversation. The important thing is that the child has your attention. You are not watching television, talking on the telephone, or fiddling with a pencil. Your child has your undivided attention.

And love language number five is Physical Touch—hugs and kisses, pats on the back, friendly wrestling on the floor. All these communicate love.

Out of the five love languages, each child has a primary love language. If you want your child to feel loved, you must give heavy doses of his or her primary love language while sprinkling in the other four as icing on the cake. If you don't speak a child's primary love language, the child may not feel loved even though you are speaking some of the other languages. This simple insight has helped thousands of parents learn to express love to their children effectively.[1]

Children Need to Know There Are Rules

A second fundamental in child rearing is to understand that there are rules. There are some things we do and some things we don't do. All societies are built on a concept of dos and don'ts. Without such rules, society could not exist. Children must learn this reality. This requires parents to decide together about the rules they intend to teach their children. Healthy rules are always reasonable. They serve some positive function. Therefore, parents need to ask themselves whether a rule is good for their child and whether it will have some positive effect on their child's life. Here are some practical questions that will help you evaluate rules:

- Does this rule keep a child from danger or destruction?
- Does this rule teach the child some positive character trait: honesty, hard work, kindness, sharing, etc.?
- Does this rule protect property?
- Does this rule teach the child to take care of his/her possessions?
- Does this rule teach the child responsibility?
- Does this rule teach good manners?

Answering questions like these will help you come up with healthy rules for your family. These are the factors about which we are concerned as parents. We want to protect our children from danger and destruction. We do not want our young children to be hit by a car in the street. And we do not want our older children to get involved in drugs. We want to teach our children positive character traits in keeping with our values. We want children to respect the property of others, so a rule about not playing baseball in the backyard may keep them from breaking the neighbor's window. We want them to learn to take care of their own possessions; therefore, a rule about putting their bicycle in the storage shed at night is a purposeful rule. We want our children to respect others, so we teach our children to look adults in the face and say yes sir and thank you.

We want our children to be responsible adults, and we know that they must learn this in childhood. Therefore, requiring a child to be responsible for making his bed or vacuuming her floor is a reasonable rule. And what of good manners? It is interesting that contemporary corporate executives are hiring etiquette trainers and consultants because instead of social graces, contemporary employees are characterized by rudeness and crudeness. I believe this can be traced to the lack of teaching manners in the home. If as parents we believe that "please" and "thank you" are better than "gimme" and "yuck," then we will have rules regarding such manners in the home. Other parents, teachers, extended family, books, and magazine articles are perfectly legitimate resources in making family rules. To have the best possible rules, parents need all the knowledge and wisdom they can get.

Once parents agree on the rules, two issues become extremely important: First, *the rules must be clearly explained to the children.* Parents often assume that children automatically know what they are to do or not to do. This is not the case. We must clearly express our expectations to children. The entire family needs to be aware of the rules. Unspoken rules are unfair rules. A child cannot be expected to live up to a standard of which he or she is unaware. Parents have the responsibility for making sure that children understand what the rules are. As children grow older, they also need to know *why* their parents have decided on these rules. If children feel genuinely loved by their parents, they will usually acknowledge and value such rules.

The second important issue with regard to rules is that once the rules are made, *the consequences for breaking the rules also need to be established.* Obedience is learned by suffering the consequences of disobedience. Effective teaching of obedience requires that consequences for breaking rules should cause discomfort to the rule breaker. It is especially helpful if the consequences for breaking family rules can be determined and discussed with the family at the time a rule is made. This has the advantage that the child knows ahead of time what the consequences of breaking a rule will be, and it delivers the parent from the peril of having to make a snap judgment about what discipline should be applied. Deciding the consequences before a child breaks a rule is also more likely to establish a reasonable consequence.

If a rule is that we don't throw a football inside the house, what are the consequences if that rule is broken? A logical consequence might be that the football is put in the trunk of the car for two days and that the child must pay from his or her allowance for anything that was broken when the football was thrown. Mr. Jones's window, broken by a baseball hit from the backyard, should require a verbal apology to Mr. Jones and payment for the window repair out of Johnny's hard-earned money.

Such consequences will likely motivate Johnny to play ball in the park and not in the yard.

If a rule is that your children do not smoke cigarettes, then if your son is caught smoking, he must immediately eat a carrot—the whole thing. This will give the body beta-carotene to overcome the nicotine, and chances are he will think twice about smoking another cigarette. If there is a second violation, having him make a $25 donation to the American Lung Association, pick up one hundred cigarette butts from the street, and read an article on the dangers of nicotine to the lungs will probably be enough to convince him that smoking is not for children.

From these illustrations, perhaps you see the emerging pattern that consequences should be as closely associated to the rule as possible.

I am often asked, "What about spanking as a consequence for disobedience?" In my opinion, it is usually far more effective to tie the consequences to the behavior. For example, in the illustration given above about Johnny's breaking the window because he broke the rule about playing baseball in the backyard, facing Mr. Jones next door and paying for the window are far more meaningful than giving Johnny some swats for disobedience. Spanking a child is not a cure for all misbehavior. In fact, it may be a reflection of a parent's unwillingness to invest time trying to teach the child obedience.

Combining Discipline with Love

When a rule is broken and the parent is required to make sure that the child experiences the agreed-upon consequence, it is extremely helpful to give your child a dose of emotional love before and after the discipline. It is most helpful when you use the child's primary love language.

For example, let's say that your son was playing football in the living room, a clear violation of rules. Let's say that the child's primary love language is Words of Affirmation. The parent might say something like this: "I think you know that I love you very much. Normally, you follow the rules quite well. I am proud of you and your many accomplishments at school and at home. You make me a very happy parent. But when you break the rules, you know that you must suffer the consequences. So, let's put the ball in the trunk and leave it there for the next two days.

And we will have to find out the cost of the vase so that you can pay for it. I just want you to know that I love you, and that's why I take responsibility to help you learn to follow the rules." The most effective way to teach a child obedience is to wrap discipline in love. Even when suffering the consequences, the child is assured of the parent's love. When a child feels loved, he is likely to receive the discipline as a fair consequence of his behavior.

Compare this to the common response of the parent who hears the vase fall from the mantel, dashes to the living room, sees the child picking up the football, and yells, "I have told you a thousand times, don't throw the football in the living room! Now look at what you've done. That vase was bought by your grandmother; it's thirty years old. It's priceless, and you destroyed it. When are you ever going to learn? You act like a two-year-old. I don't know what I'm going to do with you. Get out of here!" And the parent slaps him on the bottom as he leaves the room.

Which of these two approaches is more likely to teach the child healthy obedience? I think most parents will agree that the plan of clarifying the rule, agreeing upon the consequences of misbehavior before it happens, and lovingly but firmly applying the consequences to the child is far more productive both for the child's learning and the parents' mental health.

Children Need to Learn to Make Wise Decisions
A third foundation in child rearing is teaching children to make wise decisions. In adulthood, success or failure in life is largely dependent upon this ability.

How do children learn decision-making skills? The process begins by giving them the freedom to make decisions within boundaries. You might say to your four-year-old daughter, "Do you want to bring your tricycle inside before dinner or after dinner?" The child has a choice. Either decision is within the boundaries of her parent's desires. If, however, she chooses to wait until after dinner and then forgets entirely to bring in the tricycle, she must suffer the consequences of having the tricycle impounded for two days. And if it rains during the night, she must wipe the rain off the tricycle. In this process, she probably learns it is better to bring the tricycle in before dinner while she is thinking about it, lest she forget later.

Or take the matter of eating lunch. If a child's response to the lunch you have prepared is "Yuck! I don't like this. I'm not going to eat it," then a wise parent gives the child the freedom to make that decision. "That's fine, honey. Why don't you run along and play?" However, if later in the afternoon the child comes asking for a snack because "I'm hungry, Mommy," the mother's response should be, "I bet you are, honey. It's probably because you didn't eat your lunch. Run along and play. We will have dinner later." The child made a decision, and the child suffered the consequences. He or she will probably think twice before refusing lunch again.

Then there is the bedtime ritual. Let's say that the bedtime routine is a drink of water or milk, a bedtime story, a prayer, kisses and hugs, and being tucked in by a parent. The rule is that if the child gets out of bed after having been tucked in there is no second drink of water, no second story, no second prayer, and no second tuck in. The child must get back into bed alone and settle in. Thus, the child has the freedom to make a decision—stay in bed the first time or no tuck in the second time. Most children will learn quickly that the parental tuck in is always the better of the two choices.

Sometimes small children will throw temper tantrums in order to get parents to change the rules. If a child's temper tantrum is accompanied with demands to be taken to the parents' room or to get another drink of water, a parent can simply state, "If you want to continue yelling and screaming, you can do it for two more minutes. But if you go beyond two minutes, it means tomorrow night you will go to bed fifteen minutes earlier than your bedtime." Once children learn that all behavior has consequences, they quickly learn to change their behavior.

If a child throws a temper tantrum in the middle of the day, the parent can simply remind the child, "We don't get things by throwing temper tantrums. In fact, if you wish to continue screaming and crying, then I will put you in your room where you can do that; but you are not going to do it in my presence." Thus, the child has the freedom to throw a temper tantrum, but he or she must do it in isolation, not in your presence. Temper tantrums quickly subside when children realize that they are not acceptable behavior and they do not get the desired outcome.

As children get older, they should be assigned household responsibilities that aid in the function of the family. For example, a four-year-old can put his or her soiled clothes in the laundry hamper. As time goes on, household responsibilities expand with their expanding abilities. Once a chore is assigned and a time designated by which the chore is to be completed, a child has the choice to complete the chore or not to complete the chore. If the chore is not completed by the appointed time, then some other family member has an opportunity to do the chore and be paid out of the child's allowance. Thus, the child has a choice to do the chore on time or not to do the chore, but he or she also suffers the consequence if the chore is not done. Children learn quickly when they are held accountable for their own behavior.

What about fighting in the backseat of the car? Many parents get extremely frustrated in their efforts to stop children from fighting. My suggestion is that you give them the freedom to fight, but not in the backseat of the car. As soon as they start fighting, you remind them of the rule: no fighting in the car. They also know the consequences: If they continue to fight, you will pull the car to the side of the road. The two of them will get outside to continue their fighting. When they finish, they may get back into the car. If the family is on the way to get ice-cream cones, you can imagine how quickly the fighting will subside. The parents are not frustrated, and the children have learned a valuable lesson: We have choices, but if we make poor choices, we have to suffer the consequences.

The same principle applies in teaching children good manners. For example, if you have a rule that when someone gives your son a gift he says thank you, and the consequence of not saying it is that he doesn't get to play with the gift until he says it, the child learns to say thank you. Or, if you are at Grandmother's house and Grandmother gives him a gift, you don't prod him, you simply wait to see what he does. If he forgets to say thank you, when you get home, you take the toy, put it in your closet, and tell him he can't play with it until he writes

Grandmother a thank-you note. Children quickly learn that it pays to have good manners. If children leave the table without saying, "May I be excused, please?" they are required to come back to the table and sit while the parents wash the dishes. We are teaching children that life is composed of choices. When we make good choices, everybody is happier. When we make bad choices, the results are not pleasant.

It is this process of making choices between two alternatives that helps children learn the value of making wise decisions. You are doing them a great service, and you are removing a great deal of frustration from yourself. Forcing children to say thank you is simply getting compliance. But when they suffer the consequence of not saying thank you, they learn to say it.

When you give a child the opportunity to make decisions within boundaries, you are respecting the dignity of the child. You are recognizing that the child is a person, not a machine. People have choices, and those choices always impact themselves and others. It is a valuable lesson for a child to learn.

One of the most common mistakes that parents make is threatening their children: "If you do that again, . . ." Sometimes parents follow through with their threats if the bad behavior occurs again. Sometimes the parents do not. In my opinion, parents should never make threats; they should take loving action. Threats confuse a child; consistent action gives the child security. If a child violates a rule, the parents should administer the consequences immediately with calmness and love. An added bonus is that when a parent replaces threats with action, the parent is less likely to grow frustrated and, in the heat of anger, overreact.

There is no place for a parent to lose his or her temper with a child. Beating or yelling and screaming at a child are always negative. Calmly administering the consequences of negative behavior is the most effective way to teach children how to make wise decisions.

The pattern of discipline laid out in this chapter has helped thousands of parents learn how to effectively train their children. When a husband and wife feel that they are working together in training their children, it creates a more positive climate between them. You are working together in rearing these children, and you are consistent in applying the rules. You feel good about yourselves, and you feel good about your children. This atmosphere greatly enhances the marital relationship. If the two of you discuss and agree on the approach of child discipline as discussed in this chapter, I believe it will take you to a whole new level of effective discipline and create a much more positive climate for your marriage.

• • •

Putting the Principles into Practice

1. If you do not know the primary love language of each of your children, let me encourage you to answer the following questions:

   • Which of the five love languages does my child most often express to others: Words of Affirmation, Acts of Service, Gifts, Quality Time, or Physical Touch?

   • Which of these five does my child most often complain about?

   • Which of these five does my child most often request?

   The answers to these three questions will tell you your child's primary love language. If you and your spouse can agree to give heavy doses of the primary love language to your child while sprinkling in the other four, you can be assured your child will feel loved.

2. Make sure your child knows your rules and the consequences of breaking the rules.

   • Make a list of the rules that you have for your child. Ask your spouse to do the same. (Or perhaps you can make the list together.)
   • What would be the most logical consequence if your child broke one of these rules? Discuss it and agree on what the consequence will be.
   • Inform your child of the rules, and make clear what will happen if the rule is broken.
   • Consistently follow through by taking action when your child breaks a rule. (It doesn't matter who administers the discipline. It will be the same by both parents because you have agreed on it.)

3. Think about times in the past when you have tried to force your child to do something and it has erupted into a major battle. Now, think of a way you could have given the child a choice that would have alleviated the conflict and perhaps helped the child learn how to make wise decisions. Here are some examples to get you started: to eat or not to eat, to bring a toy in before dinner or after dinner, to complete the chores on time or not to complete the chores, to stay in bed or to get out of bed. Perhaps you can add to this list. The more choices you allow your child to make, the more quickly your child will learn the difference between poor decisions and wise decisions, and the less conflict you will have.

5

DISCOVERING
THE KEY TO INTIMACY

AT THE HEART OF A HEALTHY MARRIAGE is a deep sense of being connected, loved, appreciated, and respected—intimacy. We had it when we got married, or at least we thought we did. In the dating phase of our relationship, we spent hours talking. We respected each other's ideas. There was a sense of openness between the two of us. We felt as if we "belonged" to each other, that we were "meant" for each other. We shared our deepest secrets and believed in our hearts that we would love each other no matter what happened.

Do you remember the promises you made in those days? "Nothing you could ever tell me will cause me to stop loving you." "I'll go anywhere with you." "Whatever is best for you is what I want as long as I live." It was the belief that you had an intimate relationship unlike anything you had ever experienced before that led you to the commitment of marriage.

Sadly enough, this taste of intimacy is far too brief for many couples. Sometimes it evaporates even before the children arrive. For other couples, it begins to erode upon the arrival of the first child. As one husband said, "I don't know what happened. I thought we were doing pretty well until the baby came. After that, it has been all downhill. Before the baby, she was loving, exciting, and caring. After the baby, she became demanding and critical." His wife's response? "Before the baby, he was thoughtful. I was the focus of his life. After the baby, it was as though I didn't matter anymore. I tried to lose weight quickly. I tried to get back in shape, but nothing seemed to help. Everything else was more important to him than I am." Both of them felt disconnected, unloved, and unappreciated.

Many couples echo the sentiments of this couple. They are badgered by the secret fear, "We should not have married. We don't really love each other." They long for what they thought they had when they got married—a deeply intimate, supportive relationship.

What many couples do not understand is that love must be nurtured. Intimacy is not static. You don't "get it" and have it forever. We move in and out of intimacy based on our behavior toward each other. Chances are you would not be reading this if you had the level of intimacy you desire in your marriage. You are probably among the thousands who wish their marriage could be better. I want to assure you that your dream can come true.

The arrival of children may well have diminished your marital intimacy, but the presence of children need not keep you from building an intimate marriage. We have talked about taking control of your schedule in order to make time for each other. We have also talked about taking control of your money so that you can afford the kinds of things that build intimacy. We have discussed ideas on child rearing that will lower the stress level. The only missing ingredient is discovering the key to intimacy. How do you build or rebuild intimacy in your relationship? What do you do with the time and money you have created? Time and money alone will not build intimacy; it's how you use your time and money. In this chapter, I want to give you three essential ingredients in building an intimate marriage while at the same time being good parents.

Removing the Rubble

Perhaps you have seen houses that have been destroyed by fire, flood, or wind. Where a house once stood, there is rubble. The first step in rebuilding the house is to remove the rubble. The foundation will likely still exist, but you can't build on the foundation until you remove the rubble.

If in your marriage the dry winds have blown and the floods have come and the level of intimacy in your marriage is less than in previous years, it is extremely likely that the foundation is still there. It's time to remove the rubble.

So how do you remove the rubble? You begin by acknowledging that you are a part of the problem. Typically, we can see the failures of our spouse much more clearly than we can see our own failures. If you are going to remove the rubble, you must begin by identifying and acknowledging your part in the demolition of your intimacy. Three elements typically destroy intimacy: The first element is harsh, critical, condemning words. The second is hurtful actions. And the third is neglect. These three destroy our sense of being connected, loved, appreciated, and respected. Perhaps you would be willing to invest a few moments with God and ask him to show you the role your unkind words, hurtful actions, and neglect have played in destroying the intimacy of your marriage. If you are willing to ask God, God is willing to answer.

Another part of the rubble-removal process is confessing your failures to your spouse and asking for forgiveness. Would you be willing to say something like this to your spouse? "I know that my actions have hurt you deeply. My words have been unkind and unfair. I have neglected you. And in so doing, I have diminished what I want most in life—an intimate relationship with you. I cannot undo what I have done, but if you will forgive me, I would like to show you that I do indeed love you, respect you, and appreciate you. I know that we both have many stresses on us with the children, our jobs, and our other responsibilities. But I believe that together we can build a healthy marriage, and that is what I want." When you do this, you have taken the first step in rebuilding intimacy in your marriage.

Let me warn you that your spouse may not reciprocate quickly. He or she may not be ready to forgive you and may not admit to failing in the relationship. Don't expect too much. Rather, allow time for your spouse to see that you are sincere, that you are not simply trying to brush the past away, and that you are genuinely seeking to build a new relationship.[1]

Reaffirming Your Commitment

Perhaps you have forgotten the words, "I promise to love, honor, and keep you, in sickness and in health, in poverty and in wealth, so long as we both shall live." Perhaps on the day you married, you were so enamored by the euphoric feelings of being "in love" that you failed to reflect deeply on these words. They are heavy words, but they are the words to which you need to return if you want to renew an intimate relationship. True love is not a feeling. It is an attitude—a choice made daily to look out for the well-being of your spouse, to find ways to enhance and enrich his or her life. It is the choice to invest time, energy, and money to accomplish that goal. Bottom line—love is the commitment to be there for each other *no matter what*.

The Bible challenges the husband to love his wife as Christ "loved the church and gave himself up for her."[2] Let me remind you that Christ loved the church before the church loved him. He loved the church even when the church was rejecting his love. And he loved the church all the way to death.

The wife is challenged to "respect her husband"[3] and to allow him the privilege of loving her. Some women find this difficult because they have been reared in a culture that teaches them to be assertive and take care of themselves. However, it is the willingness to admit that spouses need each other that leads to marital intimacy. We were not made to live in isolation. We were meant to live deeply connected to each other, each of us looking out for the interests of the other and working together as a team to become the people God intended us to be. That is what marriage is all about. And the best parents are those who have this kind of marriage.

If you are willing to reaffirm your commitment, perhaps you could contact the person who performed your wedding ceremony and ask if he has a copy of the vows you made to each other. If this is not possible, I have included the vows from a typical wedding ceremony. (You will find them on page 358.) Perhaps they are close enough to the ones you made that you would be willing to verbally affirm them to your spouse. Again, let me warn you that your spouse may or may not be willing to reciprocate. The pain may be too deep, and hope may have evaporated.

Emotionally, perhaps your spouse is not presently able to affirm vows to you. Don't expect it, and don't demand it. Give your spouse time, while you continue to demonstrate that you are serious about the changes that are taking place in your own life.

Making Your Spouse Feel Loved

Finding out what makes your spouse feel loved and appreciated—and then doing it consistently—may take a while. But you can do it. Let me give you some possible approaches.

Now that you have acknowledged to your spouse your failures of the past and you have verbally reaffirmed your commitment, you are ready to say, "As you know, I am trying to become the husband/wife that you deserve. So, what could I do to help you this evening?" Whatever your spouse suggests, you not only do it to the best of your ability but you write it down in a notebook. For example:

- She likes it when I fold the towels.
- He likes it when I give him a back rub.

You ask your question every night: "What could I do to help you this evening?" And every evening, you do it and write it down, if it is not already on your list. On the simplest and easiest level, you are learning how to love and express appreciation to your spouse.

As time goes on, you ask similar questions in different social settings. For example, as you drive to church you might say, "We've been going to church a long time, but I would like to ask you, 'What could I do differently at church that would make things more meaningful for you?'" Do it, and write it in your notebook:

- She likes it when I let her talk with friends after church instead of pulling on her arm, telling her it is time to go home.
- He likes it when I sit beside him in church rather than singing in the choir.

The willingness to give, the willingness to sacrifice—this is true love, and it builds marital intimacy.

As the atmosphere between the two of you begins to improve, you might ask this question: "What could I do that would make me a better husband [or wife] to you?" With this question, you are broadening the scope for suggestions. You may address any area of life. Whatever your spouse shares you can take seriously and know that he or she is giving you valuable information on how to express love and appreciation. Do it and record it. And you will be on the road to greater intimacy.

However, not all spouses will respond positively to this approach. You may say, "What could I do to help you this evening?" and your spouse may respond, "If I have to tell you, then it doesn't mean anything to me." Or perhaps the response is "I don't want you to help me. Just stay out of my way." Either of these or similar responses indicate that your spouse has been deeply hurt and is emotionally fatigued from the lack of intimacy in the relationship. Your spouse is not highly motivated to give you an opportunity to try because there is little hope that you will be consistent.

The fact that your spouse has lost hope does not mean that you must also abandon hope. There is another approach to discovering what makes your spouse feel loved and appreciated. It's called *evaluating the criticisms*.

Look back over the years and ask yourself, "What has my spouse complained about through the years? What has my spouse nagged me about?" Perhaps at the time, you resented the criticisms and rebelled at the nagging. In fact, you were getting valuable information. Your spouse was telling you what made him or her feel loved and appreciated. This approach opens up a whole new vista of understanding your spouse.

I remember the husband who said to me after he tried this approach, "It all became so clear. In the earlier years, she nagged me about taking the trash outside every night after dinner. I wanted to wait until the trash bag was full. Finally, she started taking it out herself. Now I realize that I had blown an opportunity to express love to her. So without saying a word, I started taking the trash out every night after dinner.

"I remembered also that she used to complain that I didn't vacuum her car every time I vacuumed my truck. Personally, I didn't think her car needed it as often as my truck. Now I realize that to her that would have been an expression of love. So without saying a word, I started washing and vacuuming her car every time I washed and vacuumed my truck. I remembered a few more criticisms, and I started doing the things she had requested. After about three months, she said to me, 'What's going on with you?' I simply said, 'Remember when I told you that I was sorry for my past failures? And I told you I was committed to becoming the husband you deserve? Well, I've just been working at it. I know you deserve a whole lot more than I've given you through the years, and I intend to give it to you from this point on.' She walked away without giving me any verbal response, but within a month, one day she smiled and said to me, 'I can't believe the things you have been doing for me. I'm beginning to enjoy living with you again. You are becoming the man I married. I just hope I don't wake up and find out I was dreaming.'

"From that day, the atmosphere in our marriage has been radically different. From that point on, she would answer my question when I asked, 'What can I do to help you this evening?' She made suggestions and I did them. Before long, she started asking me what she could do to make my life better. That was the day I started having romantic feelings for her again. Once the atmosphere got better, we started talking again, looking back over the past and discussing where we both went wrong. We've learned a lot about each other. I never knew that my taking the trash out consistently made her more interested in having sex. I wish someone had told me that twenty years ago. Even the kids have noticed the difference in our marriage. Our twelve-year-old son recently said to us, 'I don't know what's going on with you two. But I want you to know I like it. I was tired of the yelling and screaming. I'm glad to see that you two are finally getting it together.' He went on to tell us how hard it was to live in the house with us when we were not getting along. Neither of us realized that our behavior had so deeply impacted him. We took the occasion to apologize to him and asked his forgiveness for our failures. I'm just glad that we are finally learning how to love each other."

In the early years of marriage, most couples are expressing love to each other. The problem is that often they are not expressing love in a way the other person understands. Typically we are doing for each other what our parents did for each other, or we are doing for them what we wish they would do for us. One young man told me that for the first six months of his marriage, every month he would bring his wife a dozen roses on the date of their anniversary. He did this because that's what his

212 || GARY CHAPMAN

father did for his mother. It took her six months to get up the courage to tell him that she didn't particularly care for roses, and in fact, she was somewhat allergic to them. He was disillusioned to find out that what was meaningful to his mother was not so meaningful to his wife. One young wife served her husband breakfast in bed every Saturday morning for the first month of their marriage because that's what her mother did. She later discovered that he much preferred eating at the table.

Sincerity is not enough. We must ask questions if we are to discover what is meaningful to the other person. What makes one person feel loved does not necessarily make another person feel loved. That is why a husband and wife can be genuinely expressing love to each other, and yet neither feels loved or appreciated. When you express love in a way that is meaningful to your spouse, you are building intimacy.

As the emotional climate between the two of you is built up, you may periodically want to ask your spouse, "What could we do to improve our marriage?" If you discover that a weekend getaway is meaningful to your spouse, then put it on your schedule and find the money to do it. If you discover that a weekly date night makes him or her feel connected to you, then by all means hire a babysitter or trade off with another couple who have children approximately the age of your children, and make it happen. If you discover that a "sit down and talk" time each evening is what makes your spouse feel loved and appreciated, then put it into your daily schedule and make it as important as reporting to work in the morning.

It's the simple things, sometimes little things, that make or break a marriage. The wise couple will discover what makes the other feel connected, loved, appreciated, and respected. And they will do it. Intimacy flourishes, and the children have the benefit of growing up in a home where Mom and Dad love and support each other. What greater gift could you give any child?

• • •

Putting the Principles into Practice
1. Removing the Rubble: If you have not already done so, why not take a few minutes to think about how you contributed to the lack

of intimacy in your marriage? Ask God to remind you of harsh, critical, condemning words; hurtful actions; and times of neglect. Once you have confessed these to God, why not acknowledge them to your spouse and ask forgiveness?

2. Reaffirming Your Commitment: Would you be willing to contact the person who performed your wedding ceremony and ask if he could send you a copy of the vows you made when you were married? If this is not possible, utilize the vows on page 358. Affirm your vows to God and then to your spouse.

3. Making Your Spouse Feel Loved: Using one of the two methods in this chapter, discover the things that make your spouse feel loved and appreciated. The first approach is to ask questions: "What could I do to help you this evening?" "How could I be a better husband/wife to you?" "What could I do at church or at the mall to make the experience more meaningful for you?" The second approach is to examine the criticisms of the past to discover what is meaningful to your spouse. What your spouse has complained about reveals his or her inner desires. In a notebook, list the things that you know are meaningful to your spouse and seek to express love in these ways on a regular basis.

• • •

Closing Thoughts on Now What?

What I have shared with you in this part of the book has helped hundreds of couples discover how to have a successful marriage and at the same time be successful parents. God never intended children to destroy marriages. On the other hand, neither do children create strong marriages. Strong marriages are created by husbands and wives who put their hands in the hand of the God who created marriage and ordained that children would flourish best in a home with a mom and dad who love, support, and encourage each other.

Many couples complain that they don't have the time or money to enrich their marriages. I believe that such complaints are ill-spoken. You have the time and you have the money to do everything you ought to do for each other and for your children. You may not yet have taken control of your schedules or taken control of your money, but you have the ability to do so. In this book, I have tried to give practical suggestions that will help you do both. If you apply these ideas, you will be able to create the time and the financial means to enrich your marriage—to keep intimacy alive while raising your children. To do so is one of the greatest things you can do for each other and for your children. I challenge you to implement the plan laid out in this book. I assure you that it works.

If you find this book helpful, I hope you will share it with a friend. If you have stories to share with me, I invite you to select the Contact link at www.garychapman.org.

• • •

Some Ideas Worth Remembering
- If an intimate marriage and parenting are both a part of God's design, then surely there is a way to do both successfully.
- What does it mean to make marriage a priority? It means, first, that we pause long enough to assess the quality of our marriage. Then we must make a conscious choice that for the benefit of our children, for ourselves, and (if we are Christians) for the glory of God, we will commit ourselves to each other and acknowledge that our marriage is important to us. Finally, we must agree that with God's help we will find a way to strengthen our intimacy.
- I believe that the answer to finding time to build a strong marriage, while at the same time being good parents, lies in taking control of our schedules.
- Getting control of your schedule means getting the right person doing the right task and deciding when it will be done, eliminating any unnecessary tasks that you are presently doing, getting your children on a schedule that interfaces positively with your schedule, and making time for yourself.
- There is a simple principle that, when applied, will keep a

marriage alive regardless of a couple's income. The principle
is this: Put your money where your priorities are.

- The best things in life are free—or at least inexpensive. Taking
time to enjoy a sunset, picking a wildflower and giving it to
your spouse, enjoying the colors of fall leaves, going to church,
taking a walk together, or sitting together on the porch while the
crickets serenade you costs nothing! Sharing ice-cream cones,
eating your favorite pizza, and taking a swim or attending a
movie together are all relatively inexpensive.
- The word *discipline* is not a negative word, nor is it to be equated
with spanking or yelling at children. The word *discipline* means
literally "to train." Most parents recognize that children need
training. Without positive discipline, children will self-destruct;
they cannot train themselves.
- In adulthood, success or failure in life is largely dependent upon
the ability to make wise decisions. How do children learn to
make decisions? The process begins by giving them the freedom
to make decisions within boundaries.
- When a husband and wife feel that they are working together
in training their children, it creates a more positive climate
between them. You are working together to rear these children,
and you are consistent in applying the rules. You feel good
about yourselves, and you feel good about your children. This
atmosphere greatly enhances the marital relationship.
- The Bible challenges the husband to love his wife as Christ
"loved the church and gave himself up for her" (Ephesians 5:25).
Christ loved the church before the church loved him. He loved
the church even when the church was rejecting his love. And he
loved the church all the way to death.
- The wife is challenged to "respect her husband" (Ephesians 5:33)
and to allow him the privilege of loving her. Some women find
this difficult when they have been reared in a culture that teaches
them to be assertive and take care of themselves. However, it is
the willingness to admit that spouses need each other that leads
to marital intimacy.

- Finding out what makes your spouse feel loved and appreciated—and then doing it consistently—may take a while. But you can do it.
- Look back over the years and ask yourself, "What has my spouse complained about through the years? What has my spouse nagged me about?" Perhaps at the time you resented the criticisms and rebelled at the nagging. In fact, you were getting valuable information. Your spouse was telling you what made him or her feel loved and appreciated.
- What makes one person feel loved does not necessarily make another person feel loved. That is why a husband and wife can be genuinely expressing love to each other, and yet neither feels loved or appreciated. When you express love in a way that is meaningful to your spouse, you are building intimacy.

Part Five

MAKING LOVE

Making Sex an Act of Love

"LET'S MAKE LOVE."

"Let's have sex."

Is there a difference? Most definitely. In fact, the two are worlds apart.

Sex is the joining of two bodies; love is the joining of two souls. When sex grows out of love, it becomes a deeply emotional, bonding experience. When having sex is viewed as nothing more than satisfying biological urges, that's all it does. It is never ultimately fulfilling. It is more animal than human.

Throughout human history, love and sex have always been related. However, in contemporary culture, love and sex have been equated. The common perception today is that *making love* means "having sex." Love is defined as a romantic feeling, and sex is its logical expression. Sex outside of marriage has become as common as sex within marriage. Sex has been separated from commitment and is viewed as a form of casual entertainment, much like being on a roller coaster or some other amusement-park ride. When it's over, we look forward to the next ride. This view of sex has left thousands feeling emotionally empty and longing for something to fill the void of the soul.

I believe that the Christian faith, which is built upon the Jewish faith, offers a wealth of insight on making love, not just having sex.

For example, both the Jewish faith and the Christian faith view sex as a gift from God. Both teach that God has given us guidelines on how to relate to each other sexually. It's interesting that recent sociological research has come to the same conclusions as those found in the ancient Jewish and Christian Scriptures. One such conclusion is that sex within marriage is much more meaningful and satisfying than sex outside of marriage.[1] While this truth is not popular in secular society, it bears the support of both research and Scripture.

The purpose of this part, "Making Love," is to explore the Judeo-Christian teachings on love and sex and on how love and sex relate to each other. I believe sex without love will never be ultimately fulfilling, but sex that grows out of love will take a marriage to a whole new level of satisfaction. I feel certain that thousands of marriages can be greatly enhanced as couples learn to make love, not just have sex.

This part of the book is not designed to be a comprehensive sex manual. My goal is to show you the difference between making love and simply having sex. Ideally, you and your spouse will read the book together, answer the questions at the end of each chapter, and then share your answers with each other. If you choose to do so, I believe you will find yourselves on the way to becoming real lovers.

However, if your spouse is not willing to read and discuss this topic with you, it will still be well worth your time to read these pages yourself. I strongly urge you to follow the suggestions made. Reach out to your spouse. Extend the opportunity for your husband or wife to respond to your efforts to stimulate growth in your relationship. I'm sure you know that you cannot force your spouse to do anything, but you can greatly influence your spouse by means of a loving attitude expressed in loving words and actions.

You can probably read this part of the book in less than two hours, and I believe you will find that reading it will be a good investment of your time. At the end of each chapter, you will find practical suggestions on how to weave these ideas into the fabric of your own marriage.

If you desire greater sexual satisfaction, you must learn to love.

1

LOVE AND SEX:
THE PERFECT COMBINATION

Contrary to popular belief, Hollywood did not invent sex. According to the most ancient Jewish writings, the Book of Beginnings, God looked at the man he had created and said, "It is not good for the man to be alone. I will make a helper suitable for him." The Creation narrative continues, "God caused the man to fall into a deep sleep; and while he was sleeping, he took one of the man's ribs and closed up the place with flesh. Then the Lord God made a woman from the rib he had taken out of the man, and he brought her to the man." The man exclaimed, "This is now bone of my bones and flesh of my flesh; she shall be called 'woman,' for she was taken out of man." Then the Creator declared that the two would "become one flesh." The account concludes with these words: "The man and his wife were both naked, and they felt no shame."[1]

Sex Is Beautiful
Based on this ancient Creation account, Jews and Christians have always viewed marriage as a sacred relationship between a husband and wife, instituted by God. The sexual union between the husband and wife is

222 || GARY CHAPMAN

seen as a living symbol of their deep companionship. That Adam and Eve were naked and unashamed indicates that from God's perspective, sex is beautiful.

Throughout the Old and New Testament Scriptures, God repeatedly affirms the beauty of sexual intercourse within the marital relationship. While the Bible records incidents of polygamy, fornication (sex outside of marriage), adultery, homosexuality, incest, and rape, these distortions of sexuality are never approved by God. Sexual intercourse from God's perspective is an act of love that binds the souls of a husband and a wife to each other in a lifelong, intimate relationship.

The Purpose of Sex

It is obvious that one of the purposes of relating to each other sexually in the context of marriage is for reproduction. God himself said to Adam and Eve, "Be fruitful and increase in number; fill the earth and subdue it."[2] Husbands and wives who love each other and express their love sexually provide the healthiest context in which to rear children. It is interesting that contemporary research supports this ancient biblical pattern.[3]

However, procreation is not the only purpose, nor the primary purpose, of sexual intercourse within marriage. Far more basic are the psychological and spiritual dimensions of making love. As a husband and wife give themselves to each other sexually, they are building a psychological and spiritual bond that unites their souls at the deepest possible level. Together they can face the challenges of life because they are soul partners. Nothing unites a husband and wife more deeply than making love.

On the other hand, if the married couple is simply having sex without love, this bonding does not take place. Thus, the couple become estranged, and their union will eventually dissipate. For some, divorce is the culmination of this estrangement. Having sex without love builds resentment and, later, hostility.

God intends marital sex to be an experience of extreme pleasure. This pleasure is not limited to the physical sensation of orgasm. It also involves the emotions, the intellect, and the spirit. Sexual intercourse within marriage is designed to give us a taste of the divine. It involves the total person and brings waves of pleasure as we make love.

An Ancient Example

The books of Hebrew poetry found in the Old Testament seek to capture this pleasure. Here are the words of a husband speaking to his bride: "You have stolen my heart, my sister, my bride; you have stolen my heart with one glance of your eyes, with one jewel of your necklace. How delightful is your love, my sister, my bride! How much more pleasing is your love than wine, and the fragrance of your perfume than any spice! Your lips drop sweetness as the honeycomb, my bride; milk and honey are under your tongue. The fragrance of your garments is like that of Lebanon. . . . You are a garden fountain, a well of flowing water streaming down from Lebanon." His bride responds, "Let my lover come into his garden and taste its choice fruits."[4]

A short time later, the wife says of her husband, "My lover is radiant and ruddy, outstanding among ten thousand. His head is purest gold; his hair is wavy and black as a raven. . . . His cheeks are like beds of spice. . . . His arms are rods of gold. . . . His legs are pillars of marble. . . . His mouth is sweetness itself; he is altogether lovely. This is my lover, this my friend."[5]

Obviously, these ancient lovers are finding great pleasure in relating to each other sexually. They are discovering what it means to make love, not just have sex.

Accentuate the Positive

Notice particularly in the passages above that the husband and the wife each accentuated the positive characteristics of the other.

Contemporary couples, in contrast, often tend to focus on the negative. Even though there were many, many positive characteristics that drew them to each other when they first met, when conflicts begin to emerge, they focus on the negative. They verbalize these by saying such things as, "I can't believe you are so lazy." "I have never known anyone as selfish as you." "You are just like your father. No wonder your mother left him." Such statements create hurt, anger, and resentment. And typically an offended spouse reciprocates with more negative statements. When we focus on the negative, we draw out the worst in our spouse.

On the other hand, when we choose to focus on the positive, we stimulate a positive response. The wife who says, "Wow. Do you ever look tough tonight!" will likely receive not only a smile but also positive words about the way she looks. The spouse who says, "Thanks for cooking the meal; it was delicious," stimulates warm, positive feelings in the heart of the one who prepared the meal. When we focus on the positive and verbalize our appreciation and admiration for each other, we create a climate in which sex can become a genuine expression of love.

Sex was designed by God to be a mutually satisfying experience whereby husbands and wives express their love, intimacy, and commitment to each other. A husband and wife may engage in sexual intercourse without feelings of love, intimacy, and commitment, but this has never been God's ideal. God's intention is for couples to make love, not just have sex.

• • •

Putting the Principles into Practice
1. How would you explain the difference between making love and just having sex?
2. On a scale of 1–10, with 10 being the highest, how would you rank your success at "making love"? How do you think your spouse would rank you?
3. What would you like your spouse to do (or stop doing) that would make the sexual relationship more meaningful for you?
4. What could you do (or stop doing) to make the sexual relationship more meaningful for your spouse?
5. Would you be willing to share your answers to the above questions with your spouse?

2

MAKING LOVE
REQUIRES PATIENCE

Sex can be quick, but love requires time. I am not denying that a "quickie" can sometimes be an expression of love. What I am saying is that finding mutual sexual satisfaction in marriage takes time. I have always found it interesting that God instructed the young men and women of Israel to take a year for their honeymoon: "A newly married man must not be drafted into the army or be given any other official responsibilities. He must be free to spend one year at home, bringing happiness to the wife he has married."[1]

The reality is that not many couples find mutual sexual fulfillment in less than a year. Just as they must grow together intellectually, emotionally, and spiritually, they must also grow together sexually. It is a process that takes time. Making love is more than inserting the penis into the vagina and having an orgasm. Making love has as its object mutual pleasure in the process.

Why does it take so much time to grow together sexually? Because males and females are different in just about every way you could imagine—physically, emotionally, and psychologically. There are key differences between men and women in the nature of the sex drive, in the ignition points that make them ready for sex, and even in their responses during intercourse. A husband and wife must discover and accept these differences before they can begin to find mutual satisfaction.

Nature of the Sex Drive

While both men and women have a biological drive to have sex, the female's drive or desire is far more tied to her emotions than is the man's. If a woman feels loved by her husband, she desires to be sexually intimate with him. However, if she does not feel loved, she may have little desire to have sex with him. (An exception might be the case in which sex is the only way she gets tender touch and kind words that speak to her emotionally.) This difference explains a lot of things for us. For example, it explains how a husband and wife can have an intense argument and say hateful things to each other, but thirty minutes later the husband wants to have intercourse. The wife will find that virtually impossible unless he apologizes in a way that she considers sincere. Then, perhaps, her sexual desire can be kindled.

A husband can desire to have sexual intercourse even when things are not right in the relationship. In fact, he often thinks that having sex will solve the problems. For the male, when the seminal vesicles are full and the testosterone level is normal, there will be a desire for sexual release. This desire is not deeply rooted in his emotions but rather in his biological urges. On the other hand, a wife wants things to be made right before having sexual intercourse. Sex itself does not solve problems for her.

Understanding this difference in the nature of sexual desire will help a husband give far more attention to his wife's emotional needs, which we will discuss further in chapters 4 and 5, pages 235–251. It will also help a wife understand why her husband's desire for sexual intimacy can be just as strong after a fight as it was before the fight.

This difference also explains why couples often disagree on the frequency of sexual intercourse. A husband's desire is guided largely by the buildup of seminal fluid, which creates a physiological need for release. This is methodical and regular and has little to do with how things are going in a couple's relationship. While the wife's biological clock is influenced to some degree by her monthly menstrual cycle, her physiological urges are often overridden by her emotions and the quality of the relationship. Couples must learn to work with this difference in the nature of sexual desire if they are to find mutual fulfillment.

Ignition Points

Another difference is in the area of ignition points, or what each finds sexually stimulating. The male is strongly stimulated by sight; the female, by touch and kind words. This explains why a husband can merely watch his wife getting ready for bed, and by the time she gets undressed, he is ready to have intercourse. On the other hand, she can watch him undress without the thought of sex ever crossing her mind. However, if the husband speaks kind words and uses tender touch, assuming that their marital relationship is fairly positive, her sexual urges will be ignited. Understanding this difference and cooperating with it will help a couple get on the same page. If they ignore this difference, a husband and wife may never find mutual fulfillment.

Incidentally, this difference also explains why men are far more tempted by pornography than women are, and why women are more likely to become emotionally involved with a coworker who speaks kind words and uses tender touch. While it's helpful to recognize these gender-specific areas of temptation, please understand that I am not offering excuses for giving in to them. Let me be perfectly clear: To yield to either of these temptations is seriously detrimental to a marriage, as well as to spiritual health. There is no place for pornography in the life of a Christian husband, and it is equally unacceptable for a Christian wife to allow herself to become emotionally attached to another man. While working on our own sexual fulfillment, we must guard our hearts from falling into these destructive patterns.

Responses

Another difference between men and women is in the context of sexual intercourse itself. The male's response tends to be fast and explosive, while the female's response tends to be slow and lasting. The male tends to reach climax quickly, and after climax, he's finished; it's all over for him—but the wife may be lying there thinking, *What's supposed to be so great about this?* She was only getting started. In order to find mutual sexual pleasure, both spouses need to understand this difference and learn to cooperate with each other. Research indicates that the average male will ejaculate after two minutes of vigorous thrusting.[2] The problem is that few women can reach orgasm in that short amount of time. Besides that, most women reach orgasm not through thrusting but through stimulation of the clitoris. This has led many couples to conclude that it is best for the wife to have orgasm as a part of the foreplay. Once she has experienced orgasm, then the husband is free to experience his own climax.

Many wives do not desire to have an orgasm every time they have intercourse. Sometimes, a wife is happy simply to experience tender touch, hear kind words, and sense her husband's love and closeness. He experiences climax and feels loved by her. They both find the experience to be satisfying even though she does not experience orgasm. A husband might object, saying, "I don't want to enjoy the sexual experience if she's not going to enjoy it." What he needs to realize is that she does enjoy making love, even if it doesn't always end in orgasm. It often requires far more energy, effort, and time for a woman to experience orgasm than it does for a man. Sometimes, because of fatigue or other distractions, a wife simply does not desire to go through the entire process. Her husband should not expect it of her. The goal is to pleasure each other. The wife should have the freedom to decide whether she desires to experience orgasm as a part of the whole sexual experience.

I have often been asked why God created men and women with all these sexual differences. I have said facetiously that if God had asked me, I would have suggested, "Don't even turn us on until we finish all our education. Then once you turn us on, let everyone get married three months later. After marriage, push both spouses' buttons every three days." Wouldn't that be a lot easier? I have concluded that God's intention, when he made us different, was for sex to be more than a reproductive act—that it would in fact be a chance to tangibly show our love. When sex is an act of love, the husband and wife approach each other and ask, "How may I pleasure you?" If we don't make it an act of love, we will never find mutual fulfillment.

If a husband and wife simply do "what comes naturally," they will never learn to make love. The best that may happen is that one of them will find partial fulfillment and the other will feel used. That is where thousands of couples are in their sexual relationship. They have sex from time to time, but they have never learned to make love. When we understand our differences, accept our differences, and learn how to work together, we can make beautiful music.

All of this takes time, patience, and understanding. If the two of you have never read and discussed a book on sexual technique, I would suggest Dr. Kevin Leman's book *Sheet Music: Uncovering the Secrets of Sexual Intimacy in Marriage.*[3] With a little information and a lot of patience, the two of you can learn to make love.

● ● ●

Putting the Principles into Practice

1. While both males and females have biological sexual drives, the female's sexual desire is greatly influenced by her emotions. Thus, if a wife does not feel loved, she may be reluctant to engage sexually with her husband. How do you experience this reality in your marriage?

   Husbands: Would you be willing to ask your wife to share with you the kinds of things you can do or say to best communicate your love to her?

   Wives: Would you be willing to share with your husband what actions on his part tend to make you feel loved?

2. The male is strongly stimulated by sight; the female, by touch and kind words. How has this difference influenced your marriage?

   Husbands: Would you be willing to ask your wife to share with you the kinds of touches and caring words that enhance her sexual desire?

   Wives: Would you be willing to ask your husband to share with you the kinds of things you could do visually to stimulate him sexually?

3. The timing of orgasm is frustrating for many couples. The most common problem is the husband's ejaculating while the wife is still warming up to the sexual experience. He is finished and she is frustrated.

    Husbands: Would you be willing to discuss with your wife a solution that has worked for many couples: the husband bringing the wife to orgasm by stimulation of the clitoris as a part of the foreplay? Then once she has experienced orgasm, he is free to experience climax.

    Wives: Would you be willing to discuss with your husband your preferences related to orgasm?

3

LOVE GIVES
BUT NEVER DEMANDS

SOME CHRISTIANS LIKE TO USE THE SCRIPTURES as a club to demand their sexual rights in marriage. One Scripture passage often used is 1 Corinthians 7:3-5: "The husband should fulfill his marital duty to his wife, and likewise the wife to her husband. The wife's body does not belong to her alone but also to her husband. In the same way, the husband's body does not belong to him alone but also to his wife. Do not deprive each other." The husband reads this to his wife and demands that she perform her "wifely duties." Or a frustrated wife will say, "All I want is for him to be a husband to me. Is that asking too much?"

The apostle Paul sets out the marital ideal: A husband will reach out and seek to meet his wife's sexual needs, and she will do the same for him. That is a picture of true lovemaking. However, we are not to *demand* the ideal; instead, we are to *create* the ideal. Most of us find it easier to preach the ideal than to practice it.

So what is the process that brings us to the point of mutual lovemaking? I believe it begins with prayer. We each ask God to give us the attitude of Christ toward our spouse. A husband is specifically challenged to love his wife as Christ loved the church and gave himself up for her.[1]

Christ loved the church before the church loved him; that is, he took the initiative. He loved the church in the face of rejection, and he loved the church all the way to death. There is no limit to his love. What is our response to such love? The Scriptures say, "We love [God] because He first loved us."[2] His love stimulated our love. God did not force us to do anything, but his love won our hearts.

This is the pattern for marriage. The husband takes the initiative to love his wife—and to persist in that love even through times of rejection. When the wife sees that he is unconditionally committed to her well-being, she respects him, and to use the language of Hebrew poetry, she invites him into her garden to enjoy the pleasures that she has ready for him.

Listen to the words of love that flow from the heart of a Hebrew husband from ancient times: "How beautiful you are, my darling! Oh, how beautiful! Your eyes . . . are doves. Your hair is like a flock of goats. . . . Your teeth are like a flock of sheep just shorn, coming up from the washing. Each has its twin; not one of them is alone. Your lips are like a scarlet ribbon; your mouth is lovely. Your temples behind your veil are like the halves of a pomegranate. Your neck is like the tower of David, built with elegance. . . . Your two breasts are like two fawns, like twin fawns of a gazelle that browse among the lilies. Until the day breaks and the shadows flee, I will go to the mountain of myrrh and to the hill of incense. All beautiful you are, my darling; there is no flaw in you."[3]

Husbands, if you want to speak words of love to your wife, you might use this as a model. Of course, you will need to update the metaphors. But I'm sure you're creative enough to do that.

What do these tender, affirming words do for a wife? They ignite her passion. She invites her husband to taste the sexual fruits of her body when she responds, "Awake, north wind, and come, south wind! Blow on my garden, that its fragrance may spread abroad. Let my lover come into his garden and taste its choice fruits."[4]

The husband responds to her invitation: "I have come into my garden, my sister, my bride; I have gathered my myrrh with my spice. I have eaten my honeycomb and my honey; I have drunk my wine and my milk."[5] Wow! That is making love, not just having sex.

The pattern is clear. The husband takes the initiative, not in demanding sex but in loving his wife. His words of affirmation describing her beauty touch her heart and make her want to be sexually intimate with him. Notice carefully that he did not enter the garden until she invited him. This is a part of lovemaking that many husbands do not understand. They are happy to take initiative—but in most husbands' minds, that means initiating a sexual encounter. The husband is sexually stimulated and assumes his wife has the same desire. So he barges ahead and enters the garden long before she is ready to invite him. The results? They end up having sex, but not making love.

Waiting for his wife's invitation can be frustrating for a man. One husband said, "I've been waiting for six months. How much longer do I wait?" The answer is not simply continuing to wait but rather giving love. The passage of time will not stimulate sexual arousal in a wife, but consistent love will.

I am fully aware that the pattern I have just presented is contrary to "what comes naturally." By nature, we tend to expect our spouse to meet our sexual needs. If our needs aren't met, then we start demanding. Such demands create resentment and drive our spouse further away. Making love is about giving, not demanding. When we focus on creating an atmosphere of love in which we are genuinely seeking to affirm our spouse, we will eventually hear the invitation.

All of this requires a change of heart. Each of us is by nature egocentric—thinking the world revolves around "me." Christ was not self-centered. He focused on his mission of loving the church and giving himself for it. When we ask God to change our perspective, then allow him to do so, we are on the road to making love, not just having sex.

•　•　•

Putting the Principles into Practice
1. Has your attitude about sex leaned more toward giving or toward demanding?
2. Would you be willing to ask God to give you the attitude of Christ toward your spouse—taking the initiative to give rather than waiting and expecting to receive?

3. Think about ways in which your words or actions may be creating frustration or resentment in your spouse. What can you say or do differently in the future?

4. Ask God to change your perspective—and then allow him to do it.

4

LOVE IS MORE THAN A FEELING

A WIFE IS SITTING IN MY OFFICE saying, "I just feel like my husband doesn't love me. He treats me like trash and then wants me to have sex with him. I don't understand that. I can't have sex with a man who doesn't love me." This wife knows deep within her heart that sex and love are supposed to go together. Sex without love seems like rape, and she cannot bear that. Many wives can identify with her pain.

On the other hand, many husbands experience the same frustration. I shall never forget the husband who said, "We had sex, but I felt like I was with a corpse." Sex without love is indeed dead.

The desire for love is universal. When we are married, the love we most long for is that of our spouse. When we feel loved, the world looks bright. Sex is the cherry on top of the sundae. All of life is sweet. Without love, the world looks bleak, and sex is at best a temporary oasis in a barren desert.

Most couples do not know how to create love when it is absent. Many feel hopeless. "We've lost our feelings for each other; maybe we shouldn't have married" is a common sentiment. The tendency is for couples to blame marriage for the loss of their euphoric feelings. In reality, they would have lost those feelings even if they had not married.

Two Stages of Love

The average lifespan of the "in love" experience is two years. We don't stay obsessed with each other forever. If we did, we would never accomplish anything. One man who was passionately in love told me, "I'm afraid I'm going to lose my job. Since I met Julie, I can't focus my attention at work." It's hard to focus on anything else when we are in love. All our energy and all our thoughts focus on being with each other. When we are together, we are supremely happy; when we are apart, we long to be together.

What many fail to realize is that there are two distinct stages of romantic or emotional love. The first stage is the super-emotional high of the "in love" obsession. In this stage, we are pushed along by our emotions. Our acts of kindness require little effort. We would gladly climb the highest mountain or swim the deepest sea for each other. Without a second thought, we buy gifts we cannot afford and make promises we can never keep. It's great fun! But it is temporary. It cannot be sustained over a long period of time.

The second stage of love is far more realistic and requires thought and effort. We are no longer caught up in the waves of strong emotion. We have lost the illusion that the other person is perfect. We have returned to the real world of preparing meals, washing dishes, cleaning bathrooms, and perhaps changing a baby's diaper. Our differences have emerged; we find ourselves in conflict over minute issues. Our emotions have plummeted and turned sour. If we let our emotions take the lead, we will begin to argue with each other. Arguments lead to resentment, and resentment destroys our intimacy. Stage 1 has come to an end, but no one has told us how to enter stage 2.

The Challenges of Stage 2

The reason stage 2 is difficult is that it doesn't begin with exciting, exhilarating emotions but rather with a conscious choice. Stage 1 begins with the tingles; stage 2 begins with choosing a positive attitude.

One husband told me of his journey: "In the early days of our marriage, we struggled greatly. I found myself with negative feelings toward my wife. She did not live up to my expectations, and I'm sure she would have said the same about me. I finally decided that I did not marry a perfect woman, and she did not marry a perfect man. It's true—we had our differences, but I didn't marry her to make her miserable. I wanted us to learn to work together as a team and enjoy life together and rear our children in a loving home. So I decided I would ask God to help me learn how to be a good husband. The next Sunday, our pastor spoke about husbands and read the verse that says we are supposed to love our wives as Christ loved the church. I figured God was answering my prayer. So I asked God to show me how to love my wife. The first thought that came to my mind was *Why don't you ask her?* So I did.

"That afternoon I said to her, 'I want to become the best husband in the world, and I'm asking you to teach me how. Once a week I want you to tell me one thing that would make me a better husband, and I will work on it.' She was eager to help me," he said with a smile. "Within two months, she asked me to give her ideas on how to be a better wife. That was fifteen years ago. Now we have a great marriage. Both of us are happy, and our children are wonderful."

"What about the sexual aspect of your marriage?" I asked. He looked at me with a twinkle in his eye and said, "It couldn't be better." I knew they were making love, not just having sex.

It All Begins with Attitude

That husband's journey illustrates the principle that the second stage of love begins with an attitude. The attitude expresses itself in acts of kindness that, in turn, stimulate warm feelings. Those couples who learn to move from stage 1 to stage 2 of emotional love are the couples who learn how to make love, not just have sex.

Too many couples simply wait, hoping that "the tingles" will return. When they don't, their attitude and behavior become negative, and they destroy what they most want— a happy marriage. Emotional love can be restored, but it doesn't happen simply with the passing of time. It comes only when couples choose the attitude of love and find meaningful ways to express it. Loving actions stimulate loving feelings.

Sexual fulfillment has little to do with technique but much to do with attitude, words, and actions. The underlying questions are, Am I expressing love to my spouse? Is my attitude characterized by love? Am I truly looking out for my spouse's interests? Is my major concern to meet his or her needs? If these are my sincere desires, then I must examine my words and my actions. Am I communicating to my spouse by the way I talk and by what I say that I am committed to his or her well-being? Do I view my spouse as a gift from God and see myself as God's agent for building him or her up to become everything he desires? Do my actions reflect my love? When I cook a meal, do I do it as an expression of love to my spouse or do I do it with resentment? When I carry out the garbage, do I do it with an attitude of love or do I complain as I do it? When my words and actions reflect the love of Christ, I am on the road to having a sexual relationship that not only brings satisfaction to the two of us but brings pleasure to God. Making life better for my spouse is the theme of love.

We choose our attitude daily. When we choose to be negative, critical, condemning, and demanding, we stimulate negative feelings in the heart of our spouse. On the other hand, when we choose to be positive, affirming, encouraging, and giving, we stimulate positive emotions.

I am convinced that the most powerful prayer you can pray for your marriage is, "Lord, give me the attitude of Christ toward my spouse." Pray that prayer daily. It is a prayer that God will answer. The theme of Christ's life was one of service to others. When that attitude permeates your behavior toward your spouse, you will be on the way to making love. The way you treat each other through the day determines whether you will make love or simply have sex. Sex without love will never give you a satisfying marriage.

A good way to express an attitude of service to your spouse is to ask what you can do to make his or her life easier, or what you can do to be a better husband or wife. Listen carefully to the suggestions offered, and you will begin to learn how to express your love in ways that are especially meaningful to your spouse.

When each of you feels genuinely loved, appreciated, and respected by the other, it brings a whole new level of love to your sexual relationship. The rewards are priceless.

• • •

Putting the Principles into Practice
1. Which of the following best describes your marital relationship?

___ We are definitely still experiencing the "in love" stage.
___ We have made the transition and are in stage 2 of romantic love.
___ We are caught in the middle, definitely out of stage 1 but not yet into stage 2.

2. If you are caught in the middle, how would you describe your present attitude?
3. Would you be willing to ask God to give you the attitude of Christ toward your spouse—an attitude of service and love?
4. Would you be willing to admit to your spouse that you have had a negative attitude and that you have asked God to teach you how to be the husband or wife that your spouse deserves?
5. Ask your spouse, "Will you give me one idea every week about how I could be a better spouse to you? I'm willing to work on it if you will tell me what you would like."

5
LOVE'S MOST
EFFECTIVE LANGUAGE

As you have been reading this part, "Making Love," perhaps you have thought, *I've tried some of these things, but they didn't seem to make a difference. No matter what I do, it doesn't seem to be enough to satisfy my spouse.* Throughout my counseling career I have encountered hundreds of couples who are sincerely trying to express love to each other and to make the sexual part of the marriage a genuine act of love. But they have been frustrated because their expressions of love haven't seemed to be "enough" for their spouses.

I remember Marc, who said, "I really wanted to do something special for Jill. I wanted her to know how much I loved her, so I spent a lot of money on a ring that I thought she would like. I planned to give her the ring at the end of a romantic evening. We had dinner together at a very nice restaurant and took a walk in a botanical garden. I told her I had a surprise for her and that I wanted her to know how much I loved her. Then I gave her the ring. She was very appreciative and gave me a big kiss and hug. I anticipated that later that evening we would have a dynamite sexual experience, but she said, 'I'm too tired.' I spent the next two hours lying in bed beside my wife wondering, *What does a man have to do to get a little love from his wife?*"

Marc genuinely desired to make sex with his wife an act of love. He thought that a romantic dinner, followed by a walk in a beautiful garden, topped off with an expensive gift would surely create the climate for a loving sexual experience. The problem was not his sincerity; he was extremely sincere. The problem was his mistaken concept of what would make his wife *feel* loved. His idea was that any woman would feel loved if a man did what he had done that evening. What he did not take into account is that people have different love languages. What makes one woman feel loved will not necessarily make another woman feel loved.

In my counseling with Marc and Jill, I found that Jill's primary love language was *acts of service*. What really made her feel loved was having Marc help her with household projects, doing something to "lighten her load." Marc was speaking the language of *quality time*, giving his wife an evening of undivided attention, and the love language of *gifts*. While both of these were appreciated by Jill, they did not deeply touch her heart as sincere expressions of love. She had been asking him for months to help her with the dishes, take out the trash, vacuum the floors, and wash her car. Her requests had fallen on deaf ears.

In Marc's mind, household chores were not the responsibility of the husband, and why should he wash her car when he didn't even wash his own? It cost only $3 to drive it through a car wash. She could do that as well as he could. But the result was that Jill didn't feel loved by Marc; rather, she was beginning to resent him. Dinner at a nice restaurant, a walk in the garden, and a nice gift did not compensate for the hurt and sense of rejection that she felt. He was sincere, but he was not expressing his love in the most effective language.

The Five Love Languages

As I have discussed in other parts of this book, I have discovered through counseling hundreds of couples that there are five fundamental ways to express love. I call them the five love languages. Several years ago I wrote a book with that title. It has now sold over five million copies and has been translated into thirty-five languages around the world.[1] In this chapter, I want to review each of these languages and discuss how they relate to this particular topic of making love.

Each of us has a primary love language; that is, one of the five languages speaks more deeply to us than the other four. It is very similar to spoken language. All of us grew up speaking a language with a dialect (I grew up speaking English Southern style). It is this language and dialect that we understand best. The same is true with emotional love. If your spouse speaks your primary love language, you will feel loved and appreciated. If your spouse does not speak your love language, you may feel unloved even though your spouse is speaking some of the other love languages.

Words of Affirmation

The Scriptures say "Love edifies."[2] That is, love builds up another person. When you speak the language of words of affirmation, you are using words to express love and appreciation to your spouse.

- "Wow! Do you ever look nice in that outfit."
- "Thanks for taking the recycling out."
- "Great meal! I really appreciate all your hard work."
- "I felt really proud of you when I saw you reading a Bible story to Jennifer tonight."
- "Thanks for putting gas in my car. That was a real help."
- "Your hair looks very nice."
- "I'm glad you volunteered to teach the five-year-olds in Sunday school. You'll do a great job. Children love you."
- "You're losing weight and looking nice. Of course, I would love you even if you didn't lose weight."

All these statements are words of affirmation. Words of affirmation may focus on your spouse's personality: "I love the fact that you're so organized. It saves us so much time." Or, "Your optimism encourages me to always try." Words of affirmation may also focus on some accomplishment your spouse has made: "I'm so pleased that you are taking that course on computers. I knew you could do it." "I was so proud of you when you caught that long fly ball in the softball game tonight. That play won the game for your team." This love language may also focus on your spouse's physical appearance: "I feel so secure when I touch the muscles in your arm." "I love your blue eyes. They are always so sparkly."

Nothing makes a person whose primary love language is words of affirmation feel more loved than the positive words you speak. Conversely, if you speak harsh, negative words, your spouse will be extremely hurt and will not quickly recover. It will be almost impossible for your spouse to make love after hearing harsh words from you. If this is your spouse's primary love language, you must learn to speak it fluently if you want to make sex an act of love.

Gifts

For some people, nothing speaks more deeply of love than a thoughtful gift. The gift communicates that someone was thinking of them. The gift may be as simple as a wildflower picked out of the yard or as expensive as the ring that Marc gave Jill. The important thing is not how much the gift cost but that someone was thinking about them. The gift is a visible indication of thoughtfulness and communicates love loudly.

If receiving gifts is your spouse's primary love language, you will need to learn to give gifts regularly. You do not need to be a millionaire to speak this language. Some gifts are free: a four-leaf clover, a coin you found in the parking lot, a "treasure" that you have saved from your childhood, a "prize" found in a cereal box. Other gifts are very inexpensive: a candy bar, an ice-cream cone, a single rose purchased from a street vendor, your spouse's favorite magazine, or a charm for her bracelet. Other gifts are much more expensive, such as tickets to a professional sports event, diamonds and rubies, membership at the local gym, or a pampering treatment at a local spa. Your spouse knows what your budget can afford. The person whose love language is gifts doesn't expect gifts that are financially unreasonable. But such a spouse does expect evidence of your love, and that means gifts.

Perhaps receiving gifts is not very meaningful to you. If so, you have probably been reluctant to give gifts to your spouse. However, if receiving gifts is your spouse's primary love language, then you have been missing out on the most effective way to express your love. It will take time to learn to "speak" this language. You may need to engage the help of your wife's sister or your husband's brother for ideas. Or you may ask your spouse to make a list of the kinds of gifts that would be meaningful.

If receiving gifts is your spouse's primary love language, then don't let a single special day pass without giving a special gift. Then sprinkle in gifts on nonspecial days too.

Acts of Service

The third love language is *acts of service*—doing things for your spouse that you know your spouse would like you to do. If you have been married for a few years, you probably know what they are because your spouse has requested them through the years:

- "Will you give the baby a bath while I finish the dishes?"
- "Would you take the trash out tonight, please?"
- "Would you mind driving my car to pick up Stephanie? Also, it would be helpful if you would stop on the way home and get some gas and wash my windshield."
- "Would you stop by the pharmacy and pick up my prescription?"
- "Would it be possible for you to mow the grass on Friday evening? My sister is coming over on Saturday."
- "Could you make a cherry cobbler this week? I love your cherry cobblers."

All these questions are requests for acts of service. If your spouse has requested something once, you can assume it is something that would be appreciated on a regular basis.

If acts of service is your spouse's primary love language, then your positive response to a request communicates your love in a powerful way. On the other hand, when you ignore a request, your spouse will feel unloved. An expensive gift will not take the place of your regularly taking out the recycling. This is the discovery that Marc made when he and Jill were in counseling.

Speaking the love language of your spouse enhances the sexual relationship because your spouse now feels loved. I remember the husband who said to me, "I wish someone had told me twenty years ago that my taking out the garbage was sexy for my wife. For me, it was just another responsibility. Had I known it was sexy, I would have taken out the garbage twice a day!" He learned a little late, but at least he learned.

Quality Time

Quality time means giving your spouse your undivided attention. If this is your spouse's primary love language, nothing is more important than the two of you having uninterrupted time together.

Some people think of quality time as simply two people being together. I remember the husband who said to me, "I knew she liked football as much as I did, so I got tickets to the game. She had told me that quality time was her love language. I expected that after a whole evening together, she would really feel loved. I was shocked when we got home that night and she said to me, 'Alex, do you really love me?'

"I said, 'You know I love you. That's why I got tickets to the game. You told me that quality time was your love language and I wanted us to have some time together.' She shook her head, walked off, and started crying.

"That's when I knew I was missing something. Later she said, 'We were together, that's true, but we were not focusing on each other. Our attention was on the game. You talked to the man beside you and the man in front of you, but you said almost nothing to me. On the way home, all we talked about was the game. We were together for four hours, but you never asked me anything about myself. Sometimes I wonder if you really care.'

"I assured her that I did care about her and that I loved her very much, but I could tell that my words sounded empty to her. That's the night I picked up the book *The Five Love Languages* and started reading it. She had been asking me for months to read it. She had told me about the concept and that her language was quality time. But I knew I was missing it.

"As I read the book, I realized that what she wanted was my undivided attention. She wanted me to sit on the couch with her, to take a walk with her, or to ask her questions and express interest in what was going on in her life. She didn't want to compete with the television or the computer. She wanted to know that she was number one in my life. I realized that my efforts to speak her language had missed the mark."

He continued, "The next day I took the book to work and finished reading it. That night I told her that I had read it and realized that I had failed to understand what she meant by quality time. I told her how sorry I was and that I wanted her to know how much I loved her. I asked her if she would like for us to initiate a 'daily sharing time' in which we would take twenty to thirty minutes every evening, sit down with the TV off, and talk with each other about what was going on in our lives. She said, 'That's what I've been wanting for so long.'

"That was the beginning of a whole new chapter in our marriage. Some nights when she felt like it, we would take a walk together. Other nights we sat on the couch and talked. Within two weeks, I saw her whole attitude toward me begin to change. Things in the bedroom changed. I had begun to think that she had lost interest in sex, but now she was taking the initiative. It was hard for me to believe that a little 'talking time' every day could make such a difference in her attitude.

"My love language is words of affirmation," he said. "And she is now speaking my language. For several months before 'the change,' she had been giving me critical words almost every day. That was one of the reasons I tried to stay away from her. I not only felt unloved, I felt like she didn't even like me, that nothing I did was enough. If only I had focused my energy on speaking her love language, things would have been different years earlier. Now that we have the love part figured out, sex has never been better."

What Alex discovered is that quality time is not simply being in the same house or at the same ball game. It is, rather, giving undivided attention, expressing interest in what is going on in the other person's life. Going to the ball game can be an expression of quality time if you spend some of that time looking into your spouse's eyes, asking questions, expressing interest so that your spouse feels more important than the game. You must talk with him or her more than with the man next to you or in front of you.

The difference is focus. Is your focus on the game, or is your focus on your spouse? The latter is quality time; the former is simply going to a ball game. Quality time involves asking questions about your spouse's activities, desires, thoughts, and feelings—and listening to the answers.

One warning: If in such a quality-time conversation your spouse shares struggles and frustrations, don't jump quickly to offer answers. When you give quick fixes, your spouse senses that you don't understand the problem. A better approach is to affirm your spouse's feelings and frustrations by saying, "I can see how that would be very frustrating. I think that would frustrate me as well." Then ask, "Is there anything I could do that might be helpful?" Be responsive to any suggestions. If your spouse asks for your advice, give it; but offer it as "something that might help," not as the thing that will solve the problem. What your spouse is looking for is understanding and support. You don't need to play the role of a parent and give instructions on what to do.

If your spouse's love language is quality time, I would encourage you to establish a daily sharing time as quickly as possible (that is, if your spouse agrees that this would be something he or she would appreciate). You will be on the road to filling the emotional love tank of your spouse—and that full love tank will spill over into the bedroom.

Physical Touch

Physical touch is a powerful communicator. We will talk in the next chapter about negative physical touch: physical and sexual abuse. Here we're talking about positive, affirming touches. Holding hands, embracing, kissing, putting your arm around her shoulder, putting your hand on his neck are all affirming touches.

For some people, physical touch is the primary method of receiving love. If such a person does not receive affirming touches from a spouse, he or she will feel unloved even though the spouse may be giving words of affirmation, gifts, acts of service, and quality time. The reasoning is, "If you seldom touch me, it means you seldom think about me. I am unimportant in your life."

These people will normally be touchers themselves. This is the man who is reaching out to give a pat on the back to everyone he encounters. This is the woman who is hugging everyone she meets. They are touching others because in their minds this is the way to express love.

Perhaps you grew up in a nontouching family. Touching does not come naturally for you. Now you find yourself married to someone for whom physical touch is the primary love language. What are you to do? The answer is simple—learn to touch. The first few times you reach out to initiate affirming touch may seem awkward or unnatural to you. I assure you it will be meaningful to your spouse. The more you do it, the easier it becomes. Make it your goal to lovingly touch your spouse every day. If your spouse's love language is physical touch, a hug before you leave the house and a kiss when you return will do wonders in the bedroom.

Sexual intercourse obviously involves physical touch. However, if you touch your spouse only when you have sex, and your spouse's primary love language is physical touch, I can tell you sex will not be an act of love. One wife said, "The only time he ever touches me is when he wants to have intercourse. I never get a kiss, he never hugs me, he never takes my hand when we get out of the car. He never holds my hand when we sit together. My primary love language is physical touch. My emotional love tank is on empty. Then he wants to have sex. It's almost more than I can bear. I feel so unloved by him." This husband is having sex, but he is not making love.

Because of the biological male sex drive, some husbands will automatically jump to the conclusion that their primary love language is physical touch, which they equate with having sex. My questions to them are: Do nonsexual touches make you feel loved? When she gives you a hug or a kiss that does not lead to sexual intercourse, do you feel loved? Do you like her to hold your hand as you walk down the sidewalk? Do you enjoy her sitting close to you on the couch? If these nonsexual touches do not communicate emotional love, then your primary love language is not physical touch.

Discovering Your Spouse's Love Language

All of us can receive emotional love in any one of the five love languages, but our primary love language is the most important. If we receive heavy doses of love in our primary language, then expressions of the other four can be sprinkled in like icing on the cake. But if we don't receive an adequate supply of our primary love language, we will not feel loved even though our spouse is sincerely speaking some of the other languages. Thus, the key to making sex an act of love is to make sure we understand and regularly speak our spouse's primary love language.

How do you discover your spouse's primary love language? Let me ask three questions. The first one is, How does your spouse most often express love to other people? If your spouse is a physical toucher, it probably means he or she receives love by physical touch. If your spouse is constantly verbally affirming people, words of affirmation is probably his or her love language. If your spouse gives gifts to others on every possible occasion, then receiving gifts may be the most important expression of love to your spouse.

A second question is, What does your spouse complain about most often? We typically get irritated when our spouse complains, but complaints reveal the need of the heart. If your husband says, "We don't spend any time together," he is telling you that quality time is his love language. When you return from a business trip, if your wife says, "You didn't bring me anything," she is telling you that receiving gifts is the most effective language to her.

A third question is, What does your spouse request of you most often? If your spouse rather regularly says, "Can we take a walk after dinner tonight?" or "Do you think we could get a weekend away within the next month?" you are being asked for quality time. If your spouse says, "Would you give me a back rub?" the request is for physical touch. If your spouse asks, "Did I do all right with that?" he or she is asking for affirming words.

The answers to these three questions will reveal your spouse's primary love language.

When you learn to speak your spouse's love language, you will see a significant difference in the emotional climate of your marriage. Remember, love's most effective language is not what *you think* would make your spouse feel loved, it is what *your spouse thinks* would make him or her feel loved. Your spouse is the expert. Don't try to impose your love language; rather, learn to speak the language that most effectively communicates love for your spouse. When you both feel loved, sex will no longer be a chore or a duty but rather a natural response. You will indeed be "making love."

· · ·

Putting the Principles into Practice
1. Do you know what your spouse's primary love language is? Do you know what yours is?
2. If you have never considered the idea of love languages before, try asking yourself the three questions suggested at the end of this chapter.
3. How might knowing your spouse's primary love language change the ways you express your love?
4. How would you like your spouse to change the way he or she expresses love to you, based on your primary love language?

6

LOVE INFLICTS NO PAIN

SHE WAS WEEPING UNCONTROLLABLY. "I've got to have help," she said. "I can't take it anymore. Last night, he pushed me onto the couch and gave me a thirty-minute lecture on how it was my fault that our children were not doing well in school, that if I would help them do their homework, they would make better grades. He accused me of watching television when I should be helping the children. I don't know how he could accuse me of that. He's never home in the evenings; he's always having a drink with his buddies and talking about sports. I don't get any help from him in rearing the children. He comes home at ten or eleven o'clock at night and wants to have sex. It's unbearable! But if I refuse, he goes into a rage. So I go along with it, but I hate it." It was obvious to me that this wife and husband, though they had sex, knew nothing of making love.

As long as one spouse is inflicting pain on the other, they will never experience the satisfaction of making love. There are many arenas in which pain can be experienced. Let me share three of the most common.

Emotional Pain

Emotional pain comes as the result of harsh language. Raised voices and condemning words are emotional bombs that explode in the human heart and destroy love.

The Hebrew Scriptures tell us, "The tongue has the power of life and death, and those who love it will eat its fruit."[1] You can kill your spouse—or you can give life—by the way you speak. When you encourage your spouse with affirming words, it creates the desire to be better. When you tear your spouse down with negative words, it creates the desire to return fire with equally damaging words.

In most marriages, emotional pain is rarely one sided. Failing to love and respect each other typically leads to condemning and berating each other. For example, the husband of the woman we met at the beginning of this chapter had this to say: "She is so critical of me, and what she says is not true. I don't hang out with the boys every night. One night a week, we enjoy *Monday Night Football* together, but the rest of the week, I'm at home working in the yard or on the house." (They were in the process of restoring an old house.) "Nothing I do is good enough for her. She blames me for all of our problems. I know I shouldn't have pushed her onto the couch, but I had had enough. When she told me it was my fault that the children were not doing well in school, I exploded. I didn't get an education. I can't help the children. She could help them, but instead, she watches television and smokes cigarettes, which I hate. The smoke is killing all of us."

Words of condemnation, like the ones this husband and wife hurled at each other, sting deeply and build more resentment. Two people who resent each other become fountains of negative words that stimulate more emotional pain. When the heart is filled with pain, there is no room left for love. The couple may withdraw from each other in order to escape the harsh words. Or, they may continue with their verbal gunfire until one of them finally capitulates. In silence they both suffer the pain of condemnation and rejection. While they may continue to have sex, they will never be able to make love until there is genuine repentance and forgiveness and until the harsh words are replaced with words of love and concern.

The good news is that if we are willing to turn from our destructive behavior and confess our own failures, not only will God forgive us, but usually our spouse will also be willing to forgive. When the walls of hurt and pain have been removed, we have the potential to learn to be lovers, to speak affirming and encouraging words that build each other up and create a desire in each other to be even better.

Some time ago, I shared the power of affirming words with a frustrated wife. She looked at me and said with all sincerity, "I hear what you are saying. I know it would be good if I could give my husband some positive words. But to be honest with you, I can't think of anything good about him."

I paused. Finally I asked, "Does your husband ever take a shower?"

"Yes."

"How often?" I asked.

"Every day," she said.

"Then if I were you, I'd start there. Tell him, 'I appreciate your taking a shower today.' There are some men who don't."

I've never met a man about whom you couldn't find *something* good to say. I've never met a wife about whom you couldn't find *something* good to say. And when you verbalize to your spouse something you like, you have taken the first step toward learning how to make love.

Physical Pain

Physical pain is experienced in two spheres. One is typically called physical abuse, and the other, sexual abuse. Physical abuse involves inflicting any type of bodily pain on another person. Pushing, shoving, shaking, hitting, and clawing are examples of physical abuse. Through the years, many people have sat in my office wearing long-sleeved sweaters or shirts designed to cover the bruises on their arms or with sunglasses hiding blackened eyes. Where physical abuse is a way of life, there will be no making love. The victim may acquiesce to avoid further abuse, but the heart is closed in pain.

Sexual abuse may or may not involve physical abuse such as that listed above. But even when it does not, pain is inflicted when one spouse treats the other as an object rather than a person. The husband who forces himself upon his wife sexually is abusing her. The husband who is insensitive when his wife has a painful physical condition, such as a vaginal infection, and insists on having sex anyway is also abusing her. On the other hand, the wife who refuses to get medical treatment for such conditions is abusing her husband. Such abuse stimulates pain and resentment, neither of which is conducive to making love.

Successful lovemaking requires the opposite attitude—one in which each expresses to the other, "The last thing I want to do is to hurt you, so please tell me if anything I do causes you physical pain. My desire is to give you pleasure, never to bring you pain." When this attitude is expressed both in your words and in your behavior, you will learn to make love, not just have sex.

Spiritual Pain

For the Christian, sex has a spiritual dimension. Recognizing intercourse as a gift from God and marriage as the setting in which God intended men and women to experience sex, the Christian comes to sex with a deep sense of gratitude to God. This gratitude may even be expressed in the middle of lovemaking. The pleasure between husband and wife is so intense that one's heart may be lifted in praise and thanksgiving to God for bringing them to each other.

However, this entire spiritual dimension is lost if one spouse chooses to walk away from God. If you are a believer and, for whatever reason, your spouse rejects God, you will experience great pain. You realize that the two of you will never reach your potential without the smile of God. If this is your situation, pray that God will give you the ability to love your spouse even when his or her behavior brings you great pain. God's love toward us is unconditional. Strive to follow his example and trust God to make your own walk with him a positive influence on your spouse.

Conversely, sexual lovemaking is greatly enhanced when a husband or wife takes the initiative to acknowledge God in all areas of life. When a husband chooses to join his wife in a time of Bible reading and prayer, he enhances their sexual experience. When she sees him taking initiative in reading Bible stories to the children and making sure the children understand the love of God, her respect for him is increased. Her spiritual hunger for God makes her want to be intimate with this man, who is seeking God. It is simply a fact. Those couples who walk closely with God will be much more successful than others in lovemaking.

● ● ●

Putting the Principles into Practice

1. Can you think of a time when your spouse inflicted emotional pain on you with harsh, condemning, blaming words? Can you think of a time in which you inflicted pain on your spouse by using such words? Have you taken the initiative to confess this painful behavior to your spouse and ask for forgiveness? If so, how did your spouse respond? If not, would you be willing to take such action today?

2. Can you think of a time in which you physically or sexually abused your spouse? Can you think of a time in which your spouse physically or sexually abused you? Have either of you taken initiative to deal with past failures in this area? If not, why not do it today?

3. Does your present walk with God create a climate that enhances your sexual relationship? Is there a decision you need to make or an action you need to take that will move you closer to being a godly husband or a godly wife? Why not do it today?

4. Consider making the following statement to your spouse:

   I want you to know that it is my desire to bring you pleasure and never pain in any area of life. So if I ever hurt you, will you please tell me so that I can apologize?

   Such a statement will greatly enhance your ability to make love, not just have sex.

7

LOVE FORGIVES PAST FAILURES

WHEN YOUR SPOUSE MADE THE DECISION TO MARRY YOU, it was likely
with the assumption that after the wedding you would behave the same
way you did before the wedding. Unfortunately, that is probably not
what happened. Once the euphoria of being "in love" evaporated, you
went back to being "normal."

When normal behavior—that is, being selfish, demanding, and critical—leads couples into anger and resentment, many conclude that they
made a mistake when they got married and that they are incompat-
ible and will never be happy together. They may give up, choose to
divorce, and set about trying to find someone better. Unfortunately,
some couples repeat this cycle two, three, and four times and are no
happier in the fourth marriage than they were in the first.

There is a better way. The secret to a loving marriage is found not
in running away but in learning to deal with our propensity for self-
centeredness. Let me share with you the process of forgiving each other,
accepting God's forgiveness, and creating a different future for your
marriage.

The First Step

The first step is to acknowledge to yourself and to God that in your efforts to meet your own needs, you have sometimes spoken and acted negatively toward your spouse. Your harsh words and hurtful behavior have created a wall between the two of you. As long as the wall exists, you will never reach your potential for making love. The walls must come down if you are to have the intimate, fulfilling relationship you desired when you got married.

In my thirty years as a marriage counselor, I have helped hundreds of couples tear down walls. It all begins with a simple spiritual exercise: Get alone with God. Admit to God that you have not been a perfect spouse. Then ask him to show you specifically where you have failed your spouse. As he brings your failures to mind, write them down. Once you have completed the list, confess these things to God, one by one. Thank him that Christ has paid the penalty for your sins and ask him to forgive you.

The Second Step

The second step may be more difficult. You must now confess these failures to your spouse and ask forgiveness. You might say something like this: "I've been thinking a lot about us lately. I realize that I am far from being a perfect spouse. In fact, the other night I asked God to show me where I have been failing you, and he gave me a rather long list. I have asked God to forgive me for these things, and if you've got a few minutes, I would like to share them with you and ask if you would be willing to forgive me, too."

If your spouse is willing to listen, then read the list and say, "I know these things are wrong. I feel bad that I have hurt you so deeply. I don't want to continue this kind of behavior. I want to be the spouse that you deserve. I'd like the chance to make it up to you, and I'm asking you if you can find it in your heart to forgive me."

Your spouse may not immediately respond with forgiveness, but at least you have opened the door for that possibility. We cannot erase our past failures, but we can confess them and request forgiveness.

After you've confessed your failures, your spouse may or may not offer a similar confession. But either way, the wall between you is not as thick because you have dealt with your side of it. When both of you confess past failures and choose to forgive each other, you will have the potential for making love, not just having sex.

God's Forgiveness

The Scriptures indicate that when we confess our sins to God, he is always willing to forgive us. "If we confess our sins, [God] is faithful and just and will forgive us our sins and purify us from all unrighteousness."[1] The moment we confess our sins to God, we experience the warm embrace of our heavenly Father. The barrier is removed, and we can now continue our fellowship with him.

As followers of Christ, we are instructed to forgive each other in the same way that God forgives us.[2] Forgiveness is not a feeling; forgiveness is a choice. We hear the confession of our spouse's failures and the request for forgiveness. Because we have been forgiven by God, we choose to forgive each other's failures.

Forgiveness does not immediately remove the pain that we have experienced, nor does forgiveness necessarily remove all the consequences of what has happened. But forgiveness does remove the barrier between us and allows us to continue our relationship.

Creating a Different Future

Now that we have dealt with past failures, we are ready to create a different future for the two of us. If we simply go back to "doing what comes naturally," we will eventually create new walls between us. Instead of living a natural life, Christians are called to live a supernatural life. We have within us the power of the Holy Spirit to change our self-centered attitudes into attitudes of unselfish love. Instead of looking out for only our own interests, we learn to look out for the interests of our spouse.

God loves your spouse unconditionally, just as he loves you. He wants you to be his channel of expressing his love to your spouse. This is true even when your spouse is not loving you.

In describing God's love, the apostle Paul says, "God demonstrates his own love for us in this: While we were still sinners, Christ died for us."[3] He is our model. He did not love us because we loved him; he loved us when we were walking away from him. That is the kind of love we are to demonstrate to our spouse. Does that sound impossible? It is, without the help of God. But again, Paul instructs us, "God has poured out his love into our hearts by the Holy Spirit."[4] We are simply passing to our spouse the love that God has poured out in our hearts.

Therefore, the daily prayer of the Christian husband or wife should be, "Lord, fill my heart with your love so I can express it to my spouse. Bring to my mind ways in which I can express your love today." That is a prayer that God will answer. You will become a channel of love to your spouse, and in due time, your spouse will likely reciprocate.

This does not mean that you will never again lose your temper or say a harsh word or treat your spouse unkindly. It does mean that whenever this happens, you will try to be quick to apologize, seek to make restitution, and ask for forgiveness. You will refuse to let the wall be erected again.

Christians are not perfect, but Christians are willing to deal with their failures and willing to forgive when there is confession and repentance. Because we have been forgiven by God, we choose to forgive each other. Practicing genuine confession and genuine forgiveness is the road to making love, not just having sex.

• • •

Putting the Principles into Practice

1. Do you sense that there is a wall between you and your spouse that hinders you from having the sexual intimacy you desire?
2. If so, would you be willing to ask God to show you your own failures in the marriage? As they come to your mind, write them down. Then confess your failures to God and accept his forgiveness.
3. Would you be willing to confess these failures to your spouse and ask his or her forgiveness? (You may want to read again the confession statement found on page 260.) Your spouse may or may not immediately forgive you. But your confession paves the way for the potential of forgiveness and reconciliation.

8

MAKING LOVE IS
A LIFELONG JOURNEY

Sexual compatibility is not something we achieve once and for all, and then forever thereafter, sex is heavenly. All of life is in a constant process of change. Our sexual desires are affected by many variables. Disease and sickness can radically impact our sexual desires and abilities. The arrival of children often upsets the sexual equilibrium between new parents. All of us experience physical and emotional stress, with our levels of stress fluctuating from time to time. Extremely stressful periods of life can greatly impact a couple's sexual relationship. Accepting too many responsibilities at work, at church, in the community, or with extended family members can also affect their level of sexual satisfaction.

When the captain of a ship realizes that he is not on course to reach his destination, he must adjust the course. In marriage, too, we must from time to time evaluate our sexual relationship and be willing to make course corrections. If we simply drift, we will drift apart. But if we put our oars in the water, we can row our way back to mutual sexual fulfillment.

The good news is that we can do it. However, it will require communication, sensitivity, and a conscious decision to make our marriages a priority.

Communication

Making necessary course corrections over time requires a couple's ongoing willingness to talk openly and honestly about their sexual relationship. Husbands and wives who take the approach that sex is not something to be talked about but just something to do will likely never become great lovers.

Marriage partners will always have different thoughts, ideas, desires, and emotions. If they are going to reach the destination of fulfilling, satisfying lovemaking, they must take the time for open communication.

I recommend that you and your spouse discuss the questions on page 266, "Putting the Principles into Practice." These questions open the door for your spouse to give you honest feedback.

Sensitivity

Once you begin communicating about your sexual relationship, it is not enough to simply listen to what your spouse says or to give a rebuttal. What is more important is that you are sensitive to your spouse's thoughts, desires, and feelings. For example, perhaps your spouse will say, "I wish you would not raise your voice and speak to me harshly. It kills my desire for sexual intimacy." Rather than being defensive, try to offer a sensitive reply, something like, "Tell me more about that. What does it sound like when I raise my voice? How does it make you feel?"

Often we are not aware of how our words or our behavior comes across to our spouse. The important thing is to be sensitive to the emotional responses our behavior creates.

If you are going to have an intimate sexual relationship with your spouse, it may well mean that you must change some behavior patterns learned in your family of origin. Many of us grew up in homes where loud talking was simply the norm. No one was especially offended by such talk. However, your spouse did not grow up in your family. Perhaps your spouse grew up in a soft-spoken family, and your loudness sounds harsh. A husband cannot treat his wife in the same way that his father treated his mother and expect his spouse to respond in the same manner as his mother. His wife is a totally different person, and his behavior affects her in a different way.

A wife may speak with sarcasm, or she may have negative responses to every idea her husband shares. To her, these are natural responses because this is how her mother spoke. But to him, they feel like a sword piercing his heart. They kill his motivation to communicate, and the two of them grow apart. The wife who wants to be a good lover must be sensitive to her husband's emotional responses to her behavior.

Remember, you are not locked into the patterns of speech and behavior that you learned as a child. As an adult you have the capacity, with the help of God, to change patterns that are detrimental to your marital relationship. If you want to make love and not just have sex, you must be sensitive to your spouse's perceptions and be willing to change.

Making Marriage a Priority

The couple who are truly following Christ will never be satisfied simply with having sex. They want to be lovers, and they are willing to take the time and effort necessary to make that a reality.

The bottom line is that both of you must make your marriage a priority. Only that decision will provide the motivation you need to do the hard work of communicating and being sensitive to each other. Under the lordship of Christ, you decide to have the kind of marriage that God intended for you. You realize that the sexual part is an extremely important part of the marriage. Thus, you are motivated to talk and listen; respect each other's ideas, desires, and emotions; and work together to create God's ideal.

God never designed sex to be put on the shelf after the honeymoon or after the children arrive or after fifteen years of marriage. You are sexual creatures as long as you live, and you need to relate to each other sexually, seeking to give each other pleasure throughout a lifetime.

The couples who will make love for a lifetime are the couples who are committed to learning. They will from time to time read a book on the sexual aspect of marriage and discuss its contents and try to make things better for each other. They will periodically attend a marriage seminar and seek to discover ideas that will strengthen their relationship. If crises develop and they realize that their relationship is in danger, they will reach out for the help of a pastor or counselor. They are mature enough to realize that everyone needs help from time to time.

The mature couple will leave no stone unturned in an effort to discover God's ideal—mutual sexual fulfillment. They will never be satisfied to simply have sex. They desire to make love and to keep love alive for a lifetime.

• • •

Putting the Principles into Practice

1. Choose one of the following questions as a means of opening communication with your spouse:

   On a scale of 1–10, how satisfied are you with our sexual relationship? If the answer is 9 or 10, follow up with this question: What can we do to keep it there? If the answer is 8 or below, follow up with this question: What can we do to enhance our relationship?

   What do you wish I would do—or stop doing—to make our sexual relationship better for you? You may wish to use the lists found in "What Husbands Wish" (pages 359–361) and "What Wives Wish" (pages 362–364) to stimulate your thinking.

   If I could make one change to enhance our sexual relationship, what would it be?

2. When was the last time you attended a marriage enrichment seminar or attended a class on marriage? If it has been more than a year, why not try to schedule such an event sometime during the next year?

3. Perhaps you and your spouse would like to select one of the books listed under "Suggested Resources," page 367, to read together. The two of you can read and discuss a chapter each week with a view toward enhancing your sexual relationship. Many couples have found such an exercise extremely helpful.

• • •

Closing Thoughts on Making Love

The challenge for many couples today is that they have had little or no training in how to love each other. They get married in the euphoria of being "in love." And they fully intend to live happily ever after. They envision sex as being heavenly and without effort. However, when they come down off the emotional high of being "in love" (the average life span of the euphoria is two years), their visions of heaven turn into nightmares of conflict. Sex becomes a battleground, and they blame each other for their unhappiness. The message of this book is that if you can learn to make love rather than just having sex, your dreams can come true and sexual union will lead both of you to the deep connection you desire.

If your sexual relationship is not what you desire it to be, don't despair. We are creatures of change, and if we make the right choices, we can change for the better. Your choices will influence the choices of your spouse, and in time, your spouse may well reciprocate. Every day our words and behavior influence our spouse in a negative way or a positive way. We determine the direction of our influence. I strongly encourage you to pray daily that God will make you a lover, not simply one who seeks to satisfy your sexual desires.

If you find this book helpful, I hope you will share it with a friend. If you have stories to share with me, I invite you to click on the Contact link at www.garychapman.org.

• • •

Some Ideas Worth Remembering
- Throughout human history, love and sex have always been related. However, in contemporary culture, love and sex have been *equated*.
- Christians have always viewed marriage as a sacred relationship between a husband and wife, instituted by God. The sexual union between the husband and wife is seen as a living symbol of their deep companionship.

- A husband can desire to have sexual intercourse even when things are not right in the relationship. In fact, he often thinks that having sex will solve the problems.
- On the other hand, a wife wants things to be made right before having sexual intercourse. Sex itself does not solve problems for her.
- It often requires far more energy, effort, and time for a woman to experience orgasm than it does for a man. Sometimes, because of fatigue or other distractions, a wife simply does not desire to go through the entire process.
- If a husband and wife simply do "what comes naturally," they will never learn to make love. The best that may happen is that one of them will find partial fulfillment and the other will feel used.
- Making love is about giving, not demanding. When we focus on creating an atmosphere of love in which we are genuinely seeking to affirm our spouse, we will eventually hear the invitation.
- Without love, the world looks bleak, and sex is at best a temporary oasis in a barren desert.
- The average life span of the "in love" experience is two years. We don't stay obsessed with each other forever. If we did, we would never accomplish anything.
- Emotional love can be restored, but it doesn't happen simply with the passing of time. It comes only when couples choose the attitude of love and find meaningful ways to express it. Loving actions stimulate loving feelings.
- Sexual fulfillment has little to do with technique but much to do with attitude, words, and actions.
- The most powerful prayer you can pray for your marriage is, "Lord, give me the attitude of Christ toward my spouse." Pray that prayer daily. It is a prayer that God will answer.
- Two people who resent each other become fountains of negative words that stimulate more emotional pain. When the heart is filled with pain, there is no room left for love.
- Forgiveness is not a feeling; forgiveness is a choice. Because we

have been forgiven by God, we choose to forgive each other's failures.

- Forgiveness does not immediately remove the pain that we have experienced, nor does forgiveness necessarily remove all the consequences of what has happened. But forgiveness does remove the barrier between us and allows us to continue our relationship.

- God loves your spouse unconditionally, just as he loves you. He wants you to be his channel of expressing his love to your spouse. This is true even when your spouse is not loving you.

- Extremely stressful periods of life can greatly impact a couple's sexual relationship. Accepting too many responsibilities at work, at church, in the community, or with extended family members can also greatly affect their level of sexual satisfaction.

- You are not locked into the patterns of speech and behavior that you learned as a child. As an adult you have the capacity, with the help of God, to change patterns that are detrimental to your marital relationship. If you want to make love and not just have sex, you must be sensitive to your spouse's perceptions and be willing to change.

Part Six

IN-LAW RELATIONSHIPS

Becoming Friends with Your In-Laws

FOR THIRTY YEARS, people have sat in my office and shared the struggles they have with in-laws. I have listened as they said,

- "My sister-in-law is driving me crazy. She is telling me how to raise my children, but she's single! What does she know about parenting?"
- "My mother-in-law and sisters-in-law exclude me. They have breakfast out each Saturday and never invite me to join them. They know that my mom and sisters live six hundred miles away. I feel left out of their girl things."
- "When my father-in-law comes to dinner, all he can talk about is sports, his work, or what he reads in the paper. He never asks about the details of our lives and seems to be totally disconnected from us emotionally."
- "My brother-in-law tries to control my husband. He is five years older and maybe he has done this all his life, but I don't like it."
- "Our son-in-law has essentially kidnapped our daughter. Since their marriage, he refuses to let her come to family events."
- "When my in-laws invite us to their home, they always include all their children and their families. Just once I wish they would have us over as a couple."
- "My wife's parents give her money to buy things we can't afford. I resent that. I wish they would let us run our own lives."

- "My husband's mother wants to tell me how to cook. I cooked my own meals for five years before we married. I think I know how to cook. I don't need her help."
- "It's awkward to invite just my brother-in-law and sister-in-law to do things. My mother-in-law is divorced, and we feel pressure to include her."
- "My husband's parents just 'drop in' unannounced. Sometimes I'm in the middle of a project I need to complete. I wish they would respect our schedule."

Perhaps you could add a few of your own complaints. In-law problems often focus on such issues as control, interference, inconvenience, and the clashing of values and traditions. The purpose of this part of the book is to provide practical ideas on how to work through these struggles and build positive relationships.

When two people marry, they don't simply marry each other; they marry into an extended family consisting of mother-in-law, father-in-law, and perhaps sister-in-law and brother-in-law. These in-laws come in all sizes, shapes, and personalities. They come with a history of family traditions and ways of relating to one another. Whatever else we say about families, we can agree that all families are different. These differences often lead to adjustment difficulties.

If we are able to make these adjustments, we can create positive in-law relationships. If we don't, in-laws can be extremely troublesome. Parental relationships—his and hers—are the most common area of in-law conflicts.

In God's plan, in-laws were not designed to be divisive. They were meant to be supportive. Freedom and harmony are the biblical ideals for in-law relationships. In order to accomplish this ideal, marriages must run on the parallel tracks of separation from parents and devotion to parents.

Separation from Parents
The Scriptures say, "For this reason a man will leave his father and mother and be united to his wife, and they will become one flesh."[1]

God's pattern for marriage involves the "leaving" of parents and the "uniting" of husband and wife. Thus, marriage involves a change of allegiance. Before marriage, one's allegiance is to parents. After marriage, the allegiance shifts to the mate.

We often call this "cutting the psychological apron strings." If there is a conflict of interest between a man's wife and his mother, the husband is to stand with his wife. This does not mean that the mother is to be treated unkindly; it does mean that she is no longer the dominant female in his life. The principle of separating from parents is extremely important. We will seek to apply this principle in the chapters that follow. No couple will reach their full potential in marriage without this psychological break from parents.

Perhaps nowhere is this principle of separation from parents more important than in decision making. Your parents and in-laws may have suggestions about many aspects of your married life. Each suggestion should be considered seriously, but in the final analysis you must make your own decisions. You must not allow parents to manipulate you into making decisions with which the two of you do not agree.

Devotion to Parents

The second fundamental principle of marriage is that we are to honor our parents. God gave to ancient Israel the Ten Commandments, one of which is, "Honor your father and your mother, so that you may live long in the land the LORD your God is giving you."[2] In the New Testament, the apostle Paul affirmed this principle: "'Honor your father and mother'—which is the first commandment with a promise—'that it may go well with you and that you may enjoy long life on the earth.'"[3]

The command to honor parents does not cease when we are married. The word *honor* means to "show respect." It involves treating others with kindness and dignity. One wife said, "My parents do not live respectable lives. How can I respect them when I don't agree with what they are doing?" It is true that not all parents live honorable lives. Their actions may not be worthy of respect. But because they are made in the image of God and because they gave us life, we are to honor them. We may not agree with their lifestyle choices, but we can respect them as people even when we don't respect their behavior. It is always right to honor our parents and the parents of our spouse. Leaving parents for the purpose of marriage does not erase the responsibility to honor them.

How do we express honor to our parents in daily life? We honor them by keeping the lines of communication open—visiting, telephoning, and sending e-mails. In such communication, you are seeking to convey the message, "I still love you and want you to be a part of my life." *Leaving* must never be interpreted as *deserting*. Regular contact is a part of what it means to honor parents. Failure to communicate says in effect, "I no longer care."

Another way of honoring parents is described in the New Testament: "If a widow has children or grandchildren, these should learn first of all to put their religion into practice by caring for their own family and so repaying their parents and grandparents, for this is pleasing to God."[4] When we were young, our parents met our physical needs. As they grow older, we may have to do the same for them. If and when the need arises, we must bear the responsibility of caring for the physical needs of our parents. To fail in this responsibility is to deny our faith in Christ. Paul the apostle said, "If anyone does not provide for his relatives, and especially for his immediate family, he has denied the faith and is worse than an unbeliever."[5] By our actions, we must demonstrate our faith in Christ by honoring our parents.

From the Parents' Perspective

If we are the parents of married children, it will help if we remember our objective. Since their birth, we have been training our children for independence—or at least, we should have been doing so. We have taught them how to cook meals, wash dishes, make beds, buy clothes, save money, and make responsible decisions. We have taught them respect for authority and the value of the individual. In short, we have sought to bring them to maturity. We want them to be able to make it on their own.

At the time of their marriage, our goal of helping them become independent reaches fruition. We have helped them move from a state of complete dependence on us as infants to complete independence as newlyweds. In the future, we must view them as adults who will chart their own course, for better or for worse. We must never again impose our will upon them. We must respect them as equals.

This does not mean that we will no longer help our married children. It does mean that when we have a desire to help, we will ask first if they want our help. An unwanted gift is not a gift but a burden. Parents sometimes give financial aid to their married children, thus helping them to establish a standard of living they cannot afford. This practice does not foster independence. Neither should parents use gifts to influence a married child. "We will buy you a new car if you will . . ." is not a gift but an effort to manipulate.

Parents sometimes want to give advice to their married children. The rule of thumb is that parents should give advice only when requested. If your children have not requested your wisdom and you feel strongly urged to share it, at least ask permission. "Would you like for me to share my perspective on that?" is a good question. Giving unsolicited advice to your married children does not develop positive relationships.

The ideals to which we aspire are freedom and harmony. The married couple needs the emotional warmth that comes from a wholesome relationship with both sets of parents. Parents need the emotional warmth that comes from the couple. Life is too short to live with broken relationships. We will not always agree with our married children, but we can offer respect and give them the freedom to make their own decisions.

So how, exactly, do we become friends with our in-laws? In the next few pages, I'm going to share seven principles that will radically change in-law relationships.

At the end of each chapter are practical suggestions on how to weave these ideas into the fabric of your own family life. Whether you are the son-in-law, daughter-in-law, mother-in-law, father-in-law, sister-in-law, or brother-in-law, these principles are for you. If you will seek to apply these principles to your in-law relationships, I predict that you will begin to see positive changes in the attitudes and behavior of your in-laws. If you will follow the suggestions in the section entitled "Putting the Principles into Practice" at the end of each of the chapters in part six, you will be on the road to positive in-law relationships.

1

LISTEN BEFORE YOU SPEAK

MARSHA'S MOTHER-IN-LAW IS AFFLUENT. Marsha, in contrast, grew up in a modest home where the emphasis was on self-sacrifice and giving. Her father was the chairman of the missions committee in their church, and her mother was actively involved in the women's ministry. Every year for as long as Marsha could remember, she had watched her parents save so they could give a significant gift to the annual missions offering. She herself had taken money out of her allowance as a child to give to this offering.

After two years of marriage, Marsha is totally frustrated with her mother-in-law. "Every month, she invites me to lunch. I'm always happy to see her. But after lunch, she insists on taking me shopping in order to buy me a new dress. At first I appreciated her generosity, but as time went on, it seemed like our lunches got shorter and shorter while our shopping sprees extended into the afternoon. She never looks for dresses on sale, and she has bought me some really expensive dresses."

Marsha continued, "I see it as an extravagant waste of money, and I feel like she is trying to buy my friendship. When I tell her that I don't need a dress this month, she says, 'Every lady needs a new dress. It lifts the spirit.'

"Well, it's not lifting my spirits," said Marsha. "It's making me resent her. Why doesn't she give that money to people who really need it? My closet is full of dresses. I don't want to hurt her feelings. I'd like for us to have a relationship that does not focus on shopping. I'd like to have a nice, quiet, extended lunch with her. I'd like to know what her childhood was like . . . what kind of struggles she and my father-in-law had in the early years of their marriage . . . how she felt about being a stay-at-home mom. All she ever talks about is her golf game and her bridge parties. I sometimes get the feeling that she's extremely lonely and that shopping is her way of trying to forget her loneliness. I don't know. I just wish our relationship could be more real."

All these thoughts and feelings Marsha had kept to herself. She tried to share them with her husband, Rob, but his response was, "Let Mom buy you dresses. It's her way of showing you that she loves you." Perhaps Rob was right, but if so, his mother is missing the mark. Marsha does not feel loved; she feels resentful.

"Have you tried to share any of these thoughts and feelings with your mother-in-law?" I asked.

"Not really," Marsha responded. "She's so overpowering. She talks most of the time and seldom asks me a question; when she does, I have the sense that she's not listening to my response. She's thinking about what she's going to say next. I feel tense when I'm around her."

It was obvious to me that Marsha had a mother-in-law problem, and it wasn't going away unless Marsha took some initiative.

"But I can't just tell her that I resent her," said Marsha. "And I can't stop having lunches with her. That's our only contact. If I tell her I don't want the dresses, I'm afraid she'll be hurt. I really don't know what to do. That's why I'm here."

"I'm glad you came," I said. "I'm not a miracle worker, but I do have an idea that I would like to suggest. The next time you have lunch with your mother-in-law, say to her, 'Before we go shopping, I want to ask you a question. On a scale of one to ten, how much pleasure do you get out of taking me shopping?' If her answer is eight, nine, or ten (which is what I would expect), then you ask, ' Tell me why you get so much pleasure out of being nice to me.'

"Listen to her answer carefully. Then tell her what you think you heard her say and ask her if that is correct. For example, you might say, 'What I hear you saying is that you enjoy buying things for me because when you were first married, your mother-in-law did nothing for you and you felt hurt. You didn't want that to happen in our relationship. Is that correct?' Continue to ask clarifying questions until you feel that you understand what is behind her desire to take you shopping.

"Then express appreciation to her for what she is doing for you. Once you understand her motivation, I think you will find that easier to do. Tell her that you really appreciate her being so kind and thoughtful of you. Then tell her how meaningful this conversation has been to you: that you feel like you know her better, and you appreciate her even more. Then go shopping with her and let her buy you whatever she wishes.

"The next month when you have lunch, ask your mother-in-law additional questions. Tell her how much you enjoyed your conversation with her last month and that if she doesn't mind, you'd like to ask her some more questions about her life. You might ask such questions as 'What was it like growing up as a child in your house?' 'What was high school like for you?' 'How did you meet your husband?' 'What made you decide to get married?' 'What were the early years in your marriage like?' 'What have been some of the things you have enjoyed most about your marriage and family?' These are probably too many questions for one conversation, but pick and choose.

"What you are trying to do is to get to know your mother-in-law better. We do this by asking questions and listening to answers. Again, ask clarifying questions to make sure you understand what she is saying. For example, 'It sounds like you had a lot of hurt from your father's behavior. Is that correct?' Whatever you hear her say, repeat it in the form of a question to give her an opportunity to clarify. Tell her how much you are enjoying the conversation and that you appreciate her willingness to share her story. Then go shopping.

"When she calls the third month and invites you to lunch, you say to her, 'I can't wait to see you. I enjoyed our conversation so much last time. I have a suggestion. I've been wanting to go to the new art exhibit downtown. What if, after lunch, we go see the art exhibit instead of going shopping?' If she accepts your suggestion, great. If, on the other hand, she says, 'Why don't we go to the art exhibit *and* go shopping,' you say to her, 'Well, maybe we would have time to do that, but could we do the art exhibit first and then play it by ear?' Chances are, she'll agree. After you have gone to the art exhibit, the two of you can decide whether or not you have time to go shopping. Maybe you can do a quick shopping trip this time or not go shopping at all. Either way, you have changed the typical pattern of lunch and shopping.

"The fourth month, you can engage her in another meaningful conversation and make the suggestion that perhaps in the future you could rotate between shopping one month and doing some other social activity together the following month. You might say, 'After all, my closet is getting full, and I really enjoy doing other things with you.' If she accepts your proposal, you have now changed the paradigm of the monthly shopping trip.

"In future months, you can be brave enough to suggest that perhaps this month, instead of buying things for you, 'We can take my friend's adopted Chinese daughter and buy clothes for her.' Or another month, perhaps you can buy groceries for a needy family or school supplies for a group of students from low-income families. Little by little, you will be helping your mother-in-law channel her giving into areas that both of you feel good about. And you will be getting to know your mother-in-law as a person, not as simply a lady with whom you have lunch and go shopping."

At the end of our conversation, Marsha was elated. She said to me, "If half of what you have described could come true in my relationship with my mother-in-law, I would be extremely happy."

Over the coming months, Marsha saw most of these visions turn into reality. She and her mother-in-law became best friends. She learned to accept her mother-in-law's gifts as expressions of love, and she taught her mother-in-law how to share life on a deeper level. Some months later, I met the mother-in-law in a social setting. She said to me, "Marsha is the best thing that ever happened in my life. Having a son is great, but having a daughter-in-law is even better." I don't know how her son would feel about that, but it is evident that she has a genuine fondness for Marsha.

Marsha's story demonstrates the power of listening. The purpose of listening is to discover what is going on inside the minds and emotions of other people. If we understand why people do what they do, we can have more appropriate responses. For example, Marsha's whole attitude toward her mother-in-law changed when she discovered that her mother-in-law's motivation for buying her dresses was because, in the early years of her marriage, she had very little money for clothes and was often embarrassed about her wardrobe. Understanding often changes our perception of people and, consequently, our negative emotions toward them.

It is a fundamental psychological principle that we cannot read other people's minds. We observe their behavior, but we do not know what is behind the behavior until we listen. Most of us have not been trained to listen. Consequently, we often misunderstand our in-laws. I want to share with you some guidelines for effective listening:

Ask Questions
The most effective way to find out what is going on in the minds of your in-laws is to ask questions. Most people do not communicate the thoughts and feelings that motivate their behavior unless they are asked. Marsha could readily observe the behavior of her mother-in-law (taking her shopping and buying her dresses), but she did not know that her mother-in-law's behavior was motivated by events that transpired in the early days of her own marriage. This information came only in response to a question.

Questions must be carefully crafted. The more specific the question, the more likely you are to receive the information you seek. You may ask preliminary questions simply to bring up the topic. For example, "Who do you think will win the pennant?" puts the topic of baseball on the table. Then you can ask, "When did you become interested in baseball? And what stimulated your interest?" The answers to these questions may let you know why your father-in-law never misses a baseball game.

Questions must always be sincere. You are not asking a series of questions in order to push your in-laws into a corner and win an argument. You are asking questions to try to understand them. When people sense that you are genuinely interested in them and want to know them better, they will typically answer your questions honestly and freely. Marsha's mother-in-law was not reluctant to talk about the early days of her marriage. Marsha had simply never expressed interest in that part of her life. When she saw that Marsha was sincerely interested, she talked openly about what motivated her interest in shopping and gift giving.

Asking your in-laws to rate their feelings on a scale of 1–10 is a quick and easy way to learn how strongly they feel about a particular subject. Jason used this technique in opening a discussion with his father-in-law. Jason was frustrated over his father-in-law's propensity for gambling. When he learned that his father-in-law had taken Jason's ten-year-old son, Bobby, to the casino, Jason was livid and told his wife, "I will never let Bobby see your father again." Two weeks later, after he'd calmed down, I challenged Jason to ask questions and listen to his father-in-law's answers.

He asked his father-in-law, "On a scale of one to ten, how much do you enjoy going to the casino?" When his father-in-law said "ten," Jason knew this was something that was extremely important to him. Jason then followed up by asking, "Why do you think you gain so much pleasure from gambling?"

His father-in-law responded, "For me, it's recreation. I'm gambling because I have money and I don't have to worry about how I spend it. When I was a child, we had very little. We never knew if we would have a meal at dinner or whether my father would say, 'Let's go to bed early, and we'll have a big breakfast in the morning.' Breakfast was always oatmeal; we could have as much as we liked. I saw my friends at school with money to burn, and I determined that when I got to be an adult, I would make money and never have to ask anyone for anything. And I have. Now I can enjoy spending my money in any way I choose. If I lose a thousand dollars, so what? I can afford it."

"So for you," Jason continued, "it's not a matter of winning or losing; it's a matter of having fun."

His father-in-law responded, "It's not just fun. It's freedom; freedom to do what I want to with what I have."

"I think I can see what you're saying," said Jason. "I think all of us want to be free, and this is one way of expressing your freedom."

In a thousand years, Jason would never have guessed what was going on in the mind of his father-in-law, but two questions, accompanied by a listening ear, helped him understand his father-in-law's motivation. He still did not want Bobby going to the casino, but having heard and understanding his father-in-law, he was able to express his concerns in a constructive way. He shared his own understanding that many people who gamble are not free but are, in fact, enslaved by gambling and have lost not only recreational money but, indeed, all their financial assets. He explained his desire to keep Bobby from being exposed to something that had the potential for becoming addictive and destroying his freedom, and he requested that his father-in-law not take Bobby to the casino in the future. His father-in-law understood and agreed.

While both Marsha's and Jason's stories have "happy endings," I do not mean to imply that asking questions and understanding the motivation of our in-laws guarantees a satisfactory solution to the issues that trouble us. But by asking questions and listening empathetically, we are much more likely to find a resolution to these issues. And in the process we will be able to preserve—or even improve—our relationships with our in-laws.

Don't Interrupt

When your in-laws are talking, the tendency is to interrupt if they say something with which you disagree. When you interrupt and give your perspective, you have taken the first step to a full-blown argument. Arguments are counterproductive. Someone wins and someone loses, and the issue is not resolved.

Remember when Marsha's mother-in-law said, "I think the reason I find so much pleasure in buying things for you is that in the first years of our marriage, we had little money and I often was embarrassed by the things I had to wear"? Suppose Marsha had interrupted and said, "*We* have *plenty* of money. Rob has a good job. You don't need to buy me things." She would have entered into an argument that likely would have further damaged her relationship with her mother-in-law. Suppose Jason had interrupted his father-in-law and said, "That's a cop-out; I don't believe that for a moment. I think you gamble because you're addicted." He and his father-in-law would likely have had a shouting match that would have further fractured the relationship.

The purpose of listening is to understand, not to make a point. Our "point" will be made much later in the conversation. In the early stages, we are trying to understand what is going on in the mind and heart of an in-law so that we then can respond appropriately. Interruptions derail the process of understanding. For some people, refraining from interrupting will be extremely difficult. They have developed an argumentative pattern of communication. They listen only long enough to gather their own thoughts; then they interrupt and disagree with whatever the other person is saying. These individuals will never have a positive relationship with in-laws—or anyone else—until they learn to break the destructive pattern of argument. Relationships are built by seeking understanding. They are destroyed by interruptions and arguments.

If you have trouble continuing to listen to your in-laws when you disagree with what they are saying, let me suggest a mental image that may be helpful. When you have asked a question and your in-laws are talking, picture yourself with huge elephant ears on both sides of your face. The ears remind you "I'm a listener. I want to understand. I will not interrupt. I will have my chance to share my ideas later. Right now, I'm trying to listen to what my in-laws are saying. I want to know where they are coming from, and I want to understand how they view their behavior. I am trying to build a relationship, not make an enemy." Learning to listen without interrupting is a foundational step to effective listening.

Clarify Meaning

Even when we are consciously focusing on listening, we often misunderstand what another person is trying to communicate. We listen through our own earphones, which sometimes distort the meaning behind another person's words. We can clarify meaning by telling the person what we think they are saying and asking if we have heard them correctly. Jason demonstrated this when he said, "So for you, it's not a matter of winning or losing; it's a matter of having fun." This allowed his father-in-law to clarify by bringing up the idea of freedom. From this feedback, Jason was able to learn more about what was going on in his father-in-law's mind.

Some people object that clarifying questions seem to be rather mechanical. One husband said, "I get tired of saying 'What I hear you saying is . . .' And I'm sure other people must get tired of hearing it." It is true that the same response, couched in the same words, can become monotonous and annoying. However, clarifying questions can be asked in many ways. Here are some examples:

- "Is this what you are saying . . . ?"
- "Do you mean . . . ?"
- "I think I understand you. Tell me if I've got it right. . . ."
- "I think what I'm hearing is . . . Is that what you're saying?"
- "I want to make sure I understand. Are you saying . . . ?"

When we learn to ask clarifying questions in various ways, the questions become a part of the natural flow of our conversation. When an in-law responds, "Yes, you understand what I'm saying," then you will know he or she feels you've heard correctly. Then you're ready for the next step.

Express Appreciation

Once your in-law has told you that you understand what he or she has said, you may say, "I really appreciate your sharing that with me. I think I understand you better, and what you are saying makes a lot of sense." With that simple response, you are no longer an enemy. You have created a positive climate.

Affirming statements do not mean that you necessarily agree with what your in-laws have said. It does mean that you listened long enough to see the world through their eyes and to understand that, in their minds, what they are doing makes good sense. You are affirming their humanity, the right to think and feel differently from other people.

Some will ask, "How can you affirm what your in-laws are saying when you totally disagree with them?" My answer is: You are not necessarily affirming the validity of what they are saying. You are affirming their right to have this perspective. You are giving them the same freedom that God gives them. You are allowing them to be human.

Affirmation does not mean that you agree with their ideas or that you like their emotions. It means that you understand how they have come to hold their ideas and how they might feel the way they feel. Given their personalities and their perspectives on issues, it's not difficult to see how they could reach their conclusions and to understand their emotions.

I cannot overemphasize the value of expressing appreciation, because it creates the climate for the next important step:

Share Your Perspective

Now that you have asked questions, allowed your in-laws to speak without interruption, clarified meaning, and expressed appreciation, you are ready to share your perspective. Because you have taken the time to treat them with dignity and respect, they are far more likely to listen to your perspective.

When Jason shared with his father-in-law why he did not want Bobby to go to the casino, his father-in-law was willing to listen and agree. Had Jason not taken the time to first listen to his father-in-law, had he simply condemned the older man's behavior and told him that Bobby would never be allowed to go with him to the casino, their relationship might have remained fractured for a lifetime. It was the process of listening that brought them to a healthy conclusion.

When Marsha began to suggest alternatives to shopping, her mother-in-law was open to the alternatives because she sensed that Marsha genuinely wanted to have a good relationship with her. Had Marsha not expressed appreciation for her mother-in-law's willingness to share information from the early years of her own marriage, the mother-in-law might never have been open to Marsha's suggestions. When we express appreciation, we are more likely to be heard by our in-laws and to reach a satisfying solution.

Your perspective on the situation is also extremely important. You are one of the key players in this in-law relationship. You need to be heard; your ideas and feelings are important. Now that you have communicated a positive respect for your in-laws, you are ready to say, "Let me share my perspective with you. Here is what I'm struggling with. Here is my objective. Here is what I think is important." And you fully explain your perspective.

Because you have listened, you are far more likely to be listened to. Because you have not interrupted, you are less likely to be interrupted. Because you have clarified meaning, your in-laws are more likely to clarify meaning. Because you have expressed appreciation, they are more likely to express appreciation to you, and together, you can accept your differences and find healthy solutions.

In this chapter we have discussed the first step in becoming friends with your in-laws. Listening has brought you deeper understanding of each other, and understanding has led you to positive conclusions that will make the future easier for all of you. In the next chapter, we will look at the power of respect.

• • •

Putting the Principles into Practice

1. Choose an in-law relationship that you would like to improve, and think about this specific relationship as you consider the following questions:

   • What questions do you need to ask in order to better understand your in-law?
   • In your conversations, do you have a tendency to interrupt? If your answer is yes, what will you do to break this pattern?
   • Try using clarifying questions in your next conversation; for example, "Is this what you are saying?"
   • Read the following statement aloud three times: "I really appreciate your sharing that with me. I think I understand you better, and what you are saying makes a lot of sense." Look for an opportunity to use this statement with your in-law.

2. When you learn to ask good questions, clarify meaning, express appreciation, and refuse to interrupt, you will then be ready to say, "Let me share my perspective." Since you have listened to them, they will likely listen to you.

2

LEARN THE ART
OF SHOWING RESPECT

RESPECT IS A MAJOR INGREDIENT in building positive in-law relationships. The word *respect* means "to consider worthy of esteem."[1] It has to do with the way we view people. For me, respect means that I choose to see you as being extremely important because you are made in God's image. My choice to respect you is not based on your character or on your treatment of me. Rather, it is based upon my perception of who you are.

Respect has nothing to do with the behavior of my in-laws or their opinion of themselves. They may see themselves as being the scum of society or as being God's gift to mankind. Thus, their view of themselves may be marred or exalted. Whatever their view of themselves, I view them as persons who have great value because they bear the image of the Creator.

I may not like their behaviors, but I respect them as being fellow humans. They are gifted by God with a level of intelligence, with the capacity to experience emotions, and with freedom of choice. Also, they are ultimately responsible to God for how they use their lives.

When I choose the attitude of respect, it will be reflected in my behavior. Respect leads me to give my in-laws the same freedom that God allows me and all humans—the freedom to be different. Therefore, I will not seek to impose my will upon my in-laws. Rather, when I find myself at odds with them, I will look for a solution that will show respect for our differences. I will not seek to control them, nor will I allow them to control me. I will give to them the same respect that I hope they will give to me.

I may well feel irritated by something my in-laws say or do. The feeling of irritation is not sinful; however, I am responsible for how I respond to my irritation. If I lash out with harsh or critical words, then I have sinned. I have failed to show respect. If, on the other hand, I treat them with dignity by seeking to understand their perspective and then looking for win-win solutions, I am showing respect.

In an effort to make this practical, let's look at five areas in which we commonly have opportunity to show respect to our in-laws.

Respecting Holiday Traditions
Marriage brings together two families, each of which has a history of celebrating holidays. It is inevitable that the manner in which they celebrate these holidays will be different. And the importance that they attach to these holiday celebrations will also differ from family to family.

For many young couples, the first Christmas becomes the first major conflict in the marriage. His mother wants the two of you at her house on Christmas Day, while her mother has the same desire. That may be possible if the parents live in close proximity and one focuses their celebration around lunch and the other around dinner. However, if they live more than a hundred miles apart, this arrangement is not feasible. If one set of in-laws insists on your presence on Christmas Day and the other set of in-laws reluctantly acquiesces, you have planted the seeds of resentment. Respect is absent in this decision. The in-laws who demanded your presence are not respecting the desires of the other in-laws, nor are they respecting your freedom as a young couple to make your own decisions.

If the art of showing respect had been applied, what might have happened? Both sets of parents would have freely communicated their personal desires to have the couple on Christmas Day. When informed that both sets of parents had the same desire, they would have encouraged the young couple to think through the situation and suggest an alternate plan. The couple are now free to explore possibilities. The couple may decide to decline both invitations and spend Christmas Day with each other. If distance is not a problem, they may suggest that they spend Christmas Eve with one set of in-laws and Christmas Day with the other, with the understanding that the following year they would switch the sequence. If distance prohibits this dual visit, they may suggest Christmas with one set of in-laws this year and the other set of in-laws next year. Who is first could be determined by the flip of a coin. If one parent is critically ill, then this may be sufficient reason to choose to be with them the first Christmas. If time and money are not a problem, Thanksgiving Day may be put into the mix so that both parents would see the couple within the space of six weeks.

You can see that there are several equally workable solutions to this holiday conflict. All of them require an attitude of respect from each of the family members. If respect is not present, then Christmas will not be a symbol of "peace on earth." I have known young couples who stayed away from both sets of in-laws at Christmas, not because they did not desire to be there, but because they felt that both sets of parents were trying to manipulate them. Manipulation is the opposite of respect. Respect says, "This is what I would like and this is why I would like it. But I also know that you must make the decision that you believe is best for you." Respect always allows freedom of choice.

I have known couples who freely admitted that they both preferred to be with one set of in-laws during the holidays rather than the other. Typically, this is because the emotional climate in one setting is extremely stressful, perhaps because of alcohol, verbal abuse, or unresolved conflicts from the past. However, I encourage young couples not to allow these feelings to lead them to write off one set of in-laws.

The Scriptures say to "honor your father and your mother."[2] We do not honor parents by writing them off. We can be honest about our feelings, honest about the stress level that we experience when we are with them, but we must not allow these realities to control our behavior. We honor parents not because we believe they are honorable but because they gave us life. Without them, we would not be here. That is a huge debt. We honor them by considering the request of one set of in-laws in the same manner that we consider the request of the other set of in-laws. We may not approve of the lifestyle of one or both sets of in-laws. We may consider their behavior not worthy of esteem. But we esteem them as persons of worth because they bear the image of the Creator.

Of course, if there is drug and alcohol abuse, profane language, and verbal or physical abuse, then you certainly must take that into account in deciding whether or not to celebrate the holidays with them, especially if you have children. One approach is to respect their freedom to make these lifestyle choices but request that while you and your children are there for the holidays they refrain from these behaviors. If they choose to respect you in the same way that you are respecting them, they may well agree, and you can have a healthy celebration of the holidays.

Showing Respect for Religious Differences

Ours is truly a global society. The couple next door may be Buddhist; the couple down the street, Hindu; the man who works with you, Muslim; and most of the rest, Christian. Within the Christian framework, there are many religious "dialects." There is the Methodist dialect, Presbyterian dialect, Baptist dialect, and so forth. Each of these dialects represents a different way of expressing and practicing the Christian faith. They all agree on a common core of Christian beliefs, but beyond that, they differ in many ways.

Most people come to marriage having grown up in a religious context. They may have deeply held personal religious beliefs, or they may treat the belief system in which they grew up rather lightly. They may even have rejected the religion or religions of their parents. Seldom do two individuals come to marriage with the same religious background and beliefs, even if they grew up in the same church. These religious differences often become divisive in the marriage. They can also create barriers to wholesome in-law relationships. I remember the Protestant couple who said, "Our daughter married a Catholic. When they were dating, he visited our church and told us that he was not strongly committed to the Catholic church. But when the children came along, he insisted that they be raised in his religion. We feel like he deceived our daughter. Consequently, we don't have a very good relationship with him."

Because religion is such a vital part of life, I strongly urge couples considering marriage to explore fully the religious foundation on which they are seeking to build their relationship. When differences on fundamental religious beliefs are greatly diverse, these issues need to be resolved before the marriage. Otherwise, they can become huge barriers to marital unity. However, even when the two of them agree on fundamental religious questions, they may find themselves in strong disagreement with their in-laws' religious perspective. One young husband said, "My sister married a Muslim. He told her that all religions were basically the same, but she soon realized that was not the case. It has been very difficult to build a positive relationship with my brother-in-law because he disagrees with almost everything I believe. Even if we try to stay away from the topic of religion, our fundamental religious beliefs tend to spill over onto the rest of life and we end up arguing about other issues as well."

It is true that when one is committed to a religious system of thought, it influences the way one views all of life. That is why the apostle Paul urged Christians not to marry non-Christians.[3] If we are going to have marital unity in the spiritual area of life, we must be close enough in our fundamental beliefs to be able to dialogue and grow together.

Because religious beliefs often go unexcavated in the dating phase of the relationship, couples often find themselves married before they realize that they have vastly different religious perspectives. These differences may be between the two of them or between them and their in-laws. So how do we process these differences, and what role does showing respect play?

Let's begin by admitting that we may never be able to resolve all our religious conflicts. Efforts at blending various religions have never been very effective. On the other hand, if we try to convince our in-laws that their religious beliefs are wrong, we will likely experience nonproductive arguments. However, if we begin with the choice to respect their religious beliefs, we create a platform on which we can have authentic dialogue. In this atmosphere, both sides can come to understand each other's beliefs more fully and even question each other's beliefs while respecting the other's right to believe what they choose.

Respect for your in-laws' religious beliefs is a foundational requirement for building positive in-law relationships. This does not mean that you will agree with their beliefs. It does mean that you will give them the same freedom of choice that God grants them. Not all religious beliefs could possibly be true, for many of these beliefs actually contradict the others. Typically, we believe that our own religious beliefs are true. However, your in-laws also have the same persuasion about their religious beliefs. Respecting an individual's freedom to choose is the foundation for all meaningful dialogue. With respect, we can have a meaningful, positive relationship even when we disagree on certain religious beliefs.

Eric and Jan were deeply committed Christians. He grew up in a Methodist home, and she grew up in a Presbyterian family. However, each of them made the discovery of a personal commitment to Jesus Christ while they were in college. They had believed the Christian faith while growing up, but their beliefs never profoundly affected their behavior. In a college classroom where the Christian faith was being questioned by an unbelieving professor, they were challenged to find answers to his attacks on the validity of the Christian faith. This pursuit led them to the personal conclusion that Jesus Christ was, indeed, divine; that his life from beginning to end gave evidence of supernatural power; and that his resurrection from the dead validated his teachings. They became involved in a Bible study group and began to invest their lives in reaching out to the troubled neighborhoods in their university town. They knew that when they finished college, their lives would never be the same.

When they got married shortly after graduation, they never anticipated that religion would be a point of conflict between them and their parents. Eric and Jan joined a community church. His father asked, "What denomination is the church?"

Eric replied, "It's not affiliated with any denomination; it's just a Christian church."

"How can it be a Christian church and not be associated with any denomination?"

"I don't know," Eric said. "I just know it's a church that teaches the Scriptures and people try to follow the teachings of Jesus. We like it and feel it's where we need to be."

"I don't know why you didn't join a Methodist church or a Presbyterian church. Why would you have to join a no-name church? It seems to me they must be hiding something. Are you sure it's not a cult?"

When Jan shared with her parents that they had joined the community church, she got a similar response. "I guess we just assumed that you and Eric would join a Presbyterian church or a Methodist church since that's what the two of you grew up in. I wish you had discussed it with us before you made your decision," her mother said. "Was this Eric's idea or your idea?"

"We both had the same idea, Mom. It's the church we believe God wants us to attend."

"I think you had better pray some more about that," her mother said as she walked out of the room.

Eric and Jan were shocked at their parents' responses. Some time later, they began to realize that her parents were blaming Eric for pulling Jan into a "no-name" church, and Eric's parents were blaming Jan. In time, religion became an "off-limits" topic with both in-laws, but this young couple had to live with the awareness that their parents disagreed with their choice of church.

When they came to my office for help, I was empathetic with their frustration. Over the past thirty years, I have encountered numerous couples who were in conflict with their parents/in-laws over religious differences.

"We really don't have that many differences," Eric said. "The basic teachings in our church are the same as in the church of my parents. It is true that our church has a more contemporary worship style and the members are more heavily involved in Bible study, prayer meetings, and getting outside the walls of the church to minister to the needs of the community. But we have the same fundamental beliefs. I don't understand why this has become such a problem with them."

I listened carefully as Jan also shared her struggles with her parents and her in-laws.

"I'm glad you came," I said. "I'd hate to see you struggle with this frustration for the next twenty years. My guess is that your parents' opposition to your being a part of the community church is based on fear and love. They love both of you very much. They want you to have a productive life. Their churches have been an important part of their lives through the years, and they want that for you, too. Their fear is based on the unknown. They know what a Methodist church is, and they know what a Presbyterian church is. But they don't know about community churches. They are fearful that this might be a cultic Christian group that will pull you into beliefs and practices that are detrimental to your well-being."

"But that's not true," said Eric.

"*I* know it's not true, but *they* don't know it's not true," I said. "All of us fear the unknown."

"So, how can we help them understand?" asked Jan.

"It all begins with respect," I said. "You must respect their choice of churches, and they must respect yours."

"We do respect their choices," Jan said, "but they don't respect ours."

"Let's hope that can change," I said.

"That's why we came," said Eric. "If they could just respect our choice and trust us the way we trust them, everything would be fine."

That was the first of several sessions I had with Eric and Jan. Within six months, they had won the respect of both sets of in-laws. The process began with an open conversation between Eric and Jan and his parents in which he was the spokesman. He shared with his parents that he and Jan really wanted to have harmony over his and Jan's choice of church and that he and Jan were willing to try to understand his parents' concerns but also wanted to share their own perspective.

He suggested that they begin by getting a list of the basic beliefs of the Methodist church, the Presbyterian church, and the community church and then compare those beliefs to see where there might or might not be genuine differences. "We really want to understand you, and we want you to understand us. We know that you love us and that you have our best interests in mind." His parents readily accepted this invitation.

The couple had a similar conversation with Jan's parents in which Jan was the spokeswoman. Her parents also were happy to discuss the matter.

When they actually compared the core beliefs of the three churches, all parties agreed that the basic beliefs were the same.

Eric also suggested that they would like to read a brief history of the Methodist church if his parents could secure it from their pastor. And Jan asked her parents for the same from the Presbyterian church. Both sets of parents agreed that they would like to read the history themselves. "The community church doesn't have much of a history," Eric said, "but we will find out how our church got started and share it with you." What they all discovered was that the motivation for starting the community church was quite similar to that of the early followers of John Wesley, who founded the Methodist church, and the followers of John Knox, who established the Presbyterian church.

In the meantime, Eric and Jan visited the Methodist church with his parents and the Presbyterian church with her parents, and each of the parents visited the community church with them. In the process, parental fears were allayed.

Eric and Jan expressed appreciation to their parents for being willing to explore the possibility that their choice of the community church was a wise choice for them. And before long, both sets of parents agreed. Now, from time to time, they visit one another's churches for special events. The parents have come to respect Eric and Jan's choice in much the same way as the young couple showed respect for the parents'.

Unfortunately, not all religious differences will be solved to this level of satisfaction. But this serves as an excellent model for how to go about addressing differences. Beginning with respect will always improve situations to some degree.

Showing Respect for Privacy

I was making a quick run to the grocery store for cereal and milk. As I made my turn into the cereal aisle, I encountered Tim and Marie. I recognized them as having attended a parenting class at which I had recently spoken. After we greeted each other, Tim said, "I know this is not the place for a counseling session, but we really need help with my mom and dad. They are driving us crazy. We don't want to hurt them, but we have got to do something."

"So, what's the situation?" I asked.

Marie responded, "We never know when they'll drop in for a visit. They never bother to call and tell us they're coming; they just show up at the door. Sometimes, it's very inconvenient. The children may be doing their homework, or I may be involved in doing laundry. I don't have time to sit down and talk with them, and the children need to get their homework done. The worst thing, and the reason we're so upset today . . ." Marie looked up at Tim, and he picked up the conversation.

"Last week, we had put the children to bed early so we could have some private time together, and just when we were about to make love, the doorbell rang and my folks walked in. As you can imagine, it destroyed our romantic evening together."

"It's just not fair," said Marie. "I'm beginning to resent them. I wish we had some scheduled times for them to visit when it is convenient for us."

"Have you talked with your folks about this?" I inquired.

Tim said, "I tried to, a couple of years ago. Mom got upset and didn't call or come by to visit for three weeks. Then all of a sudden, they showed up at our house one day as if nothing had happened. And they've been showing up ever since. We've never talked about it again."

"How often do they drop in?" I asked.

"At least once a week," Marie said, "and there's no pattern to when they show up. It can be any day, any time."

"Do you ever visit their house?" I asked.

"Yes," Tim said, "but we always call before we go. We thought that maybe our calling might give them the idea that it would be nice if they called us before they came. But obviously, this hasn't worked. In fact, Mom has told me, 'You don't have to call before you come. You can come anytime. You're family.' I guess we have a different idea of what it means to be family."

"It sounds to me like the problem is lack of respect," I said. "Your parents are not respecting your privacy as a family."

"Exactly," Marie replied. "But what do we do about it?"

"Well, you don't gain respect by being disrespectful," I said. "So, what you don't want to do is to lose your temper and lash out at them in anger, tell them how inconsiderate they are, or inform them that you are sick and tired of their messing up your plans."

"So far we have not done that," Marie said, "but believe me, I have been tempted."

"I can understand that," I said, "but I think you can see that will only make things worse."

"I don't think it could get much worse," Marie said.

"Well, let's focus on trying to make it better," I replied. "You must talk with your parents about the problem. The passing of time will not bring a resolution. I think you've seen that."

They were both nodding and saying, "Yes."

"I think Tim should be the spokesman because they are his parents. How you talk to them is extremely important. What if you begin by saying something like this: 'Mom and Dad, I love you very much. I think you know that. Marie also loves you very much, and our children think you are wonderful grandparents. We want to continue to have a good relationship with you, and we want our children to enjoy you as grandparents. I know that your intentions are good, and you really love us as we love you. I want us to find a way to do this that will be good for all of us. I know that in the past you have told me that I don't need to call when I am coming by for a visit or to pick up something from Dad's shop. But I've always felt that I should respect your privacy by letting you know that I was coming. It seems to me that a phone call makes it easier for everybody. Sometimes when you show up at our house without calling, it is at a very inconvenient time. For example, last week when you came over at eight o'clock on Tuesday night, we had put the children to bed early so that we could have a romantic time together. We were in the middle of lovemaking when the doorbell rang and you walked in. I think you can see how that was not the best time for a visit.'"

Marie interrupted and said to Tim, "Do you think you can say that to your parents?"

302 || GARY CHAPMAN

"I think so," Tim said. "In fact, that may be the one thing that may wake them up."

"Then, you can throw out some possibilities of what might be done to improve the situation, such as calling before they come and asking if it is a convenient time to come. If not, then suggest a time that would be convenient. A second idea would be to set a weekly time for them to visit. For example, Thursday night could be 'fun night with grandparents.' This will allow you to plan ahead and make it a fun evening for everyone. Of course, you could also periodically call and invite them to come over for dinner or to help you with a project you are working on. When you initiate the call, they have the choice to come or not to come. You have opened the door and let them know that you would like to have them. What you are trying to communicate to your parents is that you want them to be very involved in your lives and the lives of your children, but you want to do it in a manner that would be pleasant for everyone.

"I think if you take this approach, you may well find that your parents will be open. They may not fully understand why you would request this, but I think they would be willing to work with you. My guess is that their intention is not to make your lives miserable. They simply want to be involved in your lives and the lives of your children. It's just that the way they are doing it has become frustrating for you."

"And what if they don't pick up on these ideas and continue to show up whenever and wherever?" Marie asked.

"Then you will need to take the 'tough love' approach," I said. "At that point, you will need to make an appointment with me, and we will discuss how to show 'tough love' to in-laws who are not willing to respect your privacy. However, I really believe that if you take this approach, affirming them for their interest in your lives and expressing appreciation for all that they are doing for you, they are likely to respond to your request."

"Thanks," Tim said. "I really appreciate your taking time to talk with us."

"Let me know what happens," I said.

"We will," Marie said, "and I hope we don't have to make a visit to your office."

I nodded and reached for my Cheerios.

About six weeks later, I received a phone call from Tim. "I thought I should call and let you know how things have worked out," he said. "I had the talk with my folks shortly after we saw you in the grocery store. Dad was very understanding. Mom said she was hurt that it had come to this; she thought that family should be able to visit each other whenever they desired. I told her I understood her thoughts, but it just wasn't working for us. I think that after our conversation Dad must have talked to her, because a week later she seemed to be fine with the new arrangement. We established Thursday night as the night they would come for a visit. And so far, it seems to be working well. We did invite them over for dinner last Saturday night, and that also went well. I can sense a little tension with Mom, but I think she's coming around. I really appreciate your helping us with this because it was getting to be a real problem."

"I'm glad things are working out," I said. "When parents and their married children show respect for each other's privacy, it makes for healthy relationships. Let me know if I can ever help you in the future."

"Thanks," Tim said.

I have shared this illustration because the invasion of privacy is a common area of conflict with in-laws. Many couples wait until they are so frustrated with their in-laws that in a moment of intense anger, they lash out with harsh and condemning words and fracture the relationship. Sometimes these broken relationships stay fractured for years. But when the younger couple show respect for their parents' and in-laws' intentions and openly share with them their own frustrations, most of the problems can be resolved.

However, if in-laws insist they have a right to show up whenever and wherever, the couple will need to turn to the "tough love" approach, which may mean meeting the parents at the door and saying, "I'm sorry. But this is not a convenient time for you to visit. I'm in the midst of giving the children their baths, and then they must go to bed. I would love to have you visit, but right now is not a convenient time. If you like, I will call you tomorrow and suggest a time that would be convenient for all of us."

If the in-laws walk off in a huff, that is not your responsibility. You are doing what is best for your family and ultimately what is best for your relationship with your in-laws. If, in fact, you call the next day and suggest a time when they might come by, they have two options: They can accept your invitation, and if so, the pattern of intrusion on privacy will likely have been broken. Or they can say, "No, thank you. That is not a convenient time for us," in which case you might say, "I can understand that. Let me know when you would like to come and I will try to work it out." If they don't contact you for two or three weeks, don't panic. They are still trying to process their own feelings and thoughts. Give them time. If they don't call you, you can call them again in three weeks and give them another invitation. If they don't accept that invitation, perhaps you will want to wait until they initiate a call.

On your part, you keep the door open to have a relationship with them. If they choose to be obstinate and accuse you of pushing them out of your lives, you will know in your heart it is not true. You are simply trying to have a relationship built on respect of privacy.

Showing Respect for Their Ideas

Jeremy's brother-in-law suggested that now was a good time to sell his house and buy a bigger one, not only because Jeremy and Peggy were expecting a baby but because "the interest rates have never been lower. It's a good time to sell your house and a good time to buy another." Jeremy had not thought about moving until his brother-in-law shared the idea. As he and Peggy reflected upon the idea, they both agreed that his brother-in-law was right. They immediately started the processes of looking for a house that would meet their needs and of putting their house on the market. That was five years ago. Jeremy has often said to Peggy, "I really appreciate your brother's encouraging us to move. This house is so much better for us than the one we had, and the payments are almost the same."

Whatever the topic of discussion, we all have different ideas. Our ideas are based upon our history, education, vocation, and social experience. Because no one human can know everything, we often turn to others for ideas in areas of life where we have had little experience.

Such openness to the ideas of others is a sign of wisdom. The Scriptures indicate that when we seek the wise counsel of others, we are far more likely to make a wise decision.[4] The mature person is always looking for wisdom, even if it is spoken by a mother-in-law. When parents and in-laws make suggestions, their ideas should be given due consideration. After all, they are older and perhaps wiser than we are.

A good example of the wisdom of a father-in-law is found in Exodus 18. Moses was working from morning to evening judging the people of Israel. The waiting room was always filled, and there was no time for coffee breaks. Moses' father-in-law said, "What you are doing is not good. You and these people who come to you will only wear yourselves out. The work is too heavy for you; you cannot handle it alone. Listen now to me and I will give you some advice."[5]

His father-in-law then suggested that the crowds be divided into thousands, hundreds, fifties, and tens and that authority be delegated to other qualified men who would judge those under their jurisdiction. Moses then would be free to spend more time with God and in teaching the people the law of God. Thus, his ministry would be more "preventive" than a "crisis" ministry. Only the difficult cases would be brought to him for judgment.[6]

Moses saw the wisdom of such a suggestion and adopted it. In so doing, he revealed his own maturity. He did not have to rebel against a good idea just because it came from his father-in-law. He was secure enough in his own self-worth that he could accept a good idea regardless of its source.

Respecting the ideas of your in-laws and giving those ideas reflective thought is a sign of maturity, not a sign of weakness. On the other hand, if you are the in-law who is making the suggestion or giving advice, let me encourage you to respect the freedom of those you are advising. Don't ever seek to force your ideas upon other persons. Ideas should be shared as suggestions, not as demands. If you are receiving advice from in-laws and feel they are seeking to control your decision, then it is your responsibility to listen carefully to the suggestion; give it your best consideration and then make the decision you believe best for you and your family. If your in-laws become upset that you did not follow their idea, you can express appreciation for their being willing to share their thoughts. Let them know that you did give consideration to the idea but that you made the decision you felt was best. Respecting their ideas does not mean that you will always follow their advice. After all, the responsibility for the decision rests upon your shoulders, not upon the shoulders of your in-laws.

Showing Respect for Your In-Laws' Peculiarities

Someone has said, "All of us are different but some of us are more different than others." When you begin to know your spouse's parents and siblings, you may encounter what to you are very weird behaviors. They may not be weird to your spouse because he or she has grown up with the behavior. For example, Pam found it very strange that her father-in-law spent every Saturday alone, away from the family. During hunting season, he was hunting. When he wasn't hunting, he was fishing or golfing. He saw Saturdays as his day of recreation, which he pronounced "re-creation." "It's my way of recuperating from the hard week of work," he said.

Pam felt this was unfair to his wife and children, but his wife and children seemed to accept it as normal. Pam asked her husband, Phil, "Did your father never take you fishing?"

"He did," Phil said, "but not on Saturdays."

"How about hunting?"

"A few times, but again, not on Saturday."

"How about golfing?" she asked.

"No. He said golfing was a man's sport, not for boys."

"Did you never want to go hunting, fishing, or golfing on Saturday with your father?" Pam inquired.

"I did, but Mom told me that was his day to relax, so I spent time playing with my brother and the boys in the neighborhood."

"Do you think your mother resented his time away every Saturday?"

"Perhaps at first," Phil said, "but I think she came to accept it. I never heard them argue about it."

"Well, you do know that I would never accept that in our relationship, right?"

"Yes," Phil said. "You don't have to worry. I want to spend time with you and the children on Saturdays. I have no desire to isolate myself in recreation."

"Good," said Pam, "because if you were like your father, you and I would have a major battle."

Pam so much wanted to say to her father-in-law, "Do you know how foolish you have been over the years? Do you understand how self-centered you were? In my opinion, you were a poor model of a husband and father." However, she was wise enough to know that if she took that condemning approach, she would make herself an enemy. She also realized that it was not her place to tell her father-in-law how to live his life. She chose to accept that as a part of him that she did not understand. If her mother-in-law had been able to accept the Saturday recreational philosophy, then she would also accept it, even though in her mind it was a very strange practice.

Little things about your in-laws can be major irritants to you. Marcy was frustrated that her brother-in-law never opened the car door for her sister. Besides that, he wore a ball cap all the time, even inside the house. Her mother had taught her and her sister that ball caps were for ball games and that any gentleman should remove his hat when he walks in a house. She saw her brother-in-law as uncouth and disrespectful of her sister. She felt sad that her sister had married a man who was so inconsiderate.

When she talked with her sister about it, her sister said, "Yes. I would prefer that my husband open doors for me and that he take his ball cap off when he enters a home. But he is such a good man and treats me so well that I don't have the heart to make an issue of those things. In the big picture, they are rather small to me." Having voiced her opinion and heard her sister's response, Marcy decided to let it go. She still had her preferences, and if it were her husband, she would never accept those practices. But if it was fine with her sister, she would not wage a battle with her brother-in-law.

On a thousand fronts, we may be irritated with our in-laws. However, we must choose our battles carefully. Some things are not worth fighting over, and some things are clearly not our battles. Learning to respect the peculiarities of our in-laws is necessary if we are to have harmonious in-law relationships. In fact, if we were to fight our in-laws over every issue that strikes us as odd, we would spend the rest of our lives in battle.

In-laws were not designed to be enemies; they were designed to be friends. Showing respect for each other's holiday traditions, religious beliefs, privacy, ideas, and peculiarities is the road to friendship.

• • •

Putting the Principles into Practice
1. What struggles do you face in the following areas?

    • Respecting holiday traditions
    • Respecting religious differences
    • Respecting privacy
    • Respecting the ideas of in-laws
    • Respecting your in-laws' peculiarities

2. Discuss with your spouse how you might improve in-law relationships by showing more respect.

3

SPEAK FOR YOURSELF

THE FRUSTRATION IN IN-LAW RELATIONSHIPS often becomes so intense that we find ourselves making condemning statements. We try to listen before we speak and to respect our in-laws, but things keep getting worse. So we lose control and launch an all-out attack. I remember Margot, who said, "I can't believe I called my daughter-in-law a whore. I guess I had just had it with her little flirty, suggestive behavior. She dresses like a prostitute so I called her one. I don't know if she will ever speak to me again, and my son is also upset with me."

Margot was following a pattern that is all too common in in-law relationships. We all have our perception of what is wrong with other people. We allow our hurt and resentment to grow, and then we attack with vicious words that we later regret. Many of these condemning words are characterized by speaking for them. That is, we have reached our conclusions as to the kinds of persons they are. We have determined what we think their behavior means, and we speak for them. "You are irresponsible and disrespectful."

What Margot said in the heat of anger was, "You little whore. You dress like a prostitute, and I'm surprised you haven't been raped. You

309

are going to destroy your marriage. Why don't you think about the children?" Each "you" statement was like another exploding grenade further destroying their relationship. If Margot does not sincerely apologize, her daughter-in-law truly may never speak to her again.

When we begin a sentence with *you*, we are speaking as though we have ultimate knowledge of a person. In reality, we have only a perception. Such statements come across as condemning and will likely stimulate a defensive response from our in-laws. We end up in a major argument, and both of us go away resenting the other.

There is a simple technique that will help you break this destructive pattern. It's called "speaking for yourself." It begins by learning to make "I" statements as opposed to "you" statements. For example, "I feel hurt," rather than "You hurt me." If you begin the sentence with "I," you are reporting or revealing your feelings. If you begin the sentence with "you," it is an attack. "You" statements are like verbal grenades, which bring hurt, resentment, and often counterattacks. "I" statements reveal a problem without condemning the other person.

Margot's daughter-in-law was not an immoral woman. While her idea of modest dress was quite different from her mother-in-law's, she was not intentionally trying to attract other men. Had Margot used "I" statements in conveying her concerns, the outcome might have been totally different. She might have said, "I'm fearful for your marriage. I feel like a lot of men interpret your behavior as an invitation. I don't think this is what you want. So, I'm not being critical of you; I'm just concerned. I want the best for you and Jerry." The daughter-in-law might still have been hurt or upset, but she would likely have worked through her feelings and understood Margot's concerns. When you speak for yourself, you are making valid statements. You are revealing *your* thoughts, feelings, desires, and perceptions. "I think . . ." "I feel . . ." "I wish . . ." "My perception is . . ." All these statements are valid because they are revealing what is going on inside *you*. You are speaking for yourself.

When you make "you" statements, you are always wrong because you never fully know what is going on inside another person. Even when you make positive "you" statements, you are speaking beyond

IN-LAW RELATIONSHIPS || 311

your knowledge. "You are the most beautiful person in the world." This is certainly a positive statement but not a valid statement because you are speaking for all the people in the world. We know what you mean, and it will probably be accepted as a compliment. However, it would be more realistic to say, "I think that you are the most beautiful person I have ever seen." Now the statement seems sincere and not just flattery.

When you are expressing negative ideas, it is even more important to speak for yourself. Neal's mother, Betty, made unkind statements about his wife, Jan. She accused Jan of being lazy. "Why is she not working?" she asked Neal. "She should be helping you. Together, you could make enough money to buy a house and not have to waste money on rent." Betty continued her critical speech and concluded with, "Honey, I just want the best for you. I hate to see Jan wasting time."

Everything within Neal wanted to say, "You don't understand. You have no right to criticize Jan. You need to keep your mouth shut and stay out of our lives." Fortunately, Neal had had some training on how to speak for himself. So he began, "I'm glad you shared your thoughts with me. I did not know you were feeling that way. I can understand your concern, and I appreciate it. However, I need to share with you that Jan and I have talked about her working, and both of us have agreed that it would be best if she finished her college degree first. She is taking online classes and will finish next May. We both feel good about what we are doing, but thanks for sharing your concerns."

In speaking for himself, Neal averted an unnecessary battle with his mother. When your in-laws come at you with condemning statements, to counterattack is to start an unnecessary war. It is far better to respond with "I" statements that reveal your perspective in a positive manner.

The greatest hindrance to speaking for yourself is negative emotions. Hurt, anger, resentment, and fear push us to strike back. But striking back leads to arguments, and arguments lead to broken relationships. That is why I suggest that when you are attacked by your in-laws, take a deep and deliberate breath, followed by a moment of silence, before you speak. This may help you get on the "I" train rather than the "you" train.

Speaking for yourself is a learned pattern of speech. Most of us grew up getting "you" messages. "You disappointed me" and "You disobeyed me" were messages you heard from your parents. "You make me so angry," "You lied to me," and "You are irresponsible" are statements your parents may have made to each other.

How do you break out of this destructive, condemning pattern? By conscious choice. First, you must recognize the value of speaking for yourself; then you must try it. Perhaps it would help if you stood in front of the mirror and said, "I feel hurt," "I feel angry," "I feel disappointed," "I feel like you deceived me," or "I feel like you do not trust me." When you practice making "I" statements, you are more likely to make them in the context of live conversations.

You will not establish the art of speaking for yourself overnight. From time to time, you will hear yourself begin a sentence with "you." When you start a sentence with "You are doing . . . ," catch yourself and say instead, "Let me say that again. I feel that what you are doing . . ." When you restate your sentence with "I" instead of "you," you are not only learning to speak for yourself but also modeling the process to your in-laws.

In time, you can learn to speak for yourself. When you do, you will have learned an important skill in becoming friends with your in-laws.

● ● ●

Putting the Principles into Practice

1. Listen to yourself talk. How many of your sentences begin with "You . . . ," especially when you are upset? "You" statements start arguments.

2. The next time you have negative feelings, stand in front of a mirror and practice saying, "I feel hurt," "I feel angry," "I feel disappointed," or "I feel like you deceived me." Then, use the appropriate "I" statement when you talk to the person with whom you are angry.

3. When you start your sentence with "You make me . . . ," catch yourself and say instead, "Let me say that differently. I feel hurt when you say that."

4

SEEK TO NEGOTIATE

"WHY CAN'T WE GO SEE GRANDMOTHER?" a seven-year-old asks.

Her mother replies, "Because Grandmother doesn't want to see us right now."

"Why?" asks the child.

"Because the last time we were there, your brother marked with crayons on Grandmother's wall. She wants to wait until you and your brother get older before we go back to her house."

"I won't mark on her walls."

"I know that, honey, but Grandmother doesn't know that. It cost her lots of money to put up new wallpaper, and she is upset right now."

"When will she stop being upset?"

"I don't know. Right now we are trying to work that out."

We're trying to work that out. That is what negotiation is all about. To negotiate is to discuss an issue in order to reach an agreement. Negotiation is the opposite of withdrawal and resentment. When we negotiate, we are choosing to believe that there is an answer, and with God's help, we will find it.

Why is negotiation so important? Because without negotiation,

314 || GARY CHAPMAN

fractured relationships may continue for years. Imagine the tragedy if, at age twelve, the girl mentioned above is still asking, "Why can't we go see Grandmother?" When we do not negotiate our differences, we allow walls to stand between us and our in-laws, and the potential for becoming friends with our in-laws evaporates.

Anger is often the enemy of negotiation. Perhaps as you read the illustration above, your thoughts were, "If that's the way the grandmother feels, then forget it. I would never take my kids back to see her. If her walls are more important to her than my children, then I wouldn't care if we had a relationship." Even though these thoughts are understandable, if followed, they would sabotage negotiation and leave you with broken in-law relationships for a lifetime. Everyone loses when we allow anger to push us into an unyielding stance of opposition.

Healthy in-law relationships require negotiation for one simple reason: We are all humans. Humans think differently and experience different emotions and reactions. Without negotiation, we allow our differences to become divisive. I have experienced some of my deepest pain in the counseling office as I have listened to the stories of in-laws who haven't spoken to each other for years because someone refused to negotiate. For the sake of your spouse and your children, I urge you to abandon your stubbornness and learn the art of negotiating.

We have just looked at three essential skills that prepare you to negotiate. First, we discussed the necessity of listening before you speak. Ask questions with a view to understanding the thoughts and feelings of your in-laws. Second, show respect for their ideas. You may not agree with their ideas but you give them the freedom to be human, which means they have a perspective different from your own. Third, speak for yourself. Make "I" statements, not "you" statements. With those skills in mind, I want to share some steps in the process of negotiating:

Make Proposals

Negotiation begins with someone making a proposal; someone must break the silence. Silence indicates that something is wrong. Someone did or said something that offended an in-law. Perhaps we exchanged a few harsh words and then withdrew in silence. Or perhaps we went

immediately to the silent mode, saying nothing aloud but talking to ourselves and wallowing in hurt and anger. While momentary silence can be
a positive response to anger, silence must never become a lifestyle. Give
yourself time to cool down emotionally. Then it's time to make a proposal. Hopefully, the silence endured only for a day or two at most. The
longer a silence endures, the more difficult it is to break. But breaking
the silence is a necessity if we are going to improve in-law relationships.

Martha, the mother of the son who had marked on his grandmother's walls, called her mother-in-law and said, "I feel really bad
about Jason marking on your walls. If I had the money, I would pay
to have them repaired. I don't have the money, and that makes me feel
even worse. I do want my children to have a good relationship with
you, so I'm wondering if you could meet us at the park Thursday afternoon at two. They both really want to see you. Would that possibly
fit into your schedule?" With this proposal, Martha has apologized for
her son's behavior and has expressed her regret and her desire to make
things right. She has also offered an opportunity for the grandmother
to be with the grandchildren in a setting that has no potential for
bringing harm to her house. If the grandmother responds positively,
then the relationship is on the mend.

Proposals should be realistic and take into account the offense that
was committed. This normally means that we begin with an apology,
accepting our responsibility and being willing to make restitution when
possible. The apology is then followed with a proposal that offers an
opportunity for the relationship to continue. You may still feel hurt, and
you may not fully understand why your in-law was so offended, but you
are choosing to seek negotiation rather than withdrawing in resentment.
Your proposal opens the opportunity for the two of you to take steps in
a positive direction.

Good proposals are specific, as opposed to general. Rather than
saying, "The children really miss you, and I do hope that we can get
together soon," Martha made a proposal for a specific day, time, and
place. General proposals are too nebulous to be helpful. Had Martha
given a general proposal, it might have been several weeks or months
before her mother-in-law responded. When she made her proposal

specific, she made it easy for her mother-in-law to respond. And the process of reconciliation could begin much sooner.

John and Kim were in my office complaining that John's father had given their two children chewing gum, even after they had asked him not to. They were toying with the idea of not allowing the children to stay with their grandparents because they didn't trust John's father.

Being a grandfather myself, I was smiling on the inside, but I knew that John and Kim were serious. To them, it was not just a matter of chewing gum. It was a matter of trust. They felt that if they could not trust John's father to follow their expressed rules, then maybe it was better to keep the children away from him.

I listened to them carefully, asked clarifying questions, and then said to them, "I think I understand your concern. I'm sure that if I were in your shoes, I would feel the same way. Now let me share my thoughts." (How's that for being a good listener?)

I acknowledged that John and Kim were certainly free to keep their children away from his father, but in my opinion, negotiation was better than withdrawal. Withdrawal removes the opportunity for the relationship to improve, whereas negotiation opens the door to the possibility of a better relationship.

I suggested that they make a positive proposal to John's father. That proposal would involve expressing to him how disappointed they were that he had not honored their rules. They would also explain why they had made the rule of no chewing gum. (It had come as a recommendation from their dentist.) John and Kim knew that John's father was a Monopoly player. So they would say to John's father, "We know the children love you and you love them, and we want you to have a good relationship with them. Therefore, we are going to give you a 'Get out of jail free card' for this offense. But the next time you give them chewing gum, you will 'Go directly to jail,' you will not 'Proceed past Go,' and you will not 'Receive $200.' Do you understand?"

I encouraged them to do all this with a smile. They agreed that if John's father received their proposal in a positive way, they would continue visits as normal. However, if John's father went into an angry rage and told them that they were not going to tell him what to do with his own grandchildren and that he would give them chewing gum whenever he pleased, they would say to John's father, "If that's your decision, then we will have to keep the children away from you. If you ever change your mind, we will allow them to spend time with you."

We all knew that if this situation developed, John's mother would work on John's father and within a few weeks, he would decide not to give the children chewing gum. At that point, they could then make another proposal or his father might even call with a proposal himself.

If John's father had taken this belligerent attitude, he would have been indicating that he was not open to negotiation. In cases like this, we must withdraw for a season before making another proposal. But maybe John's father would come back and say, "Can we make two exceptions? I could give them chewing gum on their birthdays, and secondly, I could give them a cookie instead of chewing gum from time to time." That would demonstrate an openness to negotiate, which would then give John and Kim the chance to say, "We are open to chewing gum once a year on the children's birthdays. Cookies should be given only as dessert, not between meals."

John's father can accept their counterproposal or offer another proposal, and together they come to an agreement. That is the purpose of negotiating, and it brings us to the second step in the process.

Be Open to Something Different

Making a proposal is the first step in the process of negotiating. The second step is listening carefully to counterproposals. Remember, negotiating has to do with two people trying to understand each other and reach an agreement that both of them will feel good about. Because we are different, we have different ideas. A proposal opens the opportunity for dialogue. I listen carefully to your proposal. Then I bring my own thoughts and feelings to play and suggest perhaps a major or minor change to what you are suggesting. Then you have an opportunity to hear my counterproposal and perhaps make a counterproposal of your own. The process of listening, understanding, and seeking to find an agreement is the process of negotiation.

People who learn to negotiate well are people who learn to respect the ideas of others, even when they disagree. We listen because we respect them as individuals and want to understand their thoughts and feelings. If you don't fully understand their proposal, by all means ask clarifying questions.

For example, John's father might have asked, "Are you saying that you don't want the children to have chewing gum because you think the sugar is bad for them?" to which John or Kim would have replied, "Our concern is for their teeth. Our dentist advised against letting the children have chewing gum because their teeth are in a very crucial stage of development, and he felt that it would be detrimental for them to chew gum at this time." Had the father been willing to ask clarifying questions, he would have understood the situation more clearly.

When we make a proposal, we should expect a counterproposal. We must not come to negotiation with the attitude "It's my way or no way at all." We come with the attitude "Here's an idea that I think will work. What do you think about it?" We are open to hear their thoughts and open to their ideas. It is this openness to alternative ideas that gives us the ability to reach agreements.

When we are rigid in our ideas and unwilling to consider an alternative, we stymie the process of negotiation. Keep in mind that there are reasons behind your in-laws' counterproposal. If it doesn't seem logical to you, continue to ask questions of them so that they can clarify why they think their idea is workable.

Negotiation is a process of proposals and counterproposals, where all parties are seeking to find an agreement. If you are willing to continue the process of negotiation, you will likely find an agreement.

Look for a Win-Win Solution
The third step in the process of negotiating is finding a solution that both parties feel is workable. It may not be what either one of you desired at the beginning of the negotiation, but it will be a solution that addresses your key concerns. Both of you come away from the agreement feeling that you have taken a positive step in developing your relationship. This is what I like about negotiating. We end up moving in a positive direction and moving together. This is good for in-law relationships.

Betsy and Bill were at odds with Betsy's mother, Joyce. Joyce had informed them that she was taking their children to the beach for a vacation the second week in June. She was telling them in January so they would have plenty of notice. The problem was that Bill and Betsy had already enrolled the children for children's camp at their church that same week.

Joyce was shocked and angry that they had made that decision without talking with her. "I told you I wanted to take the children on a vacation to the beach this summer. Why didn't you discuss it with me before you signed them up for camp?" she asked.

Betsy responded, "Mom, there's only one week for children's camp; they either go that week or they don't go at all. We really wanted them to go to camp this year. We assumed that you could take them to the beach any week during the summer."

"Well, I could, but I have already rented this place at the beach, and I don't know if I can get my money back."

"Then maybe you should have talked with us before you rented the place," Betsy said. "It sounds like we both could have done a little better job at communicating with each other."

Both parties had good intentions. They each wanted to do something worthwhile for the children. The crisis developed because of lack of communication.

Situations like this arise regularly in in-law relationships. These situations call for negotiation. Someone needs to make a proposal and get the process started. In this case, Betsy's mother made the first proposal: "What if I check with the rental company to see if I can rent the same facility a different week?"

"That sounds like a good place to start," Betsy said. "We certainly would like for the children to have a week with you at the beach. I know they would enjoy it."

Three days later Betsy's mother came back with this report: "They will allow me to rent the facility for a different week, but there will be a $75 change fee. I tried to talk them out of it, but they say it's their policy. I hate to waste money like that. Have you checked with your church to make sure that the children's camp is that week? They are not likely to change the dates between now and then, are they?"

"I did check," Betsy said, "and they have the facility rented. It's the week they do children's camp every summer, and it's not going to change." Then Betsy made a proposal. "What if Bill and I pay the $75 change fee for you? It would be a small investment for us to have the children with you for a whole week at the beach. We wouldn't mind doing that. I know you are already paying an arm and a leg to rent the place for the week. That's the least we can do."

Betsy's mother replied, "I hate for you to do that. It's just a waste of money."

"I don't see it as wasting money, Mom. I see it as the cost of our not talking to each other before we made decisions. So, let's just look at it as a $75 learning experience on our part. I think we have both learned the importance of communication before we make commitments." Joyce agreed and the problem was solved. They both went away feeling good about the decision.

When both of us walk away as winners, we know that the negotiation has been successful. When one of us is walking away with resentment, it is a sign that we need further negotiation. Our objective should always be to reach an agreement that makes both of us winners.

Notice that I entitled this chapter "Seek to Negotiate." I would be less than honest if I did not admit that there are some in-laws who will not negotiate. These people have rigid personalities. If you do not agree with them, then you have a problem.

However, even with these individuals, I would still encourage you to seek to negotiate. Make a proposal. Who knows? Maybe they will agree with your proposal. And if so, the problem is solved. On the other hand, perhaps they will be unwilling to budge.

If you can accept their position, fine. If not, you have to make a decision. Will you simply withdraw and acknowledge that the relationship is fractured? Or will you accept something with which you disagree in order to keep the peace? You will have to decide whether or not the issue is big enough to fracture the relationship. Some things we can live with even though we don't like them. Other things are too major for us to accept. Not all in-law relationships can be healed, but it is always worth the effort to seek negotiation.

• • •

Putting the Principles into Practice

1. Is there an in-law to whom you need to make a proposal? If so, why not break the silence and share your proposal? Take the first step in negotiation.
2. Has an in-law made a proposal to you? Can you accept it, or do you need to make a counterproposal?
3. Are you willing to listen to the ideas of your in-laws, or do you have the attitude "It's my way or no way at all"?
4. To negotiate is to discuss an issue in order to reach an agreement. Ask God to help you learn the art of negotiation.

5

MAKE REQUESTS, NOT DEMANDS

In the last few years, we have been hearing more and more about "grandparents' rights." I remember one grandmother who said to me, "Our daughter will not let us see our grandchildren. We are thinking about suing her. It's just not right that they would keep the grandchildren away from us."

"What reasons do they give?" I inquired.

"They say it's because we keep beer and liquor in the house. My husband, George, is an alcoholic, and they say they don't want their children to grow up to be alcoholics. But that's absurd. George has been an alcoholic for twenty years. I don't drink alcohol at all, and I've lived with him all these years. Being around an alcoholic does not make one an alcoholic."

"How long have they been keeping the children away from you?" I asked.

"Since last Christmas," she said. "About nine months now."

"Did something happen last Christmas that influenced their decision?" I asked.

"Well, one evening, George had too much to drink. He was in a jovial mood. He poured a little beer in glasses and told the children, 'Let's make a toast to Santa Claus.' The kids went along with him, drank the beer, and then started gagging. My daughter and son-in-law rushed into the kitchen to find out what was going on. When they realized what he had done, they immediately took the children home and told us they would never return again. My husband cursed them as they left the house and told them how stupid they were. I know that what George did was wrong, but what they are doing is also wrong. Grandparents have rights too. I have told them that I would personally take all the alcohol out of the house and store it in the garage and would promise them that my husband would not drink while they were here. But that's not enough for them. I don't know what else to do; that's why I'm thinking about suing them."

"You could do that," I said, "but what if you win the suit and your daughter and son-in-law are forced to let you see the children under supervised conditions? How satisfactory would that be?"

"I know what you're saying," she said. "That's not really what I want. I just want to have a good relationship with my daughter, our son-in-law, and our grandchildren. And I don't know what to do."

"How severe is your husband's drinking problem?" I asked.

"He has been in and out of treatment programs for twenty years," she said. "He'll do fine for a while, but once he falls off the wagon, he may go on a drinking binge for a month. He's had a hard time keeping jobs. It's been really hard to live with him, but I love him and keep hoping that things will get better. I know he feels bad about not seeing the grandchildren too. We've talked about it."

As a counselor, I was deeply moved by the pain I saw in her face. I said, "Sometimes when alcoholics realize they are losing something really valuable to them, they are highly motivated to stop drinking. Do you think George would be willing to talk with me about it?"

"He might, if he thought it would help the situation," she said.

"Then tell him that I would very much like to see him, that I have some ideas I think may be helpful."

Over the next few weeks, I was able to get her husband enrolled in a Christian treatment program. I assured him that God would give him the power to conquer alcohol and that I believed this was a major step in restoring a relationship with his daughter, son-in-law, and grand-children. After the initial treatment program and while he was actively involved in a Christian support group, I began to talk with George about the power of apologizing to his daughter and son-in-law for his behavior last Christmas.

I told him apologies are only meaningful when they are sincere expressions of regret over our behavior. "An apology is accepting respon-sibility for your behavior, acknowledging that it was wrong, and request-ing forgiveness. An apology is not a demand for forgiveness," I said. "It is a request for forgiveness. Your daughter and son-in-law may not be ready to forgive you, but your request will be the first step."

Together we crafted a carefully worded apology with which he felt comfortable. I asked if he would give me permission to call his daugh-ter and son-in-law and invite them to my office so we could talk with them together about what was going on in his life. He agreed, and they accepted my invitation.

In that meeting, I shared with the young couple my involvement with the wife's father in trying to help him deal with his alcohol prob-lem. I told them that I knew he had tried to quit drinking many times through the years but I believed that this time he had truly put his trust in God and he was going to be successful. Then I gave George an opportunity to talk.

I listened as he not only shared the apology we had written but, with tears, poured out his heart. He apologized for his past failures to his daughter when she was growing up, acknowledging that he knew that he had embarrassed her many times while she was in high school, that he had failed to be the father she deserved, and that he knew that what he had done last Christmas was the most painful thing he had ever done to her. He told her how many times he had relived that scene in his mind and how bad he felt about it.

"I know I don't deserve forgiveness," he said, "but I'm asking for it. I'm not asking you to let me see the children, though I would very much like to apologize to them. I'm looking forward to my first sober Christmas in twenty years. I know that you may not be there, though I wish you would be. I would like an opportunity to make the future different. And I would like to be the kind of father that you can trust. I love you very much, and I am so sorry for what I've done to hurt you."

His daughter showed no signs of emotion. I assumed that she had heard apologies in the past but had never seen changed behavior. My guess was she questioned whether this was sincere and whether things would be different in the future.

Eventually, she said to him, "Dad, I want to forgive you. But it may take some time. I've been hurt so badly. I want to believe that what you are saying is true, and I guess the next few months will show me. I hope you understand that as much as I want to forgive you, it will take me a little time."

"I understand," her father said. "I appreciate your meeting with us today because I so much wanted to apologize to you."

The conversation ended. I offered my services to the young couple if they should ever want to talk with me further. And I told George that I would see him next week.

I never saw the young couple again, but George and his wife informed me that within a month their daughter had given her father an opportunity to apologize to the children and that the children had freely expressed forgiveness to him. After seeing the children's response, the daughter also expressed forgiveness to George. When Christmas rolled around, the daughter had given no indication that they would bring the children. But a week before Christmas, the children asked her if they could go see their grandparents at Christmas, and the mother agreed.

At first, it was a little strained since the children had not been in their grandparents' home for a year. But before the evening was over, laughter again filled the house.

As the children were leaving, George said, "I just want to thank everybody for being here. This has been the best Christmas of my life. It's been a hard year for all of us, but it has been a year of tremendous change in my life. I want to be the kind of grandfather you children deserve. And I hope you will pray for me every day because I pray for you."

When George and his wife shared the Christmas story with me,

I knew that evening marked the beginning of a new quality of relationship. And the timing reminded me that the healing of relationships is what Christmas is all about.

I share this story because it illustrates that positive in-law relationships are not built upon demands, but upon requests. Had the grandparents tried to demand their "rights" by legally forcing their daughter and son-in-law to let them see the grandchildren, it would likely have led to a lifetime of estrangement. But because they were willing to humble themselves, acknowledge their part in the broken relationship, follow the road of genuine change, honestly deal with the problem, and then request forgiveness, they found the healing desired. Good in-law relationships cannot be built on the principle of demanding our rights. The Scriptures say, "[Love] does not demand its own way."[1]

This principle is illustrated in the life of Jesus. On one occasion, after Jesus had been teaching some rather difficult things, the Scriptures tell us, "At this point many of his disciples turned away and deserted him. Then Jesus turned to the Twelve and asked, 'Are you also going to leave?' Simon Peter replied, 'Lord, to whom would we go? You have the words that give eternal life. We believe, and we know you are the Holy One of God.'"[2]

Clearly Jesus was not demanding that the twelve disciples continue to walk with him. He had invited them in the beginning to follow him. Now on this occasion, he gave them the freedom to walk away. In fact, we know that one of the twelve did eventually walk away. But at this time, Peter spoke for the others when he said, "You have the words that give eternal life." They followed Jesus because they were convinced that he was "the Holy One of God."

In-law relationships must follow this model. We cannot force our in-laws to do what we believe to be "the right thing." We can and should make requests of them. If we have desires, these desires should be verbalized. If you wish your in-laws would visit more often, invite them to come more often. If you wish that they would come less often, then request that they come only on those occasions when you have time to spend with them. We must never expect our in-laws to read our minds. Making requests is a part of any good relationship.

Jesus taught that this principle of "making requests" applies also in our relationship with God. He said, "Keep on asking, and you will receive what you ask for . . . for everyone who asks, receives." Then he moved to the human plane. "You parents—if your children ask for a loaf of bread, do you give them a stone instead? Or if they ask for a fish, do you give them a snake? Of course not! So if you sinful people know how to give good gifts to your children, how much more will your heavenly Father give good gifts to those who ask him."[3]

Does this mean that God always gives us exactly what we ask? The obvious answer is *no*. He loves us too much to give us things that he knows will be detrimental to our well-being. But as our heavenly Father, he freely gives us good gifts in response to our requests.

Will your in-laws always respond to your request in exactly the way you desire? Probably not. Nor will their response always be based on love. All of us have a tendency to be self-centered. Many times we respond to others' requests in a very selfish way. However, making requests of in-laws is an important part of building positive relationships.

Ben, who was a novice fisherman, asked his father-in-law if he could borrow certain fishing gear. His father-in-law replied, "I can't let you borrow that one, but I'd be happy to loan you this one." Ben didn't know the difference between the two; his father-in-law did, and he didn't want to run the risk of losing a $600 piece of gear to an inexperienced fisherman.

Had Ben become angry with his father-in-law because he would not loan exactly what he had requested, their relationship would have been fractured. Instead, he gladly accepted his father-in-law's offer and had a good day fishing. People are responsible for their possessions. They choose to lend or not to lend, to give or not to give. The wise in-law will not get upset when a particular request is denied but will be grateful when a request is granted or a substitute offer is made.

It is often in making requests that in-law relationships are strengthened. Brittany asked her mother-in-law, Margie, if she would teach her to knit. Margie's response was, "I can't imagine that a girl of your generation would like to learn to knit. But if you would, then I would be happy to teach you."

Brittany assured her that she was sincere. Over the next several months, not only did Brittany learn to knit, but she and her mother-in-law developed a close relationship as a unique skill was passed from one generation to the next. When they took tea breaks, Brittany learned much about her mother-in-law, including the fact that it was Margie's own mother-in-law who had taught *her* to knit. Without knowing it, Brittany was continuing a family tradition.

In time Margie, who was a gregarious, always-happy kind of person, shared with Brittany some of her health struggles through the years. Later, when Margie was diagnosed with breast cancer, it was Brittany with whom she shared the news first. And it was Brittany who was her greatest emotional support through the months of chemotherapy and recovery. And it all began with a request: "Would you teach me how to knit?"

The Scriptures say, "It is more blessed to give than to receive."[4] When you make a request of your in-laws, you are giving them an opportunity. In responding to your request, they find greater happiness than you find in receiving what you have requested.

Requesting and giving are a part of the normal cycle of good relationships. From time to time all of us need or desire certain things that another has the capacity to fulfill. If we share these desires in the form of a request and the other person chooses to respond positively, we are forging a relationship that will be strong through the years. Conversely, when we make demands upon our in-laws, telling them what they should do and making them feel guilty when they don't do what we are demanding, we destroy a relationship. Good relationships are fostered by requesting and giving, not by demanding.

●   ●   ●

Putting the Principles into Practice
1. What demands have your in-laws made of you? How did you respond?
2. What demands have you made of your in-laws? How did they respond?

3. What requests would you like to make of your in-laws? Consider making your request after expressing appreciation to your in-laws for something you admire about them.
4. What requests have your in-laws made of you? Consider responding with love to a request your in-laws have made.

6

GRANT THE GIFT OF FREEDOM

THE GREATEST GIFT THAT PARENTS CAN GIVE their married children is the gift of freedom. In the introduction to "In-Law Relationships," beginning on page 273, we talked about the biblical challenge for young couples to leave parents and establish a new family unit (see Genesis 2:24). Parents can make this easy or difficult. They can give the couple the freedom to leave, or they can continue to interject themselves into the young couple's lives and make independence extremely difficult.

Two types of individuals will have difficulty granting the gift of freedom. First are the people with a controlling personality. These are the people who think clearly, reach conclusions quickly, and assume that their ideas are always right. They are typically well-meaning people, but they are overbearing, imposing their will on anyone who will allow it. They do not see themselves as controllers. They often genuinely feel that they are looking out for the best interest of the other person. This personality type will have great difficulty releasing their children to marriage. Their tendency will be to continue to impose their ideas on their married children and the son-in-law or daughter-in-law.

There is a second type of individual who will have trouble letting go. These are the people whose self-worth is tied up in the success of their children. They have done everything in their power to help their children succeed. They have put them in the best schools, provided for every financial need, and given loads of verbal encouragement. With every educational or vocational accomplishment of the child, the mother and father feel better about themselves. This pattern will not likely change when the child gets married. They will continue to reach out, doing everything they can to help the young couple succeed. The problem is that their "help" often comes across as "intrusion" and makes it more difficult for the young couple to establish their identity. Parental efforts to help often create arguments in the marriage and, thus, are detrimental to marital unity.

Kelly and Andy were in my office expressing frustration with Kelly's mother. Andy said, "She totally decorated our apartment. She chose the colors, she chose the fabrics, and she did everything. I feel like I'm living in someone else's house. It's nice, but it's not us. I would rather have no window treatments and wait until we can afford them. She felt like we needed to have everything now. I don't like her controlling our lives."

I looked at Kelly and asked, "How do you feel about all of this?"

"I really feel that it is my mother's way of showing us that she loves us. I don't think she wants to create a problem for us. I like the way she decorated our apartment. I would like to simply accept it as a gift, but Andy doesn't see it that way. That's why we're here. We feel like this is tearing us apart. If my mother knew that we were arguing about what she had done for us, she would be devastated."

I share this story because this illustrates several principles about controlling personalities. First, controllers seldom see themselves as controllers. They see themselves simply doing what is good or right. They have great difficulty understanding how others see them as controllers. Second, a controller typically marries someone with a compliant personality. If he or she had married a person with a controlling personality, life would be one huge battlefield. The compliant person is willing to accept most of what the controller does, although eventually it often becomes a source of irritation in the marriage.

My guess was that Andy himself had a controlling personality. He

wanted to be in charge of determining how their apartment was decorated, and he wanted to pay for it. He saw this as his responsibility, and
he wanted the freedom to do it. He found his mother-in-law's actions
as an intrusion into their marriage.

Kelly, on the other hand, had a compliant personality. Through the
years, she had learned to accept her mother's acts of control as gifts
of love, which indeed they were. She had no need to be a part of the
decision-making process; she was perfectly happy letting her mother
make decisions for her. In fact, this made her life easier. It worked fine
when she lived with only one controller—her mother. However, now she
is married to another controller. Life becomes extremely difficult when
two people are trying to tell you what to do.

To the mothers-in-law and fathers-in-law who are reading this,
I urge you to learn the art of backing off. Your married children deserve
the freedom to make their own decisions. I know that your efforts to
help them are done in good faith. You are genuinely expressing love and
trying to help them have a better life.

However, your good intentions may be making life difficult for your
sons or daughters. They may be willing to receive your help, as they have
done through the years. However, their spouses may be unwilling, not
because they are contrary but simply because they are human and have
their own personality. People with similar personalities seldom marry
each other. It is highly unlikely that a compliant child will marry a
compliant spouse.

So what are in-laws to do when they genuinely want to help their
married children? You share your idea and ask if they would find this
helpful. (Make a request, not a demand.) Assure them that if they do not
see it as helpful, you will certainly understand. Then give them time to
discuss the issue and get back with you with their answer. If they accept
your offer, you may proceed. If not, you must put your idea aside, granting them the gift of freedom.

The gift of freedom is a far more valuable gift than the gift of deco-
rating an apartment. If you do not allow the couple the freedom to make
their own decisions, insisting on doing things for them that you think
will be helpful, you are in the process of creating resentment in the heart

of your daughter-in-law or son-in-law. And you are stimulating unnecessary arguments between your child and his/her spouse.

Here are some additional ideas for mothers-in-law and fathers-in-law who sincerely desire to help their married children:

Don't Make the Couple Dependent on You

Marriage is about independence, not dependence. For the first twenty or so years of life, your children were dependent on you. Through high school and perhaps college and graduate school, you made it possible for them to reach their educational objectives. However, with marriage comes a paradigm shift. No longer is an adult, married child to be dependent upon you. The couple are to establish their own place in the world, learn to work together as a team to meet their own needs. You must encourage this independence, not lessen it.

Let me give you a negative and a positive example. Bill and Alice were a fairly successful middle-class couple. They made sure that their son Ken got a college education. When Ken got married shortly after college, they realized that his entry-level job would not allow him to buy a house anytime soon. They adamantly objected to the concept of renting. They saw it as throwing money away. Therefore, they offered to make a down payment on a house and to give Ken and his new bride $500 a month toward their monthly mortgage payment. They were fully capable of doing this, and Ken and April were happy to receive it. They were thrilled to be in a house when most of their friends were living in apartments.

However, five years later, Bill died suddenly from a massive heart attack. It rocked the world of both families. When everything was settled, Alice had enough income to meet her own needs, but not enough to continue the $500 a month supplement to Ken and April.

Within two months, Ken and April were in a financial crisis. Ken's salary alone did not meet their monthly obligations. By this time, they had two small children. April really did not want to work outside the home, and Ken agreed. But they were faced with the choice of moving out of their house to something smaller or of April taking on at least a part-time job. April did in fact get a job but had a growing resentment toward Ken that she had to leave the children with a babysitter.

In retrospect, everyone realized that Bill and Alice—while sincerely trying to be helpful—had in fact created a major problem for Ken and his family. Ken and April said to me, "We wish we had started in an apartment like our friends and lived with less. I think we both would have been happier, and certainly we would not be under the stress we are now experiencing."

On the positive side, Sam and Audrey are examples of parents who discovered a way to give without making their children dependent upon their gifts. Their daughter Julie got married to Mike at the end of her junior year of college. Mike was also a rising senior. Sam and Audrey agreed to pay for Julie's final year in college, and Mike's parents did the same. After graduation, Mike started his own business, and Julie took an entry-level job with a local bank.

Mike knew he would not make much money in the first few years of his business, but they were both willing to sacrifice while Mike was getting the business off the ground. They lived in a very small apartment in a less than desirable neighborhood. They drove the old cars their parents had given them when they entered college. They bought furniture from Goodwill and lived very meagerly.

Whenever Sam and Audrey would visit with Mike and Julie, they would go home and talk about their desire to get them out of that apartment and into a respectable neighborhood. They knew that financially they had the ability to do it. On one occasion, they broached the idea with Mike and Julie and found both of them resistant to the idea of their help. Julie said, "Mother, we want to have a story to tell like you and Daddy. Remember the first place you lived after you were married? I have always admired you and your willingness to sacrifice while Dad was in the military and later when he came home to get his own business started. We know you love us and want to help us, but we would rather do it ourselves."

Audrey and Sam took Julie seriously and expressed their admiration and appreciation for her spirit. Never again did they bring up the subject. They gave the gift of freedom, and they have not regretted their choice. Today Mike's business is flourishing, and he and Julie have a nice house and a story to tell their children.

Please do not think I'm saying that you should never give gifts to your married children or help them financially. What I am saying is don't give your gift in such a way that it makes your adult children dependent on you to maintain their lifestyle. If their refrigerator goes out and you want to buy them a refrigerator, then ask if they would find this helpful and would appreciate your doing it. If they agree, then buy the refrigerator. It would be a onetime gift that meets an unexpected need and will be seen as an act of love. Your children will accept it with deep appreciation. On the other hand, I would not encourage you to agree to make the monthly loan payments if they buy a new car. Such payments normally last for a minimum of three years, and for those three years, they would be financially dependent upon your monthly help. This does not establish a pattern of independence.

Don't Give Gifts That Aren't Desired

Alan and Betsy were boat enthusiasts. When they were a young couple, they bought their first boat. Throughout the lives of their children, they had enjoyed going to the lake almost every Saturday. When their daughter Angie married Rod, they expected that Rod and Angie would regularly meet them at the lake as they had often done when they were dating. However, after marriage, Rod got a job that required him to work most Saturdays. Angie became involved in an inner-city ministry with her church. So their pattern of joining her family at the lake was broken. Her parents missed this "family time" greatly and prayed for the day that Rod would get a different job.

After about a year, Rod did in fact get a new job that did not require Saturday work. Within a week, Alan and Betsy bought a boat for Rod and Angie, invited them to the lake, and revealed their surprise gift. Rod and Angie acted excited, but when they returned home, they both agreed that the last thing they ever wanted was a boat. Rod did not enjoy water sports, and Julie had developed a sincere interest in the ministry in which she was involved on Saturdays. Neither of them wanted to spend Sundays at the lake; they much preferred to be active in their church.

When Rod and Angie's boat stayed in storage weekend after weekend, Alan and Betsy realized that they had made a mistake. They thought that the boat would lure Rod and Angie to the lake and that they could have family times like they had before. But that was not happening.

Now they faced a parental choice. They could resent Rod and Angie for not being grateful for their gift and spending time with them at the lake. Or, they could admit that buying the boat without talking with Rod and Angie about it was a mistake and perhaps even an effort to manipulate them to come to the lake. They chose to accept responsibility for their well-intended but unwise choice in buying the boat. Other than the boat issue, Alan and Betsy had a good relationship with Rod and Angie. They often had dinner together, during which the relationship was always cordial and positive.

Alan and Betsy wanted to keep this positive relationship, so they discussed a strategy to handle the boat. They agreed that if Rod and Angie were willing, they would sell the boat and give the money to Angie to use in her inner-city ministry. When they shared their idea with Rod and Angie, the young couple were elated.

Angie said, "Dad, I didn't want to tell you that we really didn't want the boat. I knew that it would hurt your feelings because I knew you bought it because you love us. But really, neither one of us is into boating. I enjoyed it as a child, but I am in a different stage of life now. I love what I'm doing on Saturdays with the kids. I can't tell you how proud I am of you for expressing this interest in what I'm doing. There are so many things that need to be done, and now, with this money, we will be able to do them. I love you so much and I appreciate your understanding." Rod affirmed Angie's comments, and the boat issue was settled.

Often our ideas of an appropriate gift will not seem appropriate to our adult children. Therefore, don't waste money on gifts that they will not appreciate. Ask before you give.

Affirm the Interests of Your Married Children

Throughout life, all of us develop interests in various pursuits. These may include educational, vocational, recreational, religious, or social interests. We all invest our time and energy in one way or another throughout life. When the children were little, we helped them explore their interests. If they wanted to play the piano, we gave them piano lessons. If they wanted to play football, we encouraged that. Why should this not continue in adulthood?

If your daughter-in-law has an interest in snow skiing, then take time to listen to her tumbles and her expressions of exhilaration. If you are looking for a gift, you might ask if there is anything in the sport that she would like to have. I suggest that you let her pick it out. Then it will be exactly what she wants and she will be appreciative.

If your son-in-law is interested in auto racing, I would encourage you not to make sarcastic comments about the stupidity of spending all day Sunday watching cars go in circles. That may be your honest opinion, but you don't build positive in-law relationships by making negative comments about someone's particular interest. If he is interested in football, I would encourage you to learn enough about football so that you can carry on an intelligent conversation with him about his area of interest. Your interest may not be in football, but I hope you have an interest in building a positive relationship with your son-in-law. Relationships are built by affirming the interests of other people.

I remember the father who said to me, "My daughter married a man from Tennessee. He is a hunter. To be honest, I had never been hunting in my whole life and had no interest in it. However, when he invited me to go deer hunting and promised me he would be sure that I wouldn't freeze to death, I accepted his invitation. It was one of the most relaxing experiences I have ever had. Sitting on the deer stand and listening to the noises of nature brought on a calmness that I had not experienced in years. Now I go with him every hunting season. I continue to have no interest in killing a deer, but I really enjoy my experience with nature. And my son-in-law and I have a great relationship. Who knows, maybe some year one of us will actually see a deer!"

It is in the exploring of other people's interests that we often expand our own world while at the same time building friendships that last a lifetime. When you express interest in that which interests others, you are giving them the freedom to be who they are. And you are choosing to enter into their world. This is the process of building friendships.

If I were to choose one word to describe the foundation upon which this nation was established, I would choose the word *freedom*. And if I were to choose one word to identify the key to unlocking positive in-law relationships, I would choose the same word. Granting young couples the gift of freedom is the most fundamental choice you can make in becoming a good mother-in-law or father-in-law.

● ● ●

Putting the Principles into Practice
Guidelines for parents:
1. Don't make your married children financially dependent upon you.
2. Don't give gifts they do not desire. Ask, "Would this be helpful?"
3. Affirm their interests by asking questions and offering encouragement.

Guidelines for young marrieds:
1. If you feel like your parents are trying to control your decisions, thank them for their interest but request that they give you freedom to make your own decisions.
2. Don't accept help that will make you financially dependent on your parents.
3. Don't presume upon your parents' freedom by expecting them to be automatic babysitters. Ask in advance if they would be free to care for the children.

7

ABOVE ALL, LOVE

THE ULTIMATE KEY THAT UNLOCKS THE DOOR to becoming friends with your in-laws is an attitude of love. By nature, we are all egocentric: We think the world revolves around us. The positive side of self-centeredness is that we take care of our needs—we protect and nurture ourselves. However, once our basic needs are met, we must learn to reach out to help others. This is the attitude of love.

The happiest people in the world are altruistic givers, not self-centered hoarders. Jesus said, "It is more blessed to give than to receive."[1] If you apply this reality to your in-laws, you will seek to enhance their lives. "What can I do to help you?" is always an appropriate question. Their answer will teach you how to express love in a way that is meaningful to your in-laws.

One mother-in-law asked this question of her daughter-in-law and received this response: "If you could teach me to cook green beans the way you cook them, I think it would greatly improve my marriage." She did, and it did!

It was asking the question "What can I do to help you?" that stimulated the daughter-in-law's memory of her husband's comments on how much he liked his mother's green beans. Since her mother-in-law was offering to help, she could make her request without embarrassment. If you want to help your in-laws, it is always better to find out what they would consider helpful rather than using your own judgment. The latter may be seen as imposition, whereas the former will be seen as an act of love.

Imagine what would happen in your in-law relationships if you began asking, "What can I do to help you?" You may find that other family members will follow your model. When families learn to love each other and express it in meaningful ways, the emotional climate is enhanced.

One young woman raised this question: "But what if my in-laws mistreat me? How can I love them when I resent them?" It is interesting that Jesus instructed us to love even our enemies,[2] and unfortunately, sometimes our in-laws qualify as enemies. When we are filled with hurt, disappointment, anger, or resentment, it is difficult to express love. But difficult is not impossible. With God's help, we can love even our enemies.

The process involves admitting your feelings but not serving your feelings. You admit them to yourself, to God, and perhaps to your spouse. But you refuse to serve negative feelings. To God, you are saying, "Lord, you know how I feel about my in-laws. You know what they've done, and you know how hurt I am. But I know it is your will for me to love them. So, I'm asking that you pour your love into my heart and let me be your channel of expressing love." God will give you the ability to ask your in-laws, "What can I do to help you?" Then in response to their answer, you can express love in a meaningful way.

Remember, love is not a feeling. Love is an attitude, a way of thinking, and a way of behaving. Love is the attitude that says, "I choose to look out for your interests. How may I help you?" A loving attitude leads to loving behavior.

The reality is that love tends to stimulate love. In fact, the Scriptures say that we love God because he first loved us.[3] It is his love that stimulates love in us. The same principle is true in human relationships. When I reach out to express love to my in-laws, something happens inside of them and they are likely to reciprocate. And when they reach out and express interest in my well-being, my emotions toward them begin to change.

Kevin is a good example of this principle. He shared his story with me while attending one of my marriage seminars. It seems that Kevin's father-in-law was not at all happy when Kevin married his daughter. Kevin was a plumber; his father-in-law was an attorney and had hoped that his daughter would marry an attorney or a physician. His father-in-law managed to be civil during the wedding festivities. But Kevin knew in his heart that his father-in-law was not happy.

About six months after the wedding, Kevin's father-in-law woke up one morning to find his front yard flooded with water from a leaking pipe. His wife encouraged him to call Kevin, so he did. "When I got there," Kevin said, "his yard looked like a rice paddy. There was water everywhere. I knew that somewhere in the line from the street to the house, there was a major leak. I turned the water off at the street and called my wife, Janet. I had promised to go shopping with her that morning, and I wanted her to know the situation. She assured me that she would rather I fix the leak for her parents. She invited the three of us to come to our house for a quick breakfast. 'Good,' I said. 'That will give time for some of this water to subside.' After breakfast, I went back and spent the next four hours locating and fixing the leak. When my father-in-law insisted on paying me for my work, I refused. I told him, 'That's what family is all about.' He was deeply appreciative."

At that point, Janet broke into the conversation and said, "Since that day, my father has never complained about Kevin. In fact, he recommends him to all his friends. 'He's the best plumber in town,' he says. 'You can't go wrong with Kevin.' I think my father finally realized that in today's world, plumbers are fully as important as attorneys and physicians. In fact, sometimes you can't live without them. As I see it, character is always more important than vocation. I think my dad would agree."

Kevin's act of love using the skills he possessed to help his in-laws stimulated a positive emotional response. Since that day, their relationship has continued to grow. Genuine love is seldom rejected, but someone must take the initiative to love.

In making love practical, two words stand out in my mind: *kindness* and *patience*. In the great "love chapter" in the New Testament, we read that love is kind and love is patient.[4]

Love Is Kind

Let me reflect first on kindness, which has to do with the manner in which we speak to people and the way we treat them. One of the ancient Hebrew proverbs says, "A gentle answer turns away wrath, but a harsh word stirs up anger."[5]

We make in-law relationships better or worse depending on how we speak to our in-laws. Loud, harsh words make things worse. Gentle, soft words make things better. When you express your anger at your in-laws by screaming at them, you are not loving them. Love is kind. When you listen empathetically and then share your thoughts in a calm and soft voice, you are expressing love even though you may be disagreeing with them. In speaking to them kindly, you are showing respect for them.

If in the past you have been quick to lose your temper and lash out with harsh, loud words to your in-laws, I urge you to apologize. You have created emotional barriers that will not be removed simply with the passing of time. Apologizing is the first step in changing your pattern of speech from harshness to kindness. In your future conversations, begin to monitor and change your pattern of speech. When you sense that you are getting angry, take a "time-out" to cool off. Then come back and, with conscious effort, speak softly to the person with whom you are angry, perhaps speaking as softly as a whisper. In the early stages of changing negative speech patterns, we must often exaggerate the change. When you learn to speak softly, you have taken the first step in learning to speak kindly.

Once you learn to speak softly, you are free to focus on affirming the intentions of your in-laws, even if you disagree with their ideas. "I can see how you would feel that way, and if I were in your shoes, I would probably feel the same. However, let me share what I was thinking and see if it makes sense to you." With such statements, you are applying the principles for deepening in-law relationships we have talked about in this part of the book. You are, in fact, learning to express love with kind speech.

Kindness is also expressed in the way we treat people. Kevin did a kind thing when he repaired his father-in-law's water leak without charge. Random acts of kindness enhance in-law relationships. However, kindness goes beyond simply performing acts of kindness. It also seeks to treat in-laws with courtesy.

Families have different ideas about what is considered common courtesy. Some families think it is discourteous to wear a ball cap inside the house. Some families think it is courteous to stand when a female enters the room. Some families believe that a man should always open a door for a woman. Then there are table manners. Some families believe it is discourteous to talk with food in your mouth and that courtesy requires the husband to seat his wife first before seating himself. Courtesy may be putting your napkin on your lap and saying "Would you please pass the potatoes?" Every family has its own set of "common courtesies." Becoming aware of these common courtesies and practicing them when you are with your in-laws enhances relationships.

Your spouse is the best source of discovering and understanding the common courtesies of his/her family. Take time to discover what your in-laws consider to be courteous behavior. Write them down as a way of reminding yourself, and seek to practice these courtesies. You will be taking positive steps toward becoming friends with your in-laws.

Love Is Patient
The second key in loving in-laws is patience. You've heard the cliché "Rome was not built in a day." This is true in relationships, as well. Patience must become a way of life. We cannot expect all our differences to be resolved overnight or with one conversation. It takes time and diligence to understand another's point of view and to negotiate answers to our differences. It is both a lifelong process and the heart and soul of relationships. We cannot build positive relationships without being diligent in the process of communicating thoughts and feelings, seeking understanding, affirming each other, and finding workable solutions.

Don't expect perfection of yourself or your in-laws. On the other hand, don't settle for anything less than a loving relationship. We must make room for momentary relapses. None of us change quickly and

346 || GARY CHAPMAN

we often revert to old patterns. Failures call for apologies, and apologies call for forgiveness. When we are willing to admit our failures and request forgiveness, it will likely be extended, and our relationships can continue on a positive track. Love is the greatest force in the world for good. Kindness and patience are two of the most important aspects of love. Learn to develop these traits and you will learn how to become friends with your in-laws.

• • •

Putting the Principles into Practice
1. Look for an opportunity to ask an in-law, "What can I do to help you?"
2. Can you remember a time when you spoke unkindly to an in-law? Have you apologized? If not, why not?
3. What acts of kindness have you done for your in-laws in the past month? What could you plan to do this month?
4. What "common courtesies" do you need to extend in order to enhance in-law relationships?

• • •

Closing Thoughts on In-Law Relationships
Positive in-law relationships are one of life's greatest assets. Living in harmony, encouraging and supporting each other in our individual pursuits, helps all of us reach our potential for God and good in the world. On the other hand, troublesome in-law relationships can be a source of deep emotional pain. When in-laws resent each other, hurt each other, or withdraw from each other, they have joined the ranks of dysfunctional families.

The seven principles I have shared with you in part six have helped hundreds of couples develop positive in-law relationships. I hope that you will not be satisfied simply to have read this part of the book. My deep desire is that you will earnestly seek to weave these principles into the fabric of your daily life. It will take time and effort, but the rewards will last for a lifetime.

Enhancing relationships is indeed a worthy endeavor. When you enhance in-law relationships, you are making life more pleasant for your children and your grandchildren. It is my sincere desire that this book will help you learn to listen, show respect, make requests, grant freedom, speak for yourself, seek to negotiate, and above all—love your in-laws. If you practice these principles, I can guarantee that your in-law relationships will be strengthened. You may even genuinely become friends with your in-laws.

If you find these principles helpful, I hope you will share them with your friends. They, too, are likely struggling with in-law relationships. I believe the principles shared in this book could help thousands of couples develop positive in-law relationships. If this happens, I will be greatly pleased. If you have stories to share with me, I invite you to click on the Contact link at www.garychapman.org.

Some Ideas Worth Remembering

- The purpose of listening is to discover what is going on inside the minds and emotions of other people. If we understand why people do what they do, we can have more appropriate responses.
- Relationships are built by seeking understanding. They are destroyed by interruptions and arguments.
- Affirming statements do not mean that you necessarily agree with what your in-laws have said. It does mean that you listened long enough to see the world through their eyes and to understand that, in their minds, what they are doing makes good sense. You are affirming their humanity, the right to think and feel differently from other people.
- Respect leads me to give my in-laws the same freedom that God allows me and all humans—the freedom to be different. Therefore, I will not seek to impose my will upon my in-laws. Rather, when I find myself at odds with them, I will look for a solution that will show respect for our differences.
- Religious differences often become divisive in the marriage. They can also create barriers to wholesome in-law relationships.

- The invasion of privacy is a common area of conflict with in-laws. But when the younger couple show respect for their parents' and in-laws' intentions and openly share with them their own frustrations, most of the problems can be resolved.
- The mature person is always looking for wisdom, even if it is spoken by a mother-in-law. When parents and in-laws make suggestions, their ideas should be given due consideration. After all, they are older and perhaps wiser than we are.
- Learning to respect the peculiarities of our in-laws is necessary if we are to have harmonious in-law relationships. In fact, if we were to fight our in-laws over every issue that we consider to be weird, quirky, or wrong, we would spend the rest of our lives in battle.
- When we begin a sentence with *you*, we are speaking as though we have ultimate knowledge of the situation. In reality, we are giving only our perception. Such statements come across as condemning and will likely stimulate a defensive response from your in-laws.
- When you speak for yourself, you are making valid statements. You are revealing *your* thoughts, feelings, desires, and perceptions. "I think . . ." "I feel . . ." "I wish . . ." "My perception is . . ." All these statements are valid because they are revealing what is going on inside *you*. You are speaking for yourself.
- To negotiate is to discuss an issue in order to reach an agreement. Negotiation is the opposite of withdrawal and resentment. When we negotiate, we are choosing to believe that there is an answer, and with God's help, we will find it.
- We cannot force our in-laws to do what we believe to be "the right thing." We can and should make requests of them. If we have desires, these desires should be verbalized.
- The greatest gift that parents can give their married children is the gift of freedom.
- Love is not a feeling. Love is an attitude, a way of thinking, and a way of behaving. Love is the attitude that says, "I choose

to look out for your interests. How may I help you?" A loving attitude leads to loving behavior.

- We make in-law relationships better or worse depending on how we speak to our in-laws. Loud, harsh words make things worse. Gentle, soft words make things better.
- We cannot expect all our differences to be resolved overnight or with one conversation. It takes time and diligence to understand another's point of view and to negotiate answers to our differences. It is both a lifelong process and the heart and soul of relationships.

Additional Tools

Part One—Everybody Wins

A Resolution by Which Everybody Wins

WHEREAS: arguing creates an adversarial relationship; and

WHEREAS: resolving conflicts is absolutely essential if we are to work together as a team:

THEREFORE, BE IT RESOLVED: That we shall commit ourselves to seek win-win solutions to our conflicts

By learning to listen empathetically:

What is my spouse saying?

What is my spouse feeling?

By choosing to respect each other's ideas and feelings,

By seeking to understand why a particular issue or point of view is so important to my spouse, and

By finding solutions that leave both of us feeling loved and appreciated.

Ratified, this _____ day of _____, 2____.

_____
HUSBAND

_____
WIFE

Part Two—Home Improvements

How to Get Your Spouse to Change without Manipulation

A THREE-STEP PLAN

Step 1. Start by admitting your own past failures and request forgiveness.

Step 2. Discover your spouse's primary love language and speak it daily.

Step 3. When making a request for change,

a. Choose your setting (time, place, emotional climate):

Time—after a meal;
Place—in private; and
Emotional climate—when your spouse gives you
permission.

b. Don't give an overdose of criticism (never more than one request per week, or according to the schedule to which you and your spouse have agreed).

c. Give three compliments before you make your request.

d. When your spouse works to make a change, *notice* and *express appreciation.* Accept those things that your spouse cannot or will not change.

What I Wish My Wife Would Change

This is a collection of what husbands have said when asked the question, "What would you like to see your wife change?" Some of these are specific and others are too general to be helpful. They are presented here simply to stimulate your thinking as you make a list of the things you would like to request of your wife. (Remember: Limit your requests to one per week, or according to your agreement with your wife.)

I wish she would not snap at our children.

I wish she would share more of her dreams and fears with me.

I wish she would spend thirty minutes a day talking with me.

I wish she would keep the kitchen desk organized.

I wish she would not clean and fuss with the house when I'm home.

I wish she would develop more confidence in her appearance and be willing to wear "sexy" clothing.

I wish she would stop bringing up the past.

I wish she would stop trying to control my thoughts and activities by making demands.

I wish she would not worry so much.

I wish she would stop being my mother (e.g., reminding me to brush my teeth).

I wish she would look for positive things rather than focusing on the negative.

I wish she would answer my questions with an answer rather than another question.

I wish she would tell me that she admires me.

I wish she would tell me that she is attracted to me.

I wish she would wash and clean the truck every week.

I wish she would talk to me.

I wish she would clean up after herself.

I wish she would stop criticizing me in front of our children.

I wish she would start getting ready earlier so we could arrive at our destination on time.

I wish she would relax and enjoy life more (e.g., watch TV with me).

I wish she would initiate sexual intercourse when she is in the mood, because I'm almost always in the mood.

I wish she would put her clothes away instead of leaving them on the floor.

I wish she would stop being so critical.

I wish she would keep the car cleaner.

I wish she would start working out at the gym and get in shape.

I wish she would learn to go to sleep with the light on so I can read.

I wish she would become more aware of the health problems related to her weight.

I wish she would get rid of some junk.

I wish she would tend to the housekeeping on a more routine basis.

I wish she would help me teach our children the value of work.

I wish she would let me cook more often.

I wish she would quit being angry all the time and have more patience with me and other people.

I wish she had a higher sex drive.

I wish she would keep the animals under better control.

I wish she would stick to her goals, even though it may be uncomfortable.

I wish she would speak kindly to me and about others.

I wish she would allow me to express my opinion even if she disagrees with me.

I wish she would not question my decisions in areas that are not her expertise, such as buying new tires for the car.

I wish she would be more intimate in bed.

I wish she would praise my hard work and say other nice things every day.

I wish she would stop putting me down.

I wish she would not be so critical and condescending toward me and start giving me more affirmation.

I wish she would not drive herself so hard—work hours, business, church.

I wish she would stop interrupting me when we have a discussion.

I wish she would give me a big kiss each morning before I leave the house.

I wish she would learn to discuss difficult issues without becoming defensive and interpreting everything as personal criticism.

I wish she would give me a back rub three times a week.

I wish she would drink Starbucks.

I wish she would stay awake when I'm talking with her

I wish she were more comfortable leaving our children with babysitters so we could do some fun things together.

What I Wish My Husband Would Change

This is a collection of what wives have said when asked the question, "What would you like to see your husband change?" Some of these are specific and others are too general to be helpful. They are presented here simply to stimulate your thinking as you make a list of the things you would like to request of your husband. (Remember: Limit your requests to one per week, or according to your agreement with your husband.)

I wish he would sit down each evening and talk with me for ten minutes.

I wish he would clean the garage and keep it clean.

I wish he would take nightly walks with me.

I wish he would watch ESPN less.

I wish he would not go from 0 to 60 miles per hour in 2.4 seconds when he is angry.

I wish he would help me give the girls a bath.

I wish he would help me pick up and keep the house cleaner.

I wish he were able to accept some feedback from me. He is extremely sensitive to any comments that may be less than 100 percent positive.

I wish he would not fall asleep when I talk.

I wish he would stop smoking.

I wish he would plan date nights once or twice a month.

I wish he would give me his undivided attention (put down the paper, crossword puzzle, etc.) when I am trying to talk with him.

I wish he would not procrastinate. "I'll do it tomorrow" is his theme.

I wish he would express appreciation for me and what I do.

I wish he would play more with the children.

I wish he would stop piling papers on the table or clear it off regularly.

I wish he would be less critical of my housework.

I wish he would stop dropping stuff all over the house, starting when he walks in the front door, and leaving stuff where it is dropped.

I wish he would spend more time considering what is important to me.

I wish he would be more frugal with our money and work with me on developing a plan to repay our debts.

I wish he would start picking up the clutter in the house instead of telling me that we need to pick up the clutter in the house.

I wish he would have a ten-minute devotional time with me each day, reading the Bible and praying.

I wish he would ask me what he could do to help me out around the house.

I wish he would let me express my feelings without reacting in anger.

I wish he would speak more kindly to me.

I wish he would turn off the TV and talk with me for a few minutes.

I wish he would exercise with me and try to get in shape.

I wish he would take more pains in washing the windshield and windows in the car.

I wish he would stop "tooting" at the table.

I wish he would pick up his shoes in the bedroom and put them in the closet.

I wish he would talk with me about decisions before he makes them. I'd like to be a partner and work as a team.

I wish he would come to bed the same time I do so that we could talk and sometimes make love together.

I wish he would make an effort to speak proper English. He frequently uses wrong tenses, which makes him appear stupid. He is very intelligent.

I wish he would learn decent eating etiquette.

I wish he would give me some time to be alone. He is wonderful and helpful. I just need some time to be by myself.

I wish he would compliment what I do and how I look, and encourage me.

I wish he would put things away when he finishes a project.

I wish he would stop rescuing our daughters (ages 18 and 20). Let them experience the consequences of their choices.

I wish he would devote as much time, energy, love, and devotion to me as he does to his work and exercise program. I feel like I get what is left at the end of a busy day—and that's not much.

I wish he would put his arms around me and hold my hand when we walk.

I wish he would initiate more dates with me.

I wish he would mow the grass before the yard becomes unsightly.

I wish he would stop swearing when he gets angry.

I wish he would spend quality time with God, me, and our children.

I wish he would hug me and touch me, even when it doesn't lead to sex.

I wish he would take the responsibility for handling our personal finances.

I wish he would find some good friends or activities that would allow him some recreational time away from me occasionally. That would allow me to have some girlfriend time without feeling guilty.

I wish he would earn enough money so that I didn't have to work full time.

I wish he would look intently into my eyes and talk for longer than five minutes.

I wish he would defend me or stand up for me with his parents.

Part Four—Now What?

Traditional Wedding Vows

The Husband Speaking:

I, _____, take thee, _____, to be my wedded wife . . . to have and to hold from this day forward . . . for better, for worse, for richer, for poorer . . . in sickness and in health. To love and to cherish . . . so long as we both shall live, according to God's holy ordinance, and hereto I pledge thee my faithfulness.

The Wife Speaking:

I, _____, take thee, _____, to be my wedded husband . . . to have and to hold from this day forward . . . for better, for worse, for richer, for poorer . . . in sickness and in health. To love and to cherish . . . so long as we both shall live, according to God's holy ordinance, and hereto I pledge thee my faithfulness.

Part Five—Making Love

What Husbands Wish

What do you wish your wife would do—or stop doing—to make the sexual relationship better for you? Check ☑ the wishes you would like to share with her.

- ☐ I wish she would learn to enjoy sex rather than looking at it as an obligation.
- ☐ I wish we would communicate our sexual interests earlier in the day. If both of us are on the same page at bedtime, it can prevent disappointments and create a great time.
- ☐ I wish she would not talk about my weight.
- ☐ I wish she would wear sexy clothes and "light my fire."
- ☐ I wish my wife wanted to have sex more often. She is so busy.
- ☐ I wish she would join me in an exercise program.
- ☐ I wish she would watch more romantic movies with me.
- ☐ I wish we could spend more quality time together.
- ☐ I wish she would be open to oral sex.
- ☐ I wish my wife would initiate sex more often. It is measurably more enjoyable for me when she is more active in getting things started.
- ☐ I wish she would open up more and talk about this part of our marriage.
- ☐ I never remember when my wife's menstrual cycle is, and I don't seem to figure it out until my motor is already running. I'm asking for a subtle little reminder.
- ☐ I wish we had sex more often and that she wanted it as much as I do.
- ☐ I wish she would take more pride in her appearance. No sweat suits in bed.
- ☐ I wish my wife would stop acting like we have to make an appointment for sex and that she would be more spontaneous.

☐ I wish my wife would be more vocal while making love. Sound is important.

☐ I wish she would be patient and release me from my obligation when her drive for sex is stronger than mine.

☐ I wish she were open to date nights where we could just enjoy doing things together.

☐ I wish there were some variety in our sexual relationship and that we would have sex more often.

☐ I wish she had a traffic light above her head that would tell me when she's "ready to go." I don't like it when I try to initiate sex and I am rejected.

☐ I wish my wife could have sex without so much romance to get it started.

☐ I wish our work schedules could be coordinated. Because we work on different shifts, we have very little time together, thus very little sex.

☐ I wish we had sex more than once a year. I wish her mind was on me rather than on her mom and dad. Maybe when they die, we can have sex.

☐ I wish my wife saw sex more as a mutual experience. It seems more and more about meeting my needs rather than an exciting experience for us.

☐ I wish I didn't have to use condoms every time we have intercourse. I wish she would take birth-control pills.

☐ I wish she would allow herself to let go of past experiences and enjoy our sexual relationship.

☐ I wish she would not go to bed early so many nights. I wish we could have time to talk and cuddle.

☐ I wish we could make love in the mornings when we are both awake.

☐ I wish my wife would seek medical advice for a physical problem she has that makes it painful for her to have sex. I'm frustrated and don't know why she won't seek help.

☐ I wish the word *no* would disappear from her vocabulary.

☐ I wish she would kick the kids out of our bedroom. I'm wondering if she is just using them to avoid having sex.

☐ I wish that my wife would not bring up problems when we are trying to have sex. We can discuss problems at another time.

☐ Over the years her lingerie closet has become fuller but is opened less often. She is a beautiful woman, and I would enjoy seeing her open that closet more often.

☐ I wish she would not have projects every night that keep us busy but apart.

☐ I wish she would stay awake when we are making love. Her pleasure is just as important as mine, and it's not fun for me when I am making love with a corpse.

☐ I wish we could dedicate more time to our physical relationship. I wish she understood the importance of it. I miss the closeness.

☐ I wish she were more open to experimentation with new ideas, would let me know what she wants, and would listen to my desires. I don't want to force anything on her.

☐ I wish she would stop chitchatting during sex and just relax and enjoy it.

☐ I wish she would not expect so much of me in the way of romantic ideas. I'm willing and I try, but it never seems to be enough.

☐ I wish she would stop telling me that I don't act like I'm attracted to her. I *am* attracted to her. I don't know what else to do.

☐ I wish my wife would allow me to pleasure her sexually. She has a general attitude that sex is "nasty." I know she was sexually abused as a child, but she refuses to go for counseling.

☐ I wish she were more comfortable with her body so we could leave the lights on when we make love. I enjoy seeing her body.

☐ I wish she would make suggestions to me about what makes the sexual experience more pleasurable for her.

What Wives Wish

What do you wish your husband would do—or stop doing—to make the sexual relationship better for you? Check ☑ the wishes you would like to share with him.

- ☐ I wish he would work with me a little more to find out what feels good for me.
- ☐ I wish he would take better care of his body so that I would be more physically attracted to him.
- ☐ I wish that he would stop coming on to me constantly so I could make the first move once in a while.
- ☐ I wish he would not rush into lovemaking—more foreplay.
- ☐ I wish he would make sex spontaneous rather than ask for it and would hold me more.
- ☐ I wish he would stop waiting for me to initiate sex.
- ☐ I wish my husband would spend more time talking and cuddling instead of just jumping right in.
- ☐ I wish he would realize that things he does throughout the day affect sex that night.
- ☐ I wish I had more say about when the sexual experience would end; often he stops too soon.
- ☐ I wish he would spend time listening to me without the computer, radio, or television competing for his attention.
- ☐ I wish he would listen to me and not criticize my thoughts and feelings.
- ☐ I wish we could have more family time together. If I feel connected, sex is better.
- ☐ I wish he would come to bed earlier—turn off the TV sooner, and just come snuggle (pre-sex), making "intimacy" a priority.
- ☐ I wish he would not come to bed thirty minutes after I've gone to sleep and start "pawing" at me.
- ☐ I wish he would touch me sometimes when he *doesn't* want sex. Throw a few hugs and kisses into the mix and I would feel more interested in sex.

☐ I wish he would let me know that he is proud of me and glad I am his wife.

☐ With a new baby, I am tired much of the time. I wish sex wasn't "expected" so often.

☐ I wish my husband would romance me again, with a flower, note, card, or small gift that says, "I love you."

☐ I wish he would sit on the couch with me, hold hands, and kiss rather than sleep in the recliner.

☐ I wish he would show more love to me before and after sex, so it's not just physical but also spiritual and emotional.

☐ I wish we had consistent date nights without discussing cost— just trying new things together.

☐ I wish my husband would stop treating sex like it doesn't mean anything but a "fix," stop asking all the time, and stop making me feel guilty when I'm not in the mood.

☐ I wish he would allow me to get into bed, touch him, or cuddle up next to him, even kiss him good night, and not have it always turn into sex.

☐ I wish he would realize that the way he acts when he comes home from work (grouchy, impatient, irritable) sets the tone for the night, and I don't have a switch that turns all that off and suddenly makes me want to have sex with him.

☐ I wish he would be okay with the fact that sex is not as enjoyable for me as it is for him. I actually love good massages without sex.

☐ I wish he would spend more time before sexual intimacy reaffirming how special I am—things like placing his arm around me, saying something nice about me, treating me in a way that makes me feel loved. Having been sexually abused as a child, I sometimes feel that when these things do not happen, he is just using me for my body.

☐ I wish my husband would remember that because I am post-menopausal, intercourse is painful for me. I want to please him because I love him very much.

☐ I wish he would arrange for a special night or weekend where it is just us so we could concentrate on sexual intimacy.

☐ I wish he would understand that my lack of interest has nothing to do with him. It has everything to do with my lack of time and energy and my stress level.

☐ I wish he would stop grabbing me in intimate places when I'm trying to cook dinner or accomplish a task.

☐ I wish my husband would continue to stimulate me throughout the sexual encounter instead of just at the beginning.

☐ I wish we had sex more often and that he was not so tired all the time.

☐ I wish he would not ask for sex when I'm not feeling well. I am pregnant and have morning sickness and just don't need to be shaken up like a soda bottle.

☐ I wish he would not tease or make "cat calls" when I undress.

☐ I wish he would work with me on our spiritual relationship.

☐ I wish my husband would seek help for impotency. It has been an issue for years.

☐ I wish we would plan intimate nights so we could both "get ready" for a fun evening. Sometimes spontaneous sexual encounters are exciting, but anticipation is fun, too.

☐ I wish he would stop playing solitaire on the computer instead of coming to bed.

☐ I wish he would feel more free to let me know what I am doing—right or wrong—in making the sexual experience good for him.

☐ I wish that my husband would compliment my physical appearance more often, but I want him to mean it.

☐ I wish he would talk about loving me as a person instead of talking about wanting and desiring sex. I want to feel desirable as a woman, not as someone to meet his needs.

☐ I wish he would believe that when I say, "I'm too tired," I really am too tired.

Suggested Resources

Part Three—Profit Sharing

Money and Finances

Crown Financial Ministries
P.O. Box 100
Gainesville, GA 30503-0100
Phone: 1-800-722-1976
Website: www.crown.org

The following is a wealth of resources covering all aspects of money management, including personal budget coaching, financial advice, seminars, workbooks, online articles, and an e-newsletter.

Larry Burkett, *The Complete Financial Guide for Young Couples: A Lifetime Approach to Spending, Saving, and Investing* (Chariot Victor Publishing, 1993)

This book covers establishing a workable budget, knowing how much insurance to purchase, recognizing economic dangers in a marriage, exploring investments, and teaching children about finances.

Howard Dayton, *Your Money Map: A Proven 7-Step Guide to True Financial Freedom* (Moody Publishers, 2006)

By revealing key biblical principles of finance through the journey of a married couple, Matt and Jennifer, *Your Money Map* steers you toward the clear biblical basics of money management and through seven financial "destinations" that anyone can reach.

Howard Dayton, *Your Money Counts: The Biblical Guide to Earning, Spending, Saving, Investing, Giving, and Getting Out of Debt* (Tyndale House Publishers, 1997)

In *Your Money Counts*, you will learn that the Bible has a lot to say about money. Indeed, the Bible is a blueprint for managing your finances. You will also discover the profound impact handling money has on your relationship with God.

Creative Spending

Ellie Kay, *Half-Price Living: Secrets to Living Well on One Income* (Moody Publishers, 2007)

A recent online survey found that 86 percent of working moms said they would stay at home if they were financially able to do so. Popular author and speaker Ellie Kay used both her financial expertise and her experience as a mom to write this step-by-step plan on how to downsize from two incomes to one.

Margaret Feinberg, Jason Boyett, Katie Meier, and Josh Hatcher, *Cheap Ways to . . .* (Relevant Books, 2003)

The authors offer fun, innovative ideas designed to help you make your resources stretch a little further while avoiding or escaping the pitfalls of mass consumerism and credit-card debt.

Living within Your Means

Howard Dayton, *Free and Clear: God's Roadmap to Debt-Free Living* (Moody Publishers, 2006)

Becoming debt free may seem an impossible dream, but it is actually an attainable goal. Howard Dayton, past president of Crown Financial Ministries, overcame his own struggle with debt by applying God's principles to managing his finances, principles he lays out in this practical and encouraging book.

Saving and Investing

Austin Pryor, *The Sound Mind Investing Handbook: A Step-by-Step Guide to Managing Your Money from a Biblical Perspective* (Sound Mind Investing, 2004)

Investment advisor Austin Pryor has carefully created the "next step" guide that helps you put godly principles of finance into motion. Each user-friendly lesson is written in everyday English and filled with helpful visual aids. You'll learn what investing is and why it's actually quite simple, important steps to take to prepare yourself financially before you invest, what mutual funds are and why they make investing easier than ever before, and how to use your personal investing temperament and present season of life to make decisions and limit your risk.

Larry Burkett, Ron Blue, and Jeremy White, *The Burkett & Blue Definitive Guide to Securing Wealth to Last: Money Essentials for the Second Half of Life* (B&H Publishing Group, 2003)

In this book Ron Blue and the late Larry Burkett, primary trailblazers and leaders in Christian financial teaching, provide direction for building a financial portfolio that will provide for your family and help you to honor God.

Part Five—Making Love

Kevin Leman, *Sheet Music: Uncovering the Secrets of Sexual Intimacy in Marriage* (Tyndale House, 2003)

Get ready to make beautiful music together! Dr. Kevin Leman's practical guide will help any couple stay "in tune" for an active, God-designed sex life. He addresses a wide spectrum of individuals—with positive, negative, or no experience—and his frank descriptions, line drawings, and warm and friendly tone will help couples find greater harmony through intimacy.

Clifford and Joyce Penner, *The Gift of Sex: A Guide to Sexual Fulfillment* (Thomas Nelson, 2003)

Internationally recognized sexual therapists Clifford and Joyce Penner draw from their vast clinical experience to help couples explore the deep, powerful, and mysterious aspects of their sexuality. Hopeful, encouraging, and highly practical, this newly revised and updated best seller is a valuable resource for any couple interested in enhancing their sexual relationship, whether newly wed or married for years.

Douglas E. Rosenau, *A Celebration of Sex: A Guide to Enjoying God's Gift of Sexual Fulfillment* (Thomas Nelson, 2002)

Dr. Douglas Rosenau is a licensed psychologist and Christian sex therapist who has for the past seventeen years used his training in theology and counseling to help Christian couples enrich and reclaim God's wonderful gift of sexuality within marriage. *A Celebration of Sex* answers specific, often unasked questions about sexual topics and presents married couples with detailed techniques and behavioral skills for deepening sexual pleasure and intimate companionship.

Ed and Gaye Wheat, *Intended for Pleasure: Sex Technique and Sexual Fulfillment in Christian Marriage* (Revell, 1997)

This is the classic manual on sex in Christian marriage, now updated and expanded. A skillful combination of biblical teaching on love and marriage, with the latest medical information on sex and sexuality. The material is presented in wholesome terms that would be of help to any married or soon-to-be-married couple.

Notes

Part One—Everybody Wins

CHAPTER 1

1. Dorothy Tennov, *Love and Limerence* (New York: Stein and Day, 1979), 142.

CHAPTER 2

1. Ecclesiastes 4:9.

Part Two—Home Improvements

CHAPTER 1

1. Author's paraphrase of Matthew 7:3-5.
2. Psalm 139:23-24, NLT.
3. 1 John 1:9.
4. For more information on the topic of rebuilding trust, see Gary D. Chapman, *The Five Languages of Apology* (Chicago: Northfield Publishing, 2006).

CHAPTER 2

1. Ollie Jones, "Love Makes the World Go Round," 1958.
2. Gary D. Chapman, *The Five Love Languages* (Chicago: Northfield Publishing, 1992, 1995, 2004).

CHAPTER 3

1. Richard M. Sherman and Robert B. Sherman, "A Spoonful of Sugar," from the movie *Mary Poppins*.
2. See 1 Peter 4:8.

Part Three—Profit Sharing

CHAPTER 1

1. Luke 12:15.
2. 1 Timothy 6:10.

CHAPTER 2

1. Genesis 1:28.
2. Genesis 2:15.
3. Exodus 20:8-10.
4. William J. Bennett, *The Book of Virtues* (New York: Simon & Schuster, 1993), 347.
5. Proverbs 13:19.
6. As quoted in George Sweeting, *Who Said That?* (Chicago: Moody Publishers, 1995), 452.
7. 1 Timothy 5:8.
8. Proverbs 6:6-11.
9. Proverbs 13:4.
10. 2 Thessalonians 3:10-12.
11. Colossians 3:23-24.

CHAPTER 3

1. James 1:17.
2. C. S. Lewis, *Mere Christianity* (New York: McMillan, 1952), 180.
3. James 1:5.
4. R. G. LeTourneau, *Mover of Men and Mountains* (Chicago: Moody Publishers, 1972), 263.
5. Matthew 6:25-33.
6. Philippians 4:6-7.
7. Matthew 6:24.
8. Joshua 1:8-9.
9. Joshua 24:15.

CHAPTER 4

1. Leviticus 27:30, 32, 34.
2. Malachi 3:8-12.
3. Matthew 23:23.
4. Luke 6:38.
5. 2 Corinthians 9:6-8.
6. Proverbs 3:9-10.
7. Philippians 4:18-19.
8. R. G. LeTourneau, *Mover of Men and Mountains*, 280.
9. 1 John 3:17-18.

CHAPTER 5

1. Proverbs 22:3, TLB.
2. Luke 14:28-30.
3. Genesis 41:34-36.
4. Proverbs 21:20.
5. Proverbs 6:6-8.

Part Four—Now What?

INTRODUCTION

1. Carolyn Pape Cowan and Philip A. Cowan, *When Partners Become Parents* (HarperCollins, 1992), 109.
2. Ibid., 89.

CHAPTER 1

1. Genesis 1:28.
2. Genesis 2:24.
3. Alice Gray, comp., *Stories for a Mom's Heart* (Sisters, Ore.: Multnomah, 2002), 29.
4. Jimmy Van Heusen and Sammy Cahn, "Love and Marriage," copyright 1955 by Barton Music Corp./Warner Chappell Music, Inc.
5. For more information on the four-seasons concept, you may wish to read *The Four Seasons of Marriage*, by Gary Chapman (Carol Stream, Ill.: Tyndale House, 2005).

CHAPTER 3

1. MSN Money staff, "Raising Your Quarter-Million-Dollar Baby," located at http://moneycentral.msn.com/content/collegeandfamily/raisekids/p37245.asp.

CHAPTER 4

1. For more information on the love-languages concept, you may wish to read *The Five Love Languages of Children*, written by Gary Chapman and Ross Campbell (Chicago: Northfield Publishing, 1997).

CHAPTER 5

1. For further help in how to apologize successfully, you may wish to read *The Five Languages of Apology*, by Gary Chapman and Jennifer Thomas (Chicago: Northfield Publishing, 2006).
2. Ephesians 5:25.
3. Ephesians 5:33.

Part Five—Making Love

INTRODUCTION

1. Linda J. Waite and Maggie Gallagher, *The Case for Marriage* (New York: Doubleday, 2000), 79.

CHAPTER 1

1. Genesis 2:18-25.
2. Genesis 1:28.
3. Waite and Gallagher, 124–140.
4. Song of Songs 4:9-11, 15-16.
5. Song of Songs 5:10-11, 13-16.

CHAPTER 2
1. Deuteronomy 24:5, NLT.
2. Kevin Leman, *Sheet Music: Uncovering the Secrets of Sexual Intimacy in Marriage* (Carol Stream, Ill.: Tyndale House, 2003), 103.
3. Ibid.

CHAPTER 3
1. See Ephesians 5:25.
2. 1 John 4:19, NKJV.
3. Song of Songs 4:1-7.
4. Song of Songs 4:16.
5. Song of Songs 5:1.

CHAPTER 5
1. Gary Chapman, *The Five Love Languages: How to Express Heartfelt Commitment to Your Mate* (Chicago: Northfield Publishing, 1992, 1995).
2. 1 Corinthians 8:1, NKJV.

CHAPTER 6
1. Proverbs 18:21.

CHAPTER 7
1. 1 John 1:9.
2. See Ephesians 4:32.
3. Romans 5:8.
4. Romans 5:5.

Part Six—In-Law Relationships
INTRODUCTION
1. Genesis 2:24; see Ephesians 5:31.
2. Exodus 20:12; see Deuteronomy 5:16.
3. Ephesians 6:2-3.
4. 1 Timothy 5:4.
5. 1 Timothy 5:8.

CHAPTER 2
1. *The New Webster's Pocket Dictionary* (New York: Lexicon Publications, Inc.), 1990.
2. Exodus 20:12; see Ephesians 6:2.
3. See 2 Corinthians 6:14-15.
4. See Proverbs 11:14.
5. Exodus 18:17-19.
6. See Exodus 18:22.

CHAPTER 5

1. 1 Corinthians 13:5, NLT.
2. John 6:66-69, NLT.
3. Matthew 7:7-11, NLT.
4. Acts 20:35.

CHAPTER 7

1. Acts 20:35.
2. See Matthew 5:43-44.
3. See 1 John 4:19, NLT.
4. See 1 Corinthians 13:4, NLT.
5. Proverbs 15:1.